JOURNAL FOR THE STUDY OF THE NEW TESTAMENT
SUPPLEMENT SERIES
258

Editor
Mark Goodacre

Figure 1. *Mark 8.10-26. The Chester Beatty Gospel Codex* (P[45]) (*Four Gospels and Acts papyrus c.* 200 CE Dublin, CBL BP I f. 6r. © The Trustees of the Chester Beatty Library, Dublin).

The Earliest Gospels

The Origins and Transmission of the Earliest
Christian Gospels – The Contribution of the
Chester Beatty Gospel Codex P45

Studies by

Barbara Aland, J. Keith Elliott, Sean Freyne,
Harry Gamble, Martin Hengel, Charles Horton,
Larry W. Hurtado, Martin McNamara,
William L. Petersen, James Robinson and
Graham Stanton

Edited by

Charles Horton

T & T CLARK INTERNATIONAL
A Continuum imprint
LONDON • NEW YORK

Copyright © 2004 T&T Clark International
A Continuum imprint

Published by T&T Clark International
The Tower Building, 11 York Road, London SE1 7NX
15 East 26th Street, Suite 1703, New York, NY 10010

www.tandtclark.com

British Library Cataloguing-in-Publication Data
A catalogue record for this book is available from the British Library

Library of Congress Cataloging-in-Publication Data
A catalogue record for this book is available from the Library of Congress

Typeset by ISB Typesetting, Sheffield
Printed on acid-free paper in Great Britain by MPG Books Ltd, Bodmin, Cornwall

ISBN 0-567-08389-6 (hardback)
         0-567-08293-3 (paperback)

CONTENTS

LIST OF ILLUSTRATIONS

FOREWORD

The Chester Beatty Library is delighted to publish, in association with T&T Clark International, *The Earliest Gospels: The Origins and Transmission of the Earliest Christian Gospels; The Contribution of the Chester Beatty Gospel Codex, P^{45}*.

This collection of essays has its origin in a conference on the theme of the origin of the New Testament organized by the Library to celebrate the Millennium Year in December 2000. The event was entitled *The Word and its beginning* a name it shared with an exhibition held simultaneously at the Library. The present volume includes all the papers delivered at the conference with one addition.

The proceedings are edited by my colleague, Charles Horton, Western Curator at the Library, and the conference was organized with the advice of our Trustee, Professor Sean Freyne of Trinity College Dublin, by Ms Veronica Ryan. The attendance was large and the discussions lively. The exhibition of New Testament manuscript materials was primarily from the Library's own collections but generous loans were given by the Vatican Library and the Library of Trinity College Dublin. We are indebted to the Provost and Board of Trinity College, the Librarian and the Keeper of Manuscripts, Dr Bernard Meehan, for their support. The Vatican Librarian, His Eminence (Cardinal then Archbishop) Jorge Meijia was unfailingly generous in his support.

The conference represents one of several efforts on the part of the Chester Beatty Library to renew its commitment to the promotion of scholarship in the areas of most interest to it. The Trustees of the Library are deeply indebted to the contributors and to those who provided generous help and support in the venture, in particular the British Council and Mr Harold Fish, Dublin, for financial support.

Michael Ryan
Director and Librarian
November 2003

ACKNOWLEDGMENTS

As curator of the Chester Beatty Biblical papyri, it has given me great pleasure to work with some of the most important Christian manuscripts in existence. Even though Alfred Chester Beatty first published his 11 Biblical papyri nearly 70 years ago (in a lavish 16 volume facsimile), this is the first occasion where many of the leading New Testament authorities were invited to contribute to a conference devoted to just one of those manuscripts. In the words of Professor Larry Hurtado, the Chester Beatty Gospel Codex (P^{45}) was 'like a flare bursting over a night-time battlefield, it cast light upon the previously darkened pre-Constantinian centuries of the textual history of the New Testament, forcing revisions of scholarly views on several major matters'.

In editing the proceedings of the conference, I am indebted to many people, mostly notably the Trustees and Director of the Chester Beatty Library for releasing me from my normal duties. To the contributors and publisher for their patience with me in guiding the texts through to publication and to my fellow reader, Professor Sean Freyne, whose eagle eyes spotted inconsistencies in my editing, for which I bear responsibility.

Note

The papyri collection in the Chester Beatty Library consists of several distinct groups based on language and other criteria. The first collection published was the Egyptian texts, bearing the *siglia Papyrus Chester Beatty I–XX* (1927–35). These were followed by the Biblical Papyri I-XII published by Frederic Kenyon (1933–58). Published citations of the Greek biblical texts are often abbreviated to Chester Beatty I, II, etc., but in this study the designation followed is the standard form in modern critical editions; P^{45}, P^{46}, or P^{47} (and Rahlf's equivalent for *Septuagint* texts), as given in N–A^{27}(*Novum Testamentum Graece* [ed. E. Nestle and K. Aland; Stuttgart: Deutsche Bibelgesellschaft, 27th edn, 1993]).

Charles Horton
Editor

ABBREVIATIONS

List of Abbreviated Titles

Kenyon I Frederic G. Kenyon, *The Chester Beatty Biblical Papyri, Descriptions and Texts of Twelve Manuscripts on Papyrus of the Greek Bible, Fasciculus I: General Introduction* (London: Emery Walker, 1933).

Kenyon II, Text *Fasciculus II: The Gospels and Acts, Text* (London: Emery Walker, 1933).

Kenyon II, Plates *Fasciculus II: The Gospels and Acts, Plates* (London: Emery Walker, 1934).

Kenyon III, Text *Fasciculus III: Pauline Epistles and Revelation, Text* (London: Emery Walker, 1934).

Kenyon III, Plates *Fasciculus III: Pauline Epistles and Revelation Plates* (London: Emery Walker, 1936).

Kenyon III, SText *Fasciculus III Supplement: Pauline Epistles, Text* (London: Emery Walker, 1936).

Kenyon III, SPlates *Fasciculus III Supplement: Pauline Epistles, Plates* (London: Emery Walker, 1937).

NA Kurt Aland and Barbara Aland, *The Text of the New Testament*, (Grand Rapids and Leiden: E.J. Brill, 2nd English edn, 1989).

N-A^{27} *Novum Testamentum Graece* (ed. E. Nestle and K. Aland; Stuttgart: Deutsche Bibelgesellschaft, 27th edn, 1993).

MH Gospels Martin Hengel, *The Four Gospels and the One Gospel of Jesus Christ* (trans. John Bowden; London: SCM Press, 2000).

ABD David Noel Freedman (ed.), *The Anchor Bible Dictionary* (6 vols.; New York: Doubleday, 1992).

ANTF Arbeiten zur neutestamentlichen Textforschung

ANRW *Aufstieg und Niedergang der römischen Welt*

ATDan Acta theologica danica

BETL Bibliotheca ephemeridum theologicarum lovaniensium

Bib *Biblica*

CJ *Classical Journal*

CSCO Corpus scriptorum christianorum orientalium

CP *Classical Philology*

CQ *Church Quarterly*

CQR *Church Quarterly Review*

ESCJ Studies in Christianity and Judaism/Etudes sur le christianisme et le judaisme

ETL *Ephemerides theologicae Louvanienses*

FRLANT Forschungen zur Religion und Literatur des Alten und Neuen Testaments

GRBS *Greek, Roman and Byzantine Studies*

HTR *Harvard Theological Review*

JA *Journal asiatique*

JBL	*Journal of Biblical Literature*
JRASS	Journal of Roman Archaeology Supplementary Series
JRH	*Journal of Religious History*
JTS	*Journal of Theological Studies*
KBANT	Kommentare und Beiträge zum Alten und Neuen Testament
MThSt	Marburger Theologische Studien
NHMS	Nag Hammadi and Manichaean Studies
NHS	Nag Hammadi Studies
NTS	*New Testament Studies*
NTTS	New Testament Tools and Studies
NovT	*Novum Testamentum*
PG	J.-P. Migne (ed.), Patrologia cursus completa…series graeca (166 vols.; Paris: Petit-Montrouge, 1857–83)
RB	*Revue biblique*
RAAN	*Rendiconti dell'Accademia di archeologia, lettere e belle arti di Napoli*
SBAW	*Sitzungsberichte der bayerischen Akademie der Wissenschaften*
SD	Studies and Documents
StPat	*Studia Patristica*
SNTSMS	Society of New Testament Studies, Monograph Series
STAC	Studien und Texte zu Antike und Christentum
TAPA	*Transactions of the American Philological Association*
TRE	*Theologische Realenzyklopädie*
TS	*Theological Studies*
TU	Text und Untersuchungen
VC	*Vigiliae Christianae*
WUNT	Wissenschaftliche Untersuchungen zum Neuen Testament
ZNW	*Zeitschrift für die neutestamentliche Wissenschaft*
ZPE	*Zeitschrift für Papyrologie und Epigraphik*

List of Manuscripts Cited

Papyri

P^4	Paris, Bibl. Nat. Suppl. Gr. 1120
P^{45}	Dublin, Chester Beatty Biblical Papyrus I / Vienna, Österr. Nat. Bibl., Pap. G. 31974
P^{46}	Dublin, Chester Beatty Biblical Papyrus II / Ann Arbor, Univ.of Michigan, Inv. 6238
P^{47}	Dublin, Chester Beatty Biblical Papyrus III
P^{52}	Manchester, J. Rylands Univ. Libr. Gr. Papyrus 457
P^{64}	Oxford, Magdalen Coll., Gr. 18; Barcelona, Fundación S. Lucas Evang., P. Barc. 1 (= P^{67})
P^{66}	Cologny, Bibl. Bodmer, P. Bodmer II
$[P^{67}]$	vide P^{64}
P^{72}	Cologny, Bibl. Bodmer, P. Bodmer VII. VIII (1.2 P nunc in Bibl. Vaticana)
P^{75}	Cologny, Bibl. Bodmer, P. Bodmer XIV
P^{77}	Oxford, Ashmolean Mus. P. Oxy. 2683
P^{101}	Oxford, Ashmolean Mus. P. Oxy. 4401
P^{102}	Oxford, Ashmolean Mus. P. Oxy. 4402
P^{103}	Oxford, Ashmolean Mus. P. Oxy. 4403
P^{104}	Oxford, Ashmolean Mus. P. Oxy. 4404
P^{105}	Oxford, Ashmolean Mus. P. Oxy. 4406

P[106]	Oxford, Ashmolean Mus. P. Oxy. 4445
P[107]	Oxford, Ashmolean Mus. P. Oxy. 4446
P[108]	Oxford, Ashmolean Mus. P. Oxy. 4447
P[109]	Oxford, Ashmolean Mus. P. Oxy. 4448
P. Oxy.30	Papyrus Oxyrhynchus 30 Latin Historical Fragment (pl.8) P. Petaus 30 Cologne, University P. Köln 376

Uncials

ℵ	Codex Sinaiticus, London, Brit Libr., Add. 43725
A	Codex Alexandrinus, London, Brit Libr., Royal 1 D. VIII
B	Codex Vaticanus, Bib Apos Vat. Gr. 1209
D	Codex Bezae, Cambridge, Univ. Libr. Nn. 2. 41
D	Paris, Bibl. Nat. Gr. 107, 107 AB
L	Paris, Bibl. Nat. Gr. 62
W	Codex Washingtonianus/Freer Gospels, Washington, Smithsonian Inst., Freer Gall. of Art, 06.274
X	Munich, Univ. Bibl., 2^0 Cod. ms. 30
Θ	Codex Koridethi, Tbilisi, Inst. rukop., Gr. 28
565	St. Petersburg, Ross. Nac. Bibl., Gr. 53
700	London, British Museum, Egerton 2610
g[1]	Codex Sangermanensis, Paris, Bibl. Nat., Lat. 11553

Fam 1	familia codd. Min. 1 et aliorum (Designates certain families of manuscripts which have been found to be closely related, and which count for text critical purposes as a single source. Families are named after their lowest-number manuscript member. Fam 1(miniscules) grouped by Kirsopp Lake in 1902, comprises codices 1, 118, 131, 209, and others)
Fam 13	familia codd. Min. 13 et aliorum (Family 13 (miniscules), four Gospel manuscripts published by T.K. Abbott in 1872 after the death of his collaborator W.H. Farrar. Comprises codices 13, 69, 124 and 346. Members later discovered include codices 543, 788, 826, 828, and others.

Professor Dr Barbara Aland, DD, DLitt, studied the Classics, Orientalism and Protestant Theology in Frankfurt, Marburg and Rome. Since 1978 she was Professor of Church History at the University of Münster, and since 1983 Director of the Institute for New Testament Textual Research in Münster. Her articles on ancient Church History focus especially on Gnosticism, and Textual Criticism. Co-editor of *Novum Testamentum Graece* by Nestle/Aland, 27th edition (1993), and *Greek New Testament*, 4th edition (1993), she is also general editor of *Novum Testamentum Graecum. Editio Critica Maior*, Installment 1, James (1997, [2]1998) and Installment 2, *The Letters of Peter* (2000).

Professor J. Keith Elliott has taught in the Department of Theology at the University of Leeds since 1967. He is Professor of New Testament Textual Criticism. He is on the Editorial Board of *Novum Testamentum* (Leiden), *Filologia Neotestamentaria* (Cordova) and *New Testament Textual Research Update* (Sydney). He is secretary of the British committee of the International Greek New Testament Project, at present working on the Fourth Gospel, having previously been the editor who published in two volumes (with Oxford University Press) the Project's previous work on Luke. He is editor of *The Apocryphal New Testament* (1993) and author of *A Bibliography of Greek New Testament Manuscripts*, 2nd edn (2000).

Until very recently Sean Freyne was Professor of Theology at Trinity College Dublin. He has been a Trustee of the Chester Beatty Library since 1984. His research is in the area of the social world of Jesus and Early Christianity, with a special emphasis on Galilee in Hellenistic and Roman times. Among his publications to do with the gospels are *Galilee, Jesus and the Gospels: Literary Approaches and Historical Investigations* (1988) and *Galilee and Gospel: Collected Essays* (2000).

Harry Y. Gamble is Professor of Early Christianity and the New Testament in the Department of Religious Studies, and Chair of the Department of Religious Studies, at the University of Virginia, Charlottesville, Virginia, USA. Professor Gamble was educated at Wake Forest University (BA), Duke University (MDiv) and Yale University (MA, PhD). He has been the Thomas Jefferson Fellow at Downing College, Cambridge University, and the Pilkington Fellow in Biblical Studies at Christ Church, Oxford. He is a member of the Society of Biblical Literature and of the International Society for New Testament Studies. Professor Gamble is the author of several books, most recently *Books and Readers in the Early Church: A History of Early Christian Texts* (1995), and a large number of scholarly articles. His special research interests are the history of the text and canon of the New Testament.

Martin Hengel is a theology educator who was born in Reutlingen, Germany. He holds a DTheol from the University of Tübingen, 1959, and numerous honary doctorates from many universities: Uppsala (1979), Strasbourg (1988), St Andrews (1981), Durham (1985), Cambridge (1989), Dublin (2000). He was Professor of Theology for the University Erlangen in the Federal Republic of Germany between 1968–72 after which he held the Professorship of Theology at the University of Tübingen, 1972–92. He became Professor emeritus in 1992. Professor Hengel is a Fellow of the British Academy (corr.); Member of the Heidelberger Akademie der Wissenschaften and a Foreign member of the Royal Netherlands Academy of Arts and Sciences.

His published works include: *Die Zeloten* (1961; 2nd edn, 1989); *Judentum und Hellenismus* (1969; 2nd edn, 1974; 3rd edn, 1988); *Nachfolge und Charisma* (1968); *Der Sohn Gottes* (1975; 2nd edn, 1977); *Studies in the Gospel of Mark* (1983); *Between Jesus and Paul* (1983); *The Cross of the Son of God* (1986); *Earliest Christianity* (1986); *The Johannine Question* (1989); *The Hellenization of Judaea in the First Century after Christ* (1989); *The Prechristian Paul* (1991); *Studies in Early Christology* (1995); *Judaica et Hellenistica,* Kleine Schriften I (1996); *Paul between Damascus and Antioch* (with Anna Maria Schwemer) (1997); *Judaica, Hellenistica et Christiana,* Kleine Schriften II (1999); *The Four Gospels and the One Gospel of Jesus Christ* (2000).

Charles Horton has nearly twenty years' experience in working for museums and specialist historical collections in Ireland. After completing his primary and post-graduate studies at Trinity College Dublin and University College Dublin, he completed further post-graduate study at University College London on the History of the Book.

Since joining the staff of the Chester Beatty Library in 1991 as Western Curator, he has been responsible for maintaining and developing the Library's famous collection of Ancient Egyptian, early Biblical papyri and other Christian collections as well as the rare printed books and European prints.

His most recent published work is on the history and development of the Chester Beatty Collection.

Larry Hurtado is Professor of New Testament Language, Literature and Theology in the University of Edinburgh, and founding Director of the University of Edinburgh Centre for the Study of Christian Origins. He received his PhD from Case Western Reserve University in 1973 and was Professor of Religion in the University of Manitoba between 1978–96, where he was also the founding Director of the Institute for the Humanities (1990–92).

His publications include *Text-Critical Methodology and the Pre-Caesarean Text: Codex W in the Gospel of Mark* (1981), *Mark: New International Bible Commentary* (1989), *One Lord, One God: Early Christian Devotion and Ancient Jewish Mono-theism* (1988; 2nd edn, 1998), and over fifty articles in scholarly journals, books and reference works in which he has dealt with the Gospel of Mark, the Epistles of Paul, the Apocalypse, early christology and text-critical issues. His most recent book is based on his 1999 Didsbury Lectures, *At the Origins of Christian Worship* (1999; 2000). He has done editorial work on several publications, including the *Dictionary of Biblical Tradition in English Literature* (1992), of which he was the Associate Editor. He has also served on the editorial board of the Canadian scholarly journal *Studies in Religion/Sciences religieuses*, and as an Associate Editor of *Critical Review of Books in Religion*.

His current research program, 'Christ-Devotion in the First Two Centuries', focuses on the origin of and developments in devotion to Christ in earliest Christianity, and he is currently writing a study on this topic.

Martin McNamara has taught scripture and related subjects at the Milltown Institute of Theology and Philosophy, Dublin, since 1972. He was Professor of Sacred Scripture until June 2000 and is currently Professor emeritus. He is a member, and one time president, of the Irish Biblical Association. Professor McNamara's early undergraduate studies were completed at the Pontifical Gregorian University, and the Pontifical Biblical Institute, Rome. He continued his biblical studies in Jerusalem at the Pontifical Biblical Institute and the École Biblique. His doctoral dissertation in Biblical Studies, entitled *The New Testament and the Palestinian Targum to the Pentateuch,* was published by the Biblical Institute Press, Rome (1966; reprint with supplements 1978).

His interest in the Bible and the Apocrypha in Ireland dates back to his student days. He has a particular interest in early Irish commentary material on the Bible, in the Apocrypha in Ireland and in the Latin text of the Bible in Ireland. He is a member of the editorial board of a Committee of the Royal Irish Academy and the Irish Biblical Association for the publication of Irish biblical commentary material by Belgian Brepols Publishers in the series *Corpus Christianorum.*

He has shown a special interest in the Psalms in the early Irish Church. He published an initial essay on this in 1973 in the *Proceedings of the Royal Irish Academy,* and a number of later studies. These were all edited in the volume *The Psalms in the Early Irish Church* published by Sheffield Academic Press (2000).

In the work *The Apocrypha in the Irish Church* (1975) he gave an overview of the extant material on the biblical apocryphal literature in Ireland (mainly in the Irish language). In 1989 Dr Máire Herbert and Professor McNamara edited the volume *Irish Biblical Apocrypha: Selected Texts in Translation.* Currently he is a member of an editorial committee for the publication of Irish New Testament Apocrypha to be published by Brepols Publishers in the series *Corpus Christianorum Series Apocryphorum.* The first volume with *Irish Infancy Narratives* was published in 2002.

He has written various essays on the text of the Latin Bible in Ireland, particularly on the Latin Gospel text, on which he has published a book in 1990: *Studies on Texts of Early Irish Latin Gospels (AD 600–1200).*

William L. Petersen is Professor of New Testament and Christian Origins at Pennsylvania State University, in the United States. He is also Director of the Religious Studies Department. He received his Doctorate in Theology from Utrecht University, in the Netherlands, where his Promotor (Doktorvater) was Professor Dr Gilles Quispel. From 1985 until 1990 he taught at the University of Notre Dame and since 1990 he has been at Penn State.

His research interests focus on the text of the New Testament, specifically its origin and evolution in the earliest Christian centuries (through 500 CE). He has also published on Syriac studies and ethics. He is the author of two books and the editor or co-editor of another three; he has written more than 30 articles and chapters in books. He reviews widely for professional journals and is frequently asked to contribute to reference works, including the *Anchor Bible Dictionary*, the *Theologische Realenzyklopaedie*, and the new fourth edition of Religion in *Geschichte und Gegenwart*. At present he serves on the editorial boards of *New Testament Studies* and of *Vigiliae Christianae*, both quarterly scholarly journals.

In 1994 he was the Jerusalem Trust Visiting Fellow at the Oxford Center for Hebrew and Jewish Studies; in 1997–98 he was a Fellow at the Netherlands Institute for Advanced Studies, where he co-directed a six person team working on the Diatessaron of Tatian – the subject of his presentation in this volume.

James Robinson was born in Gettysburg, PA. He received his DTheol at the University of Basel, Switzerland, under Karl Barth as doctoral father in 1952, his ThD at Princeton Theological Seminary 1955 in New Testament. He taught at Emory University 1952–58. He was Professor at Claremont Graduate University 1959–99, Director of the Institute for Antiquity and Christianity 1967–99. His publications include: *The Critical Edition of Q* (2000): *Documenta Q* (1996) ff (5 volumes thus far); the *Facsimile Edition of the Nag Hammadi Codices* (as Permanent Secretary of the International Committee for the Nag Hammadi Codices of the Arab Republic of Egypt), 12 volumes (1972–84). He is General Editor of *The Coptic Gnostic Library*, 14 volumes (1974–95), reprint in 5 volumes (2000) and edited *New Frontiers in Theology* (3 volumes, 1963–67) and *A New Quest of the Historical Jesus* (1959).

Graham Stanton is a New Zealander who has lived in the UK since 1965. In 1977 he was appointed to the Chair of New Testament Studies at King's College in the University of London, a post he held for 21 years. In 1998 he took up his current appointment as Lady Margaret's Professor of Divinity at the University of Cambridge. In 1996–97 he served as President of Studiorum Novi Testamenti Societas, the international learned society of New Testament scholars. For nine years he was Editor of the journal *New Testament Studies* and of the associated monograph series; both published by Cambridge University Press and considered to be the leaders in the field. He is a General Editor of the International Critical Commentaries, for over 100 years the leading set of commentaries in English on the Bible.

His publications include *Jesus of Nazareth in New Testament Preaching* (1974); The Gospels and Jesus (1989); *A Gospel for a New People: Studies in Matthew* (1992; 1993); *Gospel Truth? New Light on Jesus and the Gospels* (1995, with translations into French, Dutch, Spanish and Italian). He has edited three further books, and published numerous articles on early Christianity in symposia and learned journals. He is currently working on Justin Martyr's *Dialogue with Trypho*, and on an International Critical Commentary on Galatians.

CHRONOLOGICAL TABLE

Passover 30 CE	Death of Jesus
c. 50	1 Thessalonians, the earliest Christian literary testimony
to 57 or 62	The seven authentic letters of Paul: 1 Thessalonians; 1 Corinthians; 2 Corinthians; Galatians; Romans (winter 56/57); Philippians and Philemon either 55/56 or 58–62
62	Martyrdom of James in Jerusalem
64	Persecution by Nero. Martyrdom of Peter and Paul in Rome
66–73	Jewish War
69–70	Gospel of Mark in Rome
c. 75–85	Luke and Acts
81–96	Domitian
c. 90–95	Matthew in Syria/Palestine
98–117	Trajan
c. 100	John the Elder in Ephesus; Cerinthus; Clement of Rome; Gospel of John
c. 110	Martyrdom of Ignatius
117–138	Hadrian
c. 120–130	Papias of Hierapolis
c. 130	Basilides in Alexandria
144	Excommunication of Marcion in Rome
after 150	Justin's *Apology* in Rome
c. 160	Justin's *Dialogue with Trypho*
c. 170	Celsus
177	Persecution in Lyons: Irenaeus becomes bishop there
180	Irenaeus' *Adversus Haereses*
c. 200	Clement of Alexandria

Part I

THE EARLIEST CHRISTIAN GOSPELS AND THEIR TRANSMISSION

Early Christian Imagination and the Gospels

Sean Freyne

The Chester Beatty Gospel papyrus P^{45}, containing considerable sections of the four canonical gospels is usually dated to the early third century CE. However, the emergence of the fourfold gospel is much earlier still. Thus the papyrus is a direct witness to choices that were made at a very early stage of the new movement's development, choices favouring the codex, or book, rather than the more usual scroll form and opting for the fourfold gospel rather than a single composite version as the more appropriate witness to the good news with which the movement had been entrusted.

These and other aspects of the papyrus will be discussed in other essays in this volume. In this study I wish to discuss the prior choice of the narrative mode as the most appropriate genre for expressing and disseminating the gospel or good news about Jesus of Nazareth. Was the decision influenced by factors operative in the world in which they sought to enculturate both Jewish and Græco-Roman, or was it the result of inner Christian dynamics? What, if any, were the theological points they sought to make in opting for the narrative mode? Did they feel free to adapt existing forms or was the gospel form a purely Christian creation? If we can see creative, yet practical minds at work in the later development of Christian identity as reflected in the production of gospel books such as P^{45}, it is worth exploring the ways in which this same creativity expressed itself from the very beginning of the movement as it took the momentous step from oral to written communication.

1. The Uniqueness of the Christian Gospels

In speaking of his own teaching in comparison with that of other Jewish teachers Jesus is reported as having said: 'No one puts new wine into old wine-skins; otherwise the wine will burst the skins and the wine is lost and so are the skins; but one puts new wine into fresh wine-skins' (Mk 2.23). The sense of newness about Jesus and his message was highly significant for him and for his followers and expressed itself in many different ways from the very beginning. Yet, this originality has to be balanced against other sayings attributed to Jesus, in which continuity with the received traditions of Judaism was also affirmed. The Christian scribe was expected to bring forth from his treasure both the new and the old (Mt. 13. 51). While these and other sayings now occur in polemical situations in the gospels, reflecting later debates with the parent religion, they are for that very reason also highly relevant to a consideration of the status of the Christian gospels as literary productions within their own environment.

The description 'unique' is one that has been frequently employed by those who wish to highlight the originality of the early Christian gospels. Yet on reflection this may be deemed something of an overstatement when applied to any literary work. It is not necessary to agree fully with the post-modern literary theory that claims that every literary production participates in all previous writings, in order to acknowledge that a 'unique' literary production that breaks totally with the conventions of genre and language operative in a given culture would scarcely be intelligible. Perhaps that may explain why many of us have great difficulty in reading James Joyce's *Ulysses*, even though we are generally familiar with the world behind the text, namely early twentieth-century Dublin.

It is worth exploring further some expressions of those who have spoken of the uniqueness of the gospels. One such is the highly influential German New Testament scholar Rudolph Bultmann, whose reasons could be described as theological rather than literary. According to him, the first three gospels are collections of oral material that had been shaped in the context of early Christian faith and worship. While the various units from the pre-gospel stage (miracle stories, parables, wisdom sayings and the like) should be compared with extra-biblical parallels from the surrounding culture, any such comparison of the complete gospels serves 'only to throw the uniqueness of the gospels into stronger relief'.[1] However, for him this does not warrant the claim that a unique literary genre has been created. That would only arise if a history of similar works could be shown to have developed directly from the Synoptic gospels, something which in Bultmann's view did not occur, with the single exception of the Fourth Gospel.[2] Only in this work can one detect a genuine authorial presence that developed the possibilities for a spiritual biography from what the Synoptic writers had accomplished in their compilations. However, this development was terminated by the emergence of a Christian canon, which cut short the process of gospel writing. The Synoptists, by contrast were 'completely subordinate to Christian faith and worship', merely providing 'receptacles' for the collection of pre-formed units of Christian piety. In a word, the 'uniqueness' of the gospel was for Bultmann based on their content, not their form.

The North American poet-scholar, Amos Wilder, adopts a more literary perspective in his discussion of the Gospel genre, in contrast to Bultmann's heavily kerygmatic/dogmatic approach. He writes as follows:

> All the literary forms of the New Testament, even those that seem to have a Christian background, fall definitely outside the categories of formal literature, as practised in the world of culture of that time [...] The gospel form is the only

---

1.   Rudolf Bultmann, *The History of the Synoptic Tradition* (trans. John Marsh; Oxford: Basil Blackwell, 1968), pp. 373–74.

2.   For a critique of this claim by Bultmann cf. Hubert Cancik, 'Die Gattung Evangelium: Das Evangelium Markus im Rahmen der antiken Historiographie', in *idem* (ed.), *Markus-Philologie* (WUNT, 33; Tübingen: Mohr, 1984), pp. 85–114, especially pp. 91–92, who claims that in the period 50–400 CE, as many as fifty works dealing with the deeds and words of Jesus can be documented and ascribed to a genre based on the gospels.

wholly new genre created by the Church, and the author Mark receives the credit for it. Yet this anonymous work is in large degree a group project [...] As a type of composition it is not like ancient biography or tragedy. Dibelius has shown how different it is from narratives, perhaps superficially similar, of the fate of the hero or of the life and death of a saint or a martyr. Yet all such accounts were written with an appeal to sentiment, with sharper portraiture or with fuller biographical details. Mark represents a divine transaction whose import involves heaven and earth, and even the scenes of the passion are recounted with a corresponding austerity. The gospel action is not so much a history as a ritual re-enactment or mimesis. The believer did not hear it as a record of the past.[3]

Even though Wilder is more oriented to the literary aspects of the gospels than was Bultmann, and is, therefore, prepared to speak of them as a new literary genre, he too regards the gospels as being a quite different type of literature from any of the contemporary analogues, especially ancient biography. Neither scholar seems interested in the representational nature of the gospels in terms of their biographical aspects, since for both they are the products of Christian faith and reflect the ethos of Christian worship. Comparison with other writings only serves to highlight their distinctiveness. Even though Wilder has a keener literary sense than Bultmann, in terms of style, tone and characterization, the absence of the distinctive authorial presence of an individual writer is lacking, and it is this aspect that makes these works quite unique. For him the individual voice of an author is drowned by the sound of the utterly new voice of the Christian communal experience that has given rise to a 'new style of utterance'.[4]

It is clear that whether one speaks of a theological or literary approach to the gospels the designation 'unique' presents difficulties. The Bultmannian uniqueness was only gained at the cost of separating content and form, with the consequent devaluation of the achievement of the gospel writers. Subsequent gospel scholarship over the past half century has redressed this situation with the advent of Redaction and Narrative criticism.[5] On the other hand Wilder's enthusiasm for the newness and creativity of the early Christian movement has caused him to overstate the case for their difference from all analogous forms of ancient narratives, especially, as we shall see, ancient biography. A more fluid understanding of uniqueness, both theological and literary is called for, since otherwise, the early Christian movement could scarcely have captured the imagination of such a large and diverse public so quickly.[6] The Christian scribes were indeed charged with combining the old and the new in communicating the good news that they themselves had experienced. It could scarcely have been otherwise.

3.   Amos Wilder, *Early Christian Rhetoric: The Language of the Gospel* (Cambridge, MA: Harvard University Press, 1971), p. 28.

4.   Cf. Amos Wilder, *Jesus' Parables and the War of Myths: Essays in Imagination in the Scriptures* (London: SPCK, 1982), especially pp. 121–32, 'The New Voice'.

5.   Cf. Stephen D. Moore, *Literary Criticism and the Gospels: The Theoretical Challenge* (New Haven: Yale University Press, 1989).

6.   Cf. Mary Ann Tolbert, *Sowing the Gospel: Mark's World in Literary-Historical Perspective* (Minneapolis: Fortress Press, 1989), especially pp. 49–50.

2. *The Genre of the Gospels and Ancient Narrative*

An alternative approach to the set of questions outlined earlier is to view the gospels in the context of ancient narratives, especially historiography and biography. In their helpful book entitled *The Nature of Narrative*,[7] Robert Scholes and Robert Kellogg talk about the gradual emergence of history as a particular form of narrative, which could be distinguished from mythic accounts which were concerned with the affairs of the gods and heroes rather than the causal relationships between the acts of humans, which is the proper subject of history writing. An interest in human affairs independently of the gods or of fate marked a major shift in human self-understanding. Yet the ancients never quite forgot, in the way that moderns are all too liable to do, that the enterprise in which they were engaged was *mimesis* or re-presentation of the past, that is, in the words of a modern critic 'a telling not a showing'. This awareness made them at once more realistic, but also more creative than some moderns who live under the tyranny of nineteenth-century ideas of 'the past as it really was'. We shall return to that point in the final part of this paper, but in order better to address the questions posed we must first discuss the gospels within the context of ancient narrative. Three issues call for a brief discussion: namely, defining genre; the nature and functions of biography in the ancient world; and the gospels as types of ancient biography.

a. *Defining Genre*
'Genre functions as a norm or expectation to guide the reader in his/her encounter with the text', according to one account. In the words of another theorist there is a 'generic contract' between author and reader, whereby the author shows that s/he intends to follow some at least of the recognized conventions of a particular genre, and the reader engages with the meaning of the text on that assumption. Insofar as the question of genre has been raised in gospel studies, a much more rigid understanding than that suggested by these definitions has been operative, however, namely, one in which genre is seen as a set of fixed rules to which an author is expected to adhere, leading to firm boundaries between different, but related types of writing. Such an understanding has its origins in ancient theory going back to Aristotle, who speaks of genres as *eide* or forms, thus implying an ideal type according to the Platonic notion of abstract forms. While theoretic discussions continued in the Roman period along these lines, nevertheless it is quite clear that in practice many authors operated with mixed genres, allowing for variety and creativity to play a role.[8]

In contrast to this taxonomic or classificatory understanding of genre, theologian David Tracy calls for a productive understanding of the notion, which refuses to separate form and content, and so shares in and contributes to the imaginative

7.   Scholes, Robert, and Robert Kellogg, *The Nature of Narrative* (London: Oxford University Press, 1966).
8.   Richard Burridge, *What are the Gospels?: A Companion with Graeco-Roman Biography* (SNTSMS, 70; Cambridge: Cambridge University Press, 1992), pp. 26–38.

enterprise that produces any work of literature, be it historical or romantic. Tracy writes as follows:

> Genre does not merely classify, anymore than the power or impetus behind it, namely the imagination, merely reproduces. Genre produces the meaning of the text. It accomplishes this not by remaining in the participatory understanding of the original experience. Rather the ability to employ a genre distances the author from the original experience into an expression of its meaning, by way of the production of a structured whole, a work, which allows the meaning to become shared.[9]

In line with his philosopher colleague, Paul Ricoeur, Tracy, therefore, rescues imagination from notions of the fanciful, and locates it in its rightful place in the production of meaning. This includes also the choice, use and to some extent exploitation of the various options available within any given cultural setting for bringing foundational experiences to language. While indications of genre choices presume certain expectations in the reader/hearer, they also demand careful attention to the individual adaptations that a writer may have undertaken, especially in the case of mixed but related genres. In the case of a 'great work', Tracy's 'classic', this will often mean that the author plays on the reader's expectations in order to change, or even subvert them by the use of what Tracy describes as 'the analogical imagination'. Thus understood, the creative use of genre needs not exclude the 'newness' at the heart of the Christian story, something that caused the kerygmatic school to claim the gospels as a 'unique genre'. Even though Tracy's own treatment of the gospel narratives leans towards this kerygmatic rather than an historical approach with his interpretation of the Christ event as Manifestation and Proclamation, his views on genre are highly significant for our discussion of the gospels. In order to understand this phenomenon properly we must abandon the notion of an intricate, standard biographical form, developed and passed on through the centuries, and instead see the range of features that could be employed and the functions that they served.

b. *The Development of Biography*
It is generally recognized that biography developed within the broader category of historiography, but also had close associations with the encomiastic tradition whereby men of renown were given public honour for their service to the city, either during their life or after their death. Thus, while Herodotus, 'the father of history', was interested in the causes and sequence of the Persian War, at various points in the work he breaks off to deal with the character and exploits of important individuals engaged in the action on both sides of the conflict. From this interest in individuals and their roles in determining human affairs, fourth-century Athens saw the emergence of the *Bios* or Life as a discrete genre, which could apply to philosophers as well as statesmen and military leaders. Socrates in particular proved to be a fitting and an enduring subject for praise because of his nobility, steadfastness

---

9.   David Tracy, *The Analogical Imagination: Christian Theology and the Culture of Pluralism* (London: SCM Press, 1981), pp. 127–30, especially p. 129.

and in particular because of the manner in which he faced his death. He had also to be defended against his detractors who accused him of subverting the best interests of the state. The towering figure of Alexander the Great and his exploits was also to prove a highly suitable subject for biography in the Hellenistic period, one that lent itself to many different treatments – philosopher-king, military leader of a pan-hellenic movement, great explorer, founder of cities and bringer of culture, the ideal ruler. The biographic genre was highly congenial to the Romans also, because of their respect for familial traditions as well as the exigencies of the honour/shame culture, where the propaganda value of biography was fully exploited, especially with regard to the imperial court. Yet in Plutarch's *Parallel Lives* of Greek and Roman characters the most enduring legacy of Roman biography is achieved. Here the *Bios* genre is employed for moral exhortation, presenting examples of the virtuous life to be imitated, a facet that is not unimportant in discussion of the gospels also.

It has sometimes been said that the Jewish tradition was not interested in biography. Certainly, later Rabbinic literature shows little inclination for the biographical as such. Anecdotal and typical stories, mainly about Rabbis, are scattered throughout this corpus of literature, but they are mostly subservient to the need for expounding some point of *halacha*, and show little interest in dealing with a character in a particular social or historical setting.[10] It is quite remarkable, and indeed ironic, that we know so little about Rabbi Judah ha-nasi, the editor and propagator of the Jewish law-book, the *Mishnah*, almost contemporaneous with the consolidation of the fourfold gospel with its four different portraits of Jesus circa 200 CE. In the various accounts of early Israel of the Pentatuech and the Deuteronomic and Chronicler's Histories, the achievements of such important characters as Moses, Joshua, the Judges, David and Solomon form part of the larger narratives, and the perspective is on the fate of all Israel rather than on any individual. These various agents merely direct the destiny of the nation on Yahweh's behalf as his representatives.

With the prophets, on the other hand, one encounters a strong sense of the individual, who often stands over against the unfaithful people, and whose task it is to remind Israel of its calling. Already in the books of Amos and Hosea, biographical elements are interwoven with the collection of oracles which form the prophet's message. But it is with the figures of Jeremiah and Ezekiel that the biography of the prophet and his message can be said to shape the work as a whole. The life experiences of other prophetic figures such as Jonah and Daniel are also intimately bound up with their mission. Only recently has scholarly attention been directed to the collection known as the *Vitae Prophetarum*, to be dated probably to the first century CE. These consist of biographical information about various prophets, especially their deaths, and were possibly intended as accompaniments to the reading of the prophetic books in the synagogue prayer service.[11] Philo's *Life of Moses* from

10. William Scott Green, 'What's in a Name? The problem of Rabbinic Biography', in *idem* (ed.), *Approaches to Ancient Judaism: Theory and Practice* (Brown Judaic Series, 1; Missoula, MT: Scholars Press, 1978), pp. 77–96.

11. Anna Marie Schwemer, *Studien zu den frühjüdischen Prophetenleben* (2 vols.; Texte und Studien zu Antiken Judentum, 49 and 50; Tübingen: Mohr, 1995–96), I (1995), pp. 51–52.

the Hellenistic milieu of first-century Alexandria, is the outstanding example of Jewish historiography, and one that can throw considerable light on the gospels also. The beginning and end of the work reflect many of the traditional features of the *Bios* genre, yet the work as a whole is thematically rather than chronologically arranged and Moses is presented in a thoroughly Platonic colouring in line with the author's own philosophical and apologetic interests.

c. *The Gospels and Ancient Biography*
This sketch of the development of ancient biography as it emerged in Greece and Rome as well as among the Jews bears out the contention that the genre was indeed a flexible one, touching on several other types of literature and capable of serving various functions in ancient societies. Inevitably, this raises the question as to what are the distinguishing features, and in particular what criteria should be applied in deciding whether or not the gospels also can be seen within this larger framework. In this regard two recent studies of the problem adopt a comparative approach that seeks to be more exhaustive than any that have so far been attempted. Significantly, both acknowledge the need to avoid rigid categories of what constitutes an ancient Life, and aim to focus instead on features that are shared by a large array of writings from the ancient world that would generally be regarded as biographical in some sense, writings that have a 'family resemblance' to each other, therefore.

Richard Burridge in his monograph, *What are the Gospels?* identifies four characteristic sets of features common to a wide range of ancient biography that he has examined. These are (1) *Opening features*: title and prologue; (2) *The subject*: a single individual as the main focus of attention and the centre of the action as indicated by the frequency with which this person is the subject of verbs in the work, in contrast to the amount of space allotted to other characters; (3) *Internal features*: topics to do with the main character (birth, ancestry, education, deeds, virtues, death), style, tone, characterization, values, setting and chronology and declarations of authorial intention; and finally (4) *External features*: use of sources, size, structure, smaller literary units (anecdotes, sayings, speeches dialogues etc.).

In the light of categories such as these the gospels fit well within the parameters of what might be described as a *Bios* in the ancient world. Most striking perhaps is the high percentage of verbs in all the gospels of which Jesus is the subject. This indicates how much the various writers focus on the person and deeds of the main character. Another feature that the gospels have in common with ancient biography according to Burridge's description is the variation in terms of the amount of space within the work devoted to certain aspects of the main subject's life, for example, the passion stories, whereas other aspects receive only cursory treatment.

Burridge's analysis is based on a representative sample of ancient literature and draws attention to various features of ancient biography not usually considered in comparisons with the gospels. His method allows for considerable variation within the overall genre but has been criticized for being somewhat vague and for not dealing adequately with certain topics which are highly distinctive features of ancient Lives, namely those listed by him under 'internal features'. The 1996 Heidleberg dissertation of Dirk Frickenschmidt, *Evangelium als Biographie*[12] attempts to address this very issue, again drawing on a very wide sample of ancient lives, 142 in all. According to Frickenschmidt, from an early stage of the development of biography there existed a brief biographical outline with a three part structure which was intended to summarize the details of an individual's life, either in the context of history-writing or for encomiastic purposes. This formed the basis for the subsequent development of the full-blown *Bios* genre, and it offered plenty of opportunity for development in various directions in all three parts.[13]

The *first* part covers the person's life from birth and background to their appearance in public, covering as many as 19 different *topoi* or themes – birth, genealogy, ancestry, omens or prophecies of greatness to come, name, education and training, physical attributes, nearness to the gods, test of character through a first temptation, travels – all aspects that can be echoed if not actually paralleled in the gospels. The *middle* part of the biography allows for a chronological or thematic development, or a combination of both. Here deeds and sayings (*chreiai*) of the person are recounted, reactions of wonder and praise registered, but also the negative reaction of enemies acknowledged. It is in this section that the essential aspect of the character of the subject is developed through the narrative mode rather than by a simple listing of virtues. Deeds and words reveal (*apokalyptein*) or manifest (*deloun*) the hidden quality of the person and there is a special emphasis on wondrous deeds (*thaumata*) which can also be described as signs/*semeia*.

Here Frickenschmidt makes some very interesting observations about different emphases in Greek, Roman and Jewish biography. The Greek version is based on an Aristotelian anthropology which identifies the universal virtues, such as moderation, courage, the practice of asceticism etc. of the subject, based on his *physis* or nature, whereas the Roman approach is more pragmatic and places greater emphasis on the public rather than the inner side of the personality. Virtues like liberality and humanity, especially when exercised for the good of the Roman people are to be admired, but also the courage to resist tyrants, even if this brought about banishment or death. In the Jewish context one can see a special emphasis on the subject's closeness to God and their endowment with the spirit of God in their actions and utterances. Philo's *Life of Moses* can stand for all in this respect with its extraordinary description of Moses' intimacy with God: 'As a friend of God Moses entered into the very same darkness within which God was; that is, into the formless, invisible, non-corporeal pattern of existing things, where he perceived what is forever invisible to natural sight' (*Life of Moses* 1.158). At the same time, Philo's Moses is the epitome of Greek virtue, so that the work exemplifies just how eclectic an ancient author could be in drawing on various styles of biographic portraiture to depict their subject adequately in terms of the *akme* or peak of their life.

12.   Dirk Frickenschmidt, *Evangelium als Biographie: Die Vier Evangelien im Rahmen antiker Erzählkunst* (Tübingen: Franke Verlag, 1997).
13.   The speeches in the early chapters of Acts of the Apostles provide a possible example of such early summaries of the life of Jesus. Thus, e.g. Acts 10.37–42 forms an accurate summary of Mark's Gospel in terms of the three stages of the unfolding story – 'beginning in Galilee', going around 'doing good' and the death and resurrection in Jerusalem.

Finally there is the *third* part of the biography dealing with the death and vindication of the subject. Here again themes familiar from the gospels can be readily
identified. These include prophecies and portents of doom; betrayals, plots and
intrigues; arrests and escapes; trials and pseudo-trials; farewell speeches and last
words; detailed description of the last days of the subject and their attitude to death;
reactions of bystanders and miraculous signs; and finally, heavenly ascensions and
assumptions.

There can be little doubt that once one examines the range of themes and motifs
associated with ancient biography, especially as these have been investigated by
Burridge and to a greater extent still by Frickenschmidt, the gospels do fit into this
general category of ancient biography. The 'family likenesses' are real and there is
no reason to question the conclusion of an eminent ancient historian, Günther Zuntz,
that any ancient reader/hearer of these works would undoubtedly have recognized
them as belonging to the *Bios*/Life category, and have judged them accordingly.[14]
And yet there are real differences that should not be overlooked, not least the fact
that several different lives of Jesus appeared quite early and that from these a fourfold gospel emerged and established itself within the first hundred years. This multiplicity and variety of Lives of Jesus clearly points to something distinctive about
the significance of his career for various groups of followers. The only remotely
comparable examples in that regard in antiquity are Socrates and Alexander the
Great, but apart from the fact that these were both public figures in a way that Jesus
was not, one has to ask why the multiplicity of gospels so early and what kind of
imaginative freedom allowed for such a development within less than a century
after his death.

Burridge suggests that what makes the case of Jesus different is the fact that the
gospels belong to a particular type of Life, namely, the philosophical rather than
the political, and this explains why discourse is so important but not a precise
chronology. In other words, within the general classification *Bios,* certain types of
biographic narration occur and these can be distinguished in terms of the subject to
be treated and the combination of the motifs that are appropriate in any particular
instance. Others, most notably C.H. Talbert, have sought to distinguish various categories of Lives in terms of the functions that they served and to classify the different gospels accordingly.[15] While Talbert's proposal of five different types of ancient
Lives, each with its own specific purpose has been criticized for its over reliance on
function to the neglect of formal aspects of biography, he has nevertheless high-
lighted the need to explore the setting and purpose of biography in antiquity, and
by association the same applies to the gospels also. One assumption of Redaction
Criticism of the Synoptic Gospels has been that the evangelists sought to speak to
specific 'situations in the life of the community'. This makes it possible to explain
why more than one gospel was required, since social, cultural and religious situ-

    14.   Günther Zuntz, 'Ein Heide las da Markusevangelium', in Cancik (ed.), *Markus-Philologie,*
pp. 205–22.
    15.   Charles H. Talbert, 'Biographies of Philosophers and Rulers as Instruments of Religious
Propaganda in Mediterranean Antiquity', in *ANRW* II, 16.2 (1978), pp. 1619–51.

ations varied considerably within early Christianity as we can also see from the Pauline letters with their different emphases in addressing the various churches.

3. *Creative Imagination, Genre and History*

The argument of this study has been that the creative imagination behind the early Christian experience expressed itself not in the development of a *sui generis* type of writing as Bultmann and Wilder had claimed, but rather in the ability of certain people to adopt a form that was well established in the Graeco-Roman world and adapt and mould it to various specific situations, drawing on the rich repertoire of motifs available. In doing so there was no constraint to conform rigidly to a set pattern or to restrict themselves to one single account, in the way that nineteenth-twentieth century sensibilities about history-writing demanded. Luke, the most self-conscious of these early Christian biographers of Jesus, is aware that many before him had undertaken the task of producing an account of the things that had been accomplished among them, and yet this did not preclude him from engaging in the same enterprise. In terms of David Tracy's account of genre, Luke has his own in-sightful experience of the meaning of those events and wants to share that with Theophilus and the readership that he represents. This very formal introduction to his work which Luke constructs along classical lines evokes suitable expectations from the outset, and yet, as a Graeco-Roman reader, Theophilus would not have been at all surprised that the subsequent account differed from others he may have read/heard previously. Indeed he would have been surprised if such had not been the case.

The fact that the gospels are to be judged in the context of ancient biography can throw an interesting light on the age-old problem of their historical reliability. This was not a new problem when in the eighteenth century it arose in the context of debates about the historical Jesus. Already in the second century pagan detractors like Celsus had spotted the differences between the different accounts of Jesus' life that were in circulation, and sought to discredit him and the Christian movement accordingly. Indeed the impulse for Tatian to produce his famous *Diatessaron* or harmony of the four gospels almost certainly arose in the context of the need to refute such detractors. For the most part modern debates about the gospels' his-toricity have been concerned with the pre-gospel traditions and their formation, and the question of genre has not featured in discussions about the historical character of the completed works. That is because the modern notion of history as 'hard facts' obscures the mimetic dimension of history-writing, which implies distance from the original experience of the event or person, and therefore calls for an active imagination in order to represent the subject adequately.

As well as the historiographical there are also the biographical and the encomi-astic aspects to be considered. Plutarch, one of the best known of the ancient biog-raphers was well aware of the apparent conflicts between these different modes. 'I am writing biography, not history', he states in the introduction to his *Life of Alexander*, explaining his task in terms of a portrait painter who brings his own particular insight to bear on the character of his subject, a character that could be discerned from small details or words more than from famous battles and sieges, which are the stuff of history. In another place he again resorts to the same image of the portrait painter in describing the task of the encomiast, who must follow the truth exactly and give it fully, even when it involves narrating some blemishes in the character of the subject, 'lest one abuse the memory of the subject with a false and counterfeit narration' (*Life of Cimon* 2).

It is not difficult to envisage the role of imagination in the encomiastic and biographical dimensions of the gospels. Praise is close to worship, and certainly the early Christian literary achievement took place in an atmosphere of worship. 'Let every tongue confess that Jesus Christ is Lord to the glory of God the Father' (Phil. 2.11) is generally recognized as reflecting early Christian hymnody, echoing what the pagan writer Pliny reports about the Christians' eucharistic gatherings in the province of Bithynia: 'they sing hymns to Christ as to a God' (*Letters* 10.96). This is the atmosphere of awe and austerity which Wilder detected in the Passion story, and which pervades the whole. To acknowledge this background of the gospels' narratives is not, however, to identify the works as 'cult legends' as Bultmann and Wilder would have it. Rather, it reflects the overall context within which early Christian imagination was nurtured, namely, a context of belief in Jesus as the long-awaited Messiah of Jewish hopes, and the need for a coherent account of salient aspects of his deeds and words for the cultic re-enactment of his life 'in memory of him'. The uniqueness of the gospels is that that memory was given definitive and lasting expression in a *Bios*-like narrative that was written from the post-resurrection perspective that heightened the encomiastic aspect, without excluding the historical and biographical also. Thus the gospels were intelligible for both Christian and non-Christian readers alike, representing a highly significant dimension of early Christianity's adaptation to the larger environment in which they found themselves.

Underlying the whole enterprise of early Christian gospel-production is the historical dimension of the new movement based on the memory of a real human being who had walked among them. Jesus of Nazareth was no mythical figure or demi-god, but one of them. Biography as a narrative form may have evolved from ancient myth and epic, and later developed into romance and novel, but in the Greek and Roman periods it dealt with historical characters, those who were deemed to have influenced history in important ways. That was the daring aspect of the early Christian self-expression, namely the claim that Jesus of Nazareth, a Jew from an outlying region who had died a criminal's death at the hands of the Romans, had in fact changed history – and changed it irrevocably. It was that understanding that impelled those who did not represent the literate and political elites to co-opt a genre which had previously been employed in the celebration of 'great ones', and adapt it to their particular needs, historical as well as kerygmatic. Therein lay the inspiration for their daring act of literary as well as theological imagination that gave new vitality to an ancient genre. In line with their new understanding of themselves came a new understanding of time, so that past, present and future could now be blended into a single multi-dimensional type of narrative in which all aspects of human life are concentrated.

THE FOUR GOSPELS AND THE ONE GOSPEL OF JESUS CHRIST*

Martin Hengel

1. *The Aporia*

As is shown by the beginning, ἀρχὴ τοῦ εὐαγγελίου Ἰησοῦ Χριστοῦ, Mark, the earliest evangelist, calls his narrative of Jesus εὐαγγέλιον, message of salvation.[1] He uses a word, which had already been a key term of Paul for his missionary, *oral* preaching.[2] According to Galatians Paul received his 'Gospel', which was not narrated but proclaimed as teaching, through a special revelation, and according to him there is no other 'message of salvation' than this one.[3]

It is part of the riddle, of the New Testament that this *one* message of salvation has found written expression in *four* writings of a biographical kind, which often differ. Each of them bears the designation τὸ εὐαγγέλιον, supplemented by the author: κατὰ Μαθθαῖον, κατὰ Μάρκον, κατὰ Λουκᾶν, κατὰ Ἰωάννην. Thus we have four written versions of the one message from *very* different authors. Only later did the church speak of four 'Gospels' in the plural: τὰ εὐαγγέλια. Up to the middle of the second century Christian texts use only the singular, because there can be only one εὐαγγέλιον Ἰησοῦ Χριστοῦ.[4]

* This lecture is a summary of my book *The Four Gospels and the One Gospel of Jesus Christ* (trans. John Bowman; London: SCM Press, 2000), hereafter Hengel, *Gospels*. Evidence and arguments, which the reader may miss here, may be found in the book. I confine myself here to the most important information.

1. Mark 1.1. About the philological roots of the earliest Christian use of εὐαγγέλιον which itself depends on the verb εὐαγγελίζεσθαι, see Hengel, *Gospels*, pp. 3.210–11 n. 9. It is found in the Old Testament and Jewish usage of the verb *biśśar*, for instance in Deutero-Isaiah and the Psalms and of the derived substantive *bᵉśôr á ṭôbá*. It is independent from the use in regard to the Emperor Cult, which has been exaggerated in research. The famous inscription of Priene has, like most examples of Greek usage the plural εὐαγγέλια, which is not found in the New Testament. Cf. P. Stuhlmacher, *Das paulinische Evangelium* (FRLANT, 95; Göttingen: Vandenhoeck & Ruprecht, 1968).

2. The seven definitely genuine letters of Paul (Rom., 1 and 2 Cor., Gal., Phil., 1 Thess., Phlm) use it sixty times, a usage which is unique in the whole of ancient literature. Mark follows with eight times (including the secondary 16.15). Otherwise it is rare in the New Testament: Mt., four times, Acts, twice; 1 Pet. and Apocalypse, once. In Lk., Jn (Gospel and Letters), Heb., Jas and Jude it is missing completely. In Apoc. 14.6 the word has the neutral meaning of 'message' and is not specifically Christian.

3. Gal. 1.6–8.11f.

4. Before Irenaeus it is found only twice: once in Justin, *1 Apol.* 66.3. ἐν τοῖς [...] ἀπο-μνημονεύμασιν, ἃ καλεῖται εὐαγγέλια and in Apollinaris of Laodicea, in Dindorf (ed.), *Chronicon*

Only in Justin do we find a single occurrence of the plural εὐαγγέλια for our four Gospels. Elsewhere he avoids it and prefers to use the formula 'reminiscences of the apostles'.[5]

That brings us to our topic: How is it that we have the narrative of Jesus' activity in a fourfold and often contradictory form in the New Testament and what is the origin of these texts? A single Gospel about Jesus would have already spared the church – to the present day – much soul-searching.

2. Harmonization or Radical Reduction?

This question is not new; it was already a preoccupation of the early church. Around 180 CE, Irenaeus was the first to use something like a 'canon' of recognized apostolic writings. That he had to defend the fact of *four* 'apostolic' Gospels with a variety of arguments indicates not only that the existence of the Four-Gospels-Collection was older, but also that it had been attacked. He makes a virtue of necessity and argues, that the εὐαγγέλιον τετράμορφον expresses the perfection of apostolic tradition, since the Gospel in its divinely willed fourfold form is: 'held together by *one spirit*'.[6]

When Justin, around 150 CE, says that the reminiscences 'were composed by apostles and their successors', he is already thinking of the two 'apostolic' Gospels of Matthew and John and of the two successors Mark and Luke.[7] That there was a dispute about the number four later still is shown by the Roman presbyter Gaius, who denied the authenticity of the Gospel of John, claiming it to be a product of the arch-heretic Cerinthus. So, for Gaius the Fourth Gospel was an impudent forgery by John's opponent. The reason given was 'historical-critical': it deviated all too much from the Synoptics.[8]

Celsus, the first pagan literary opponent of Christianity, read all four Gospels and found rich ammunition in them. His accusation against the Christians was that 'some of the faithful, as though coming from a drinking bout, fought one another and altered the Gospel after it had first been written down three or four times, indeed many times, and falsified it, so that they could better reject arguments against it'.[9]

Paschale ad exemplar Vaticanum (Bonn: Weber, 1832), 1, pp. 13–14. Only Irenaeus, in connection with his 'fourfold Gospel', uses the plural 'the Gospels' a few times.

5. Ἀπομνημονεύματα τῶν ἀποστόλων which he uses 15 times, much more than εὐαγγέλιον which appears only twice in the singular and once in the plural. The non-Christian readers understood the literary meaning of ἀπομνημονεύματα better, which he took from Xenophon, whose ἀπομνημονεύματα Σωκράτους he quotes in *2 Apol.* 11.3 (= Xenophon, *Memorabil.* 2.1.21ff.,) see Hengel, *Gospels,* pp. 212 n. 13.

6. *Adv. Haer.* 3.1.1; 3.11.8: τετράμορφον τὸ εὐαγγέλιον, ἐνὶ δὲ πνεύματι συνεχόμενον, see Hengel, *Gospels,* pp. 10ff., 214–17 n. 29–47. Even in Irenaeus the singular is still much more usual. The plural is found only in connection with the defense of the four-Gospel-collection.

7. *Dial.* 103.8; Hengel, *Gospels,* pp. 20.221f. n. 83–85. In *Dial.* 106.3 he mentions Mk 3.16 as 'reminiscences of Peter'.

8. Hengel, *Gospels,* pp. 21.222 n. 86; *idem, Die Johanneische Frage* (WUNT, 67; Tübingen: Mohr, 1993), pp. 26–27.

9. Origen, *Contra Celsum* 2.27; Hengel, *Gospels,* pp. 22.222. n. 89-90.

Here he was arguing that the Christians altered their original 'message' to avoid accusations. The 'three' or 'four times' is a reference to the Gospel-collection, the number of which was not yet clearly recognized everywhere, while the manifold forgeries refer to the 'apocryphal Gospels' written in the second century. Such charges are continued by later enemies, from Porphyry and Julian up to Faustus, Augustine's Manichaean opponent; it compelled Augustine to write his defence, *De consensu evangelistarum.*[10]

It is all the more surprising, therefore, that the early church resisted the temptation to replace the four Gospels with a Gospel Harmony, which would have done away with all these problems. Around 170 CE, Tatian, from Syria, a pupil of Justin, created such a harmony, the so-called διὰ τεσσάρων (εὐαγγελίων), the One Gospel from the Four, by working the Gospel material into the framework of John. Initially the Diatessaron became established in the Syriac-speaking East, but later it was displaced by the four 'separate' Gospels of the mainstream church. However, revised versions of the Diatessaron were translated into numerous languages ranging from Persian and Arabic to Middle English, since a unitary work continued to be popular.[11]

This means that in this early period the texts of the Gospels could still be changed. That is also evident from the numerous harmonizing parallel supplementations. Moreover during the first half of the second century sayings of Jesus were still being quoted with a relative freedom: they were not yet untouchable 'sacred text' in the strict sense. However, that does not mean that the textual tradition in the manuscripts was arbitrary. The text of the Gospels is the best-transmitted text in antiquity. We possess approximately thirty-five Gospel papyri of the pre-Constantine era and about seven or eight of them may go back to the very early third or to the second century. Nearly all the alterations and interpolations can be picked up in the multiple textual tradition. The most important of all is the famous Chester Beatty Biblical Papyrus I (P[45]) with all four Gospels and Acts in one large codex. In size, age and importance, it is an unique text-witness.[12]

This freedom in dealing with the earlier Gospel writings, which was still widespread in the second century, may have caused Tatian to compose his Harmony, which was worked out with scrupulous accuracy. He wanted a complete summary of the 'apostolic testimony' about Jesus, which had been split into four versions, as a *really unitary work* and thus create a superior counterpart, much richer in content, to a quite different unitary Gospel, that of Marcion, who around 144 CE had been expelled from the church in Rome because he claimed that all apostles except Paul had falsified Jesus' message of the 'gracious Father'. Marcion's approach was not that of synthesis, but of rigorous reduction: he wanted to purge the Gospel of Luke

10. See the fundamental book of H. Merkel, *Die Widersprüche zwischen den Evangelien* (WUNT, 13; Tübingen: Mohr, 1971). Cf. also John Granger Cook, *The Interpretation of the New Testament in Greco-Roman Paganism* (STAC, 3; Tübingen: Mohr, 2000), pp. 26–27, 197.

11. For Tatian see William L. Petersen, *Tatian's Diatessaron. Its Creation, Dissemination, Significance and History in Scholarship* (VCSup, 25; Leiden: Brill, 1994) and his contribution to this volume.

12. Hengel, *Gospels*, pp. 26–31. See B. Aland's article in this volume.

of all 'Jewish leaven', claiming it as the only true one, which Paul had received from Christ. Thus Marcion too wanted radically to do away with the offensive multiplicity and through 'literary criticism' to regain the original form of the gospel revealed by Christ to the one true apostle, Paul.[13]

3. *The Testimony of Irenaeus*

Around 180 CE, Irenaeus opposes what in his view is real 'apostolic tradition' against radical reduction. This tradition is the divinely willed *unity* of the four Gospels, the Acts of the Apostles, the letters of the three most significant apostles and the Apocalypse.

According to him, the apostles first preached the Gospel 'but later by God's will also handed it down to us in scriptures'.

> Matthew composed his Gospel among the Hebrews in their language, when Peter and Paul were preaching the Gospel in Rome and founding the church (there). After their death, Mark, the disciple and interpreter of Peter, handed down to us the preaching of Peter in written form. Luke, the companion of Paul, set down the Gospel preached by him in a book. Finally John, the disciple of the Lord, who also reclined on his breast, himself composed the Gospel when he was living in Ephesus in Asia.[14]

Scholars have been fond of describing this account as a late apologetic legend. However, it is a tradition, which must be taken seriously, written from a Roman perspective. Its form corresponds to the short notes about authors in the catalogues of ancient libraries. Presumably it came from a Roman church archive. In Rome, where after the destruction of Jerusalem all threads of the communities came together, they already had the four Gospels. These short notes about each writing and its author were kept in the archive there; they were important for reading them aloud in worship, since people had to know what was being read there. From the beginning the Gospels required a title for their use in worship, similar to the Old Testament scriptures.[15] This is confirmed by Justin about 150 CE according to whom the 'reminiscences of the apostles', that is three (or already four?) Gospels or the books of the prophets, that is Old Testament texts were read at the Christian services on Sunday morning, a custom which may go back to the beginning of the second or the end of the first century.[16]

---

13. For Marcion see the unsurpassed work of Adolf von Harnack, *Marcion: das Evangelium vom fremden Gott; eine Monographie zur Geschichte der Grundlegung der katholischen Kirche* (Wissenschaftliche Buchgesellschaft, 1921; reprint Darmstadt, 1960) and the informative article of Barbara Aland, 'Marcion/Marcioniten', *TRE* 22 (1992), pp. 89–101.

14. *Adv. haer.* 3.1.1.

15. Hengel, *Gospels*, pp. 34–38: About the Roman perspective and the Church-archives in Rome see C.-J. Thornton, *Der Zeuge des Zeugen: Lukas als Historiker der Paulusreisen* (WUNT, 56; Tübingen: Mohr, 1991), pp. 10–54.

16. *1 Apol.* 67, 3. Justin, a former Platonic philosopher, converted to the Christian faith about 130 CE in Asia Minor. The form of the service he describes is in its first part the 'service of the word' and nearly identical with the Synagogue-Service: it therefore must be old. See e.g. the

4. *The Order of the Gospels*

The *order* of the four Gospels according to Irenaeus is an indication of the age of the collection. If we leave aside the problematical 'Hebrew' Matthew, it corresponds precisely to the chronological order of their origin: Mark, Luke, and John. Mark is the earliest, followed by Luke, who uses it; John presupposes both but gives a quite different account. The Gospels were composed between around 70 and 100 CE. The Hebrew Matthew of Irenaeus, apparently the earliest, remains a riddle, because our Greek text of Matthew is not older than about 90–95 CE and is dependent on Mark and probably on Luke.[17] So on the whole Irenaeus, or better the Roman archive, seems to be rather well informed about the circumstances of the composition of the Gospels.

It is known by these sources that Mark wrote his Gospel after the deaths of Peter and Paul. Irenaeus does not say that Mark wrote his Gospel in Rome, as Clement of Alexandria shortly later reports, since that was generally known there; this is pre-supposed in the statement that Mark wrote his Gospel after the death of Peter and Paul (64 CE) and 'handed down to us', namely the Roman community. On the other hand, he correctly reports the origin of the fourth Gospel in Ephesus in Asia. Here for Christians in Rome a geographically more exact information was necessary.

This order of the Gospels in Irenaeus, based on the chronological order of their composition, is confirmed by the order in most of the great uncials since the fourth century, Vaticanus, Sinaiticus, Alexandrinus. This order appears already in an early papyrus, P^{75}, a Codex which dates from the end of the second century, with Luke followed by John, thus confirming the already traditional order. It was probably the second codex following a first one containing Matthew and Mark. Further witnesses are the Muratorian Canon and the earliest prologues of the Gospels.[18] Three different texts in a collection of books have six possibilities of sequence and four already have twenty-four. So this order cannot be pure chance.

It is striking that not all four Gospels are attributed to apostles, but – as Justin already emphasizes – also to (at least two) of their disciples, namely as we know Mark and Luke, and further that their works were manifestly *older* than John. It is also striking that the so-called Western order as in Codex D with the apostolic Gospels

synagogue-like community prayer at the end of *1 Clem.* 59.2–61.3 which surely comes from the Roman liturgy. See now the *Habilitationsschrift* of H. Löhr, *Studien zum frühchristlichen und frühjüdischen Gebet: Eine Untersuchung zu 1 Clem 59 bis 61 in seinem literarischen, historischen und theologischen kontext* (WUNT, 160; Tübingen: Mohr, 2003). Cf. also *1 Clem.* 2.1: The words of Christ and his sufferings presuppose the reading of the Gospel.

17. About Matthew see Hengel, *Gospels*, pp. 68–78 and about his relation to Luke, pp. 169–207. The Greek Matthew (written *c.* 90–95 CE) is surely no translation from 'Hebrew' (i.e. 'Ara-maic). Papias, two generations earlier than Irenaeus, knows about a collection of *Logia of Jesus* in Aramaic by Matthew. But this collection had not the title 'εὐαγγέλιον' which was first given to Mark (see above p. 14). The name of Matthew was conferred upon the first Gospel (coming from an anonymous Jewish-Christian scribe and able theologian) to give him apostolic authority, which was an innovation.

18. Hengel, *Gospels*, pp. 38–47, 233–38 n. 159–94. Cf. M. Hengel, *Studies in the Gospel of Mark* (London: SCM Press, repr. 1997 [1983]), pp. 64–84.

Matthew and John at the beginning followed by and then the apostle-disciples Luke
and Mark did not prevail. The 'historical' order was stronger because it was older.

5. *The Superscriptions of the Gospels*

The unusual list in Irenaeus already presupposes the superscriptions of the Gospels.
They are attested by a few early papyri, P[75], P[66] and P[64], reports of second- and
third-century church fathers and by the earliest translations.

Their original form is uniformly εὐαγγέλιον κατὰ Μαθθαῖον, and so on, 'the
Gospel *in the version* of Matthew, Mark, Luke or John'. Here the form customary
in ancient book titles, in which the name of the author is put first in the genitive and
followed by the title of the work, is deliberately avoided.[19]

The evangelists are not meant to appear as biographical authors, like others, but
to bear witness in their works to the one saving message of Jesus Christ, each in his
own version. The genitive was only possible for the name of Jesus Christ: εὐαγγέλιον Ἰησοῦ Χριστοῦ (Mk 1.1). He is the real author and the contents of the
Gospel.[20]

This means that these superscriptions were not added to the Gospels secondarily,
long after their composition, say when the four Gospels were first brought together
in a great codex; since in the second century they primarily still circulated as individual writings. The codex form, which was still very rare in the ancient world at
that time, was above all a Christian achievement. It set the sacred books of the new
community apart from the scriptural scrolls of its Jewish mother. The collection of
the four 'Jesus biographies' into a collection of church scriptures developed only
step by step in the libraries of leading communities and by using them in worship.
We must therefore distinguish between the collection of the four in one codex,
which is later, and the collecting them as single codices in the book cupboards of
the church libraries. From the thirty canonical Gospel manuscripts which Lührmann
counts up to the end of the third century, sixteen are from John, twelve from Matthew, seven from Luke and only one from Mark in P[45] (our Chester Beatty Biblical
Papyrus I). This shows that in the Pre-Constantinian era the single Gospel codex prevailed and that Matthew and John had totally superseded Mark. Obviously Mark
survived only in the bookcases of large communities but very seldom in the Egyptian Chora.[21]

This also excludes the possibility that for a long time the Gospels had been
circulating *anonymously* in the communities. For if they had only been given their

---

19.   In the New Testament e.g. Ἰακώβου ἐπιστολή or for biographies Πλουτάρχου βίοι
παράλληλοί, Φιλοστράτου βιοὶ σοφιστῶν or τὰ ἐς τὸν Τυάνεα Ἀπολλώνιον etc. This usual
form of a book title was generally accepted since Hellenistic times by its use in the famous library
of Alexandria.
20.   Hengel, *Gospels*, pp. 48–49, 239–40 n. 196–202.
21.   D. Lührmann and E. Schlarb (eds.), *Fragmente apokryph gewordener Evangelien in
griechischer und lateinischer Sprache* (MThSt, 59; Marburg: Elwert, 2000), see the schedule p. 22.
Besides that he enumerates fourteen all of them very fragmentary texts older than the fourth century from 'apocryphal Gospels' or from a similar genre [p. 23].

titles at a secondary stage in quite different communities, this must necessarily have resulted in a multiplicity of titles. There is no trace of that. Not only their uniformity from Alexandria to Lyons and from Antioch to Carthage before the end of the second century but also references in the second century itself, show their great age.[22]

Moreover, contrary to a widespread view, Marcion with his one purified Gospel was not the first to prompt the bringing together of the four-in-one collection. It was the other way round. As the examples of Justin and Tatian show, Marcion's radical reduction furthered the production of Gospel Harmonies on the basis of three or four texts. However, after Marcion such harmonies could no longer establish themselves, since the plurality of the gospels had already largely found recognition before him, and since from the beginning, names from the apostolic age were connected with them.[23] The 'apostolic' authority of the four (or three) Gospels is not therefore a consequence but the presupposition of the Marcionite reduction to one Gospel.

Already before Marcion, Basilides of Alexandria wrote 'Twenty-Four Books on the Gospel'; the singular 'Gospel' is typical of this early period. But already Basilides seems to have known several Gospels. According to Origen there was even an εὐαγγέλιον κατὰ Βασιλίδην. Possibly the Gospel text of his work was, like that of Justin, a harmonizing mixture, disseminated as εὐαγγέλιον κατὰ Βασιλίδην. This too as the simple title εὐαγγέλιον with Marcion is a sign that this form of title was already a model in the first decades of the second century. That also follows from the titles of individual apocryphal Gospels, the majority of them gnosticizing. They imitate an already recognized form of title, as in the case of the 'Gospel according to Peter', 'to Thomas', 'to Philip', 'to Mary' and others.[24] 'Apocryphal Gospel texts', that were produced up to the Middle Ages, received specially the names of 'apostolic' authorities.

6. Papias' Note about Mark and Matthew

In the time of Hadrian (117–38 CE), the Bishop of Hierapolis composed an 'Exegesis of the Sayings of the Lord' in five books, which Eusebius quotes in his *Church History*. In it, Papias is the first to speak of two Gospel authors, Mark and Matthew. He made enquiries about the oral traditions of the disciples of Jesus from the 'elders', who include two otherwise unknown figures, Ariston and 'John the elder', 'the disciple of the Lord', whom he himself had heard.[25] From him he has this report about Mark:

22.   Hengel, *Gospels*, pp. 50–58; pp. 240–47 n. 203–41.

23.   Already Justin used some sort of harmony from three Gospels for catechetical purposes. But only his pupil Tatian took the fourth Gospel as a frame for his whole harmony. The tendency for harmonization leads to many harmonizing additions in the text of the four Gospels especially in the second century.

24.   Hengel, *Gospels*, pp. 57–60; pp. 245–49 n. 230–51. The title 'Gospel' was sometimes secondarily added, so e.g. in the gospel of Thomas. This shows how strong the importance of this title had become in the second century. See J.M. Robinson's article in this volume.

25.   Eusebius, *Hist. Eccl.* 3.39.1-7; Hengel, *Johanneische Frage*, pp. 75–95.

This also the 'elder' says: Mark, who was the interpreter of Peter, wrote down carefully, but not in the right order, everything that he remembered. For he had neither seen the Lord, nor had he followed him, but later (he followed) Peter, who shaped his teachings to the needs (of the hearers), however, not in such a way that he gave an orderly account of the sayings of the Lord. So Mark did not make a mistake in writing down some things as he remembered them. For he had one concern, not to omit anything that he had heard or to falsify anything in it.[26]

This is not an apology, but a moderate criticism, probably from the 'higher' standpoint of the Gospel of John, which has the right 'order', and, unlike Peter's presentation of Jesus' teaching, gives an 'ordered account'. This Mark was not an eyewitness and wrote down only 'some things', 'as he remembered them'. So the tone is more negative. Papias wants better accounts about Jesus. Presumably his informant, 'John the elder', is identical with the 'elder' of 2 and 3 John, the author of 1 John and the Gospel.[27] He emphasizes the importance of Peter, but stresses the superiority of the 'ideal' Beloved Disciple. 1 Peter (5.13), 'She who is also elect in Babylon sends you greetings; and so does my son Mark', also indicates a connection between Peter and Mark in Rome. 'John the elder' is here handing on to Papias, probably a younger member of his wider circle of disciples, a tradition which extends well back into the first century and confirms Irenaeus' report of the 'origin' of the second Gospel.

The note about Matthew seems to deal with his Gospel even more critically: Matthew compiled the sayings (of the Lord) in the Hebrew language; but everyone translated them as he was able.[28]

It is impossible for this to refer to the canonical first Gospel, since that was originally written in Greek and not translated from an Aramaic original; the addition about the arbitrariness of different translations is even more incomprehensible. The Greek Matthew is based on Mark and reproduces more than eighty percent of it. This shortened story of Mark is supplemented with the birth narrative, and expanded with five great discourse complexes. Matthew is said to have worked into these besides his special material primarily material from the problematic *Logia Source*. Here, I suppose that he also used the earlier Luke.[29] Probably the information of Papias, like the note on Mark, also goes back to John the 'elder', who knew that there was a collection of sayings of the Lord in Greek which circulated in

26. Eusebius, *Hist. Eccl.* 3.39.14-15.
27. Hengel, *Johanneische Frage*, pp. 96–119.
28. Eusebius, *Hist. Eccl.* 3.39,16: Ματθαῖος μὲν οὖν Ἑβραΐδι διαλέκτῳ τὰ λόγια συνετάξατο, ἡρμήνευσεν δ'αὐτά, ὡς ἦν δυνατὸς ἕκαστος.
29. Matthew written between 90 and 95 CE or even 100 CE is about 10–15 years later than Luke and presupposes the institutions of the 'Rabbinate' founded by the Synhedrium of Jabne. Luke is much better informed about details of the Jewish war 66–70 CE (and deeply moved by it) and also about its prehistory since the procurator Felix and its consequences. Matthew writes like John in a rather large temporal distance from the catastrophe. Besides that the 'non-apostolic' Gospels of Mark and Luke are older than the 'apostolic' ones. In the second century Mark would have received the title 'Gospel according [to] Peter' and Luke 'Gospel according [to] Paul'. Marcion preferred a 'corrected' Luke, because he believed him to be the pupil and travel companion of Paul. About the whole problem see the last chapter of Hengel, *Gospels*, pp. 169–207; 303–23 n. 663–807.

different versions, since 'each had translated them as he was able', and which ultimately went back to an Aramaic original attributed to the apostle Matthew.[30]

Papias' enigmatic negative note did no harm to the first Gospel. On the contrary, of all the four Gospels, Matthew quickly gained the strongest influence on the church for it contained what the communities needed.[31] Only at the end of the second century is it equalled by John with its christological orientation as the εὐαγγέλιον πνευματικόν of which Clement of Alexandria speaks. A further reason why the first Gospel established itself so quickly was its allegedly direct apostolic origin. This gave it, as later with John, a greater authority than its forerunners Mark and Luke, who were only known as disciples of the apostles.

In all probability the unknown Jewish-Christian teacher from the borders of Palestine circulated his work, modelled on the earlier Mark, as εὐαγγέλιον κατὰ Ματθαῖον, perhaps with the indication that it was based ultimately on a very early collection of 'sayings of the Lord' by the apostle Matthew. We must assume that such works were sent soon after their completion to the most important communities with covering letters. In other words, the self-confident evangelist gave his work an apostolic name and wrote it for the whole church; this is shown by the universal mission command at the end to all apostles or by the *introitus* of the Sermon of the Mount: 'You are the salt of the earth [...] You are the light of the world'.[32]

7. The Evangelist Mark and the Peter Tradition in Rome

In reality the Gospel of Mark is the earliest Gospel written in Rome shortly before the conquest of Jerusalem. Its Roman origin is indicated by an unique number of Latinisms.[33] Such an accumulation of Latinisms (and of Aramaisms) are quite unusual in pagan and Christian literature. The only exception is Hermas which was also written in Rome. The eschatological discourse (ch. 13) reflects the evangelist's experiences of the Neronian persecution and the confusion of the Roman civil war. The martyrdoms under Nero influence the invitation to take up the cross and follow Jesus. Nero was the first to have Christians crucified and burned as nocturnal torches. Peter is said to have been crucified at that time.[34] Such connections make it probable that the earliest 'evangelist', Mark, was really a companion and interpreter of Peter. Probably the Greek-Palestinian John Mark from Jerusalem is to be seen as the author. He was acquainted with both Paul and Peter, but was closer to Peter. It is quite understandable that the Galilean fisherman needed an interpreter on his

30. The τουθ' [...] ἔλεγεν of the presbyter at the beginning of *Hist. Eccl.* 3.39.15 corresponds to the ταῦτα ἱστορῆται [...] at its end and to the ταῦτ' εἴρηται of Papias at the beginning of 3.39.16. The 'presbyter' is the most important informant of Papias.

31. See W.-D. Köhler, *Die Rezeption des Matthäusevangeliums in der Zeit vor Irenäus* (WUNT, 2.24; Tübingen: Mohr, 1987).

32. Mt. 5.13–16; 28.18–20.

33. Hengel, *Gospels*, pp. 78–89, 259–66 n. 318–67.

34. Mk 8.34; Tacitus, *Ann.* 15.44.4: aut crucibus adfixi atque flammati. About the crucifixion of Peter see already Jn 21.18, for later evidence see Hengel, *Johanneische Frage* (n. 9), pp. 210–11 n. 19: Tertullian, *Scorp.* 15.3; *Acta Vercell.* 35–41; Porphyrius according Macarius Magnes 3.22 etc.

missionary travels because he spoke only broken Greek. After the deaths of the leading men of the first generation, Peter, Paul and James the Lord' s brother, between
62 and 64 CE, Mark must have gained a special reputation. His writing, quite novel in
earliest Christianity, managed to establish itself in the communities and to be used
by Luke and the author of the first Gospel only because a recognized authority and
not an anonymous gentile Christian stood behind it. This first 'Gospel', revolutionary
in its form and content, was not written by a person of no standing. Critical New
Testament scholarship seems here to be too uncritical in regard to real history. Earliest Christianity was bound by authority, beginning with the unique personality of
Jesus. Nothing has led research into the Gospels so much astray as the romantic
superstition involving creative community collectives and anonymous 'ghostwriters'
that are supposed not only to have formed the oral tradition but also to have produced whole writings. The fact that Simon Peter stands behind the Gospel of Mark
follows from the Gospel itself, since he is given unique significance in it only a few
years after his death. He is not only the first disciple, but also the one whose name
appears last – quite unnecessarily. The angel at the tomb gives the women the
instructions: 'But go and tell his disciples and Peter that he will go before you into
Galilee'. The 'and Peter' is superfluous. It is a clear *inclusio:* Simon Peter is named
first and last in the Gospel to show that it is based on his authority.[35] He is the only
disciple on whom Mark puts special emphasis; he is mentioned twenty-five times,
stands at the head of all the lists of disciples, and has received the honorific title
'Rock' by Jesus, which displaces his personal name. With two exceptions, he is the
only disciple to appear as a conversation-partner of Jesus. These multiple mentions
of Peter were intended by the author.

It should further be noted that the period of transmission between Jesus and the
author of Mark is less than 40 years. He is not too far removed from the original
events, and he has emphasized the name of Simon Peter as his most important
bearer of his tradition. However, his 'Gospel' is not to be understood as a simple
historical report to satisfy the curiosity of its hearers and readers. All his narratives
are intended as proclamation, but nowhere is there mere 'proclamation' without a
concern to offer a dramatic '(hi)story' of Jesus. And as a narrator he also remains
aware throughout of the chronological distance between him and the fundamental
Jesus event.

8. *Mark's Narrative about Jesus as 'Gospel'*

Because 'biography' and 'proclamation' are fused in his work, Mark can call his narrative about Jesus 'saving message', that is, an account of Jesus' activity which
brings about faith and thus salvation. Accordingly the narrative about John the Baptist is the 'beginning of the Gospel of Jesus Christ': ἀρχὴ τοῦ εὐαγγελίου. In

---

35.   Mk 1.16 Simon is mentioned twice and also 16.7: εἴπατε τοῖς μαθηταῖς αὐτοῦ καὶ τῷ
Πέτρῳ. Mt. 28.7 omits this superfluous καὶ Πέτρῳ. Cf. also Mk 1.36 for the group of the earliest
disciples: Σίμων καὶ οἱ μετ᾽ αὐτοῦ and the unique story about the healing of his mother in law
1.29ff.

contrast to all the later evangelists, Mark uses the word εὐαγγέλιον seven times.[36] The last mention (Mk 14.9) is the most illuminating; here Jesus rejects the disciples' indignation about the woman who anoints him: 'Truly, I say to you, wherever the Gospel is preached (κηρυχθῇ) in the whole world, what she has done will also be told (λαληθήσεται) in memory of her'. Here the unity of narrative and proclamation is evident. Mark presupposes that this story of the anointing is not an unimportant episode but belongs to the Gospel, which is preached and narrated 'in all the world'. Given the towering significance of Peter, we may see him as the most important 'narrator' of this saving message for the author, Mark.[37]

This dramatic 'kerygmatic-biographical Jesus story' that is closely connected with Simon Peter is not just meant to inform but also to win over the hearts of hearers to belief in the Messiah Jesus. Mark's work, despite his quite different account, has the same aim as the fourth Gospel: 'But this is written that you may believe that Jesus is the Christ, the Son of God' (Jn 20.31). Here the misunderstanding, indeed the egoistical self-centredness, of the disciples and especially that of Peter, in Mark are emphasized even more unsparingly: the vicarious atoning death of Jesus is for them all.[38] The sinful disciple Simon Peter has experienced the salvation brought about by Jesus to which Mark, his own disciple, bears witness, just as much as the former persecutor Paul.

9. The Origin and Dissemination of the 'Gospels' and their Uniform Title

There are some indications that this work, so revolutionary in content, grew out of a living oral presentation and from the beginning was intended to be read out in worship. Johann Herder, the friend of Goethe, already saw this: 'His Gospel is written to be read out aloud' for it 'is a church Gospel written from living narrative for public reading in the community'. The majority of early Christians could not read and needed the Gospel to be read to them in worship. We should therefore speak rather of 'hearers' of the Gospels of Mark, Matthew and John than of 'readers'.[39] Luke is a special case: It was written originally for 'the most excellent Theophilus, and for his relatives and necessary friends' (Acts 10.24).[40] All the points mentioned, make it probable that Mark, the first kerygmatic 'biography' of Jesus was put into circulation relatively quickly from Rome under the title εὐαγγέλιον κατὰ Μάρκον. So it became – necessarily – known to the later evangelists, first of all Luke, then to the anonymous author of the first Gospel and last to John. But the later Gospels no longer have this accumulated, sevenfold use of εὐαγγέλιον: the term does not appear at all in Luke and John, and in Matthew it appears only four

---

36.   Mk 1.14; 8.35; 10.29; 13.10; 14.9; (16.15).
37.   Hengel, *Gospels*, pp. 90–96; 266–69 n. 368–95.
38.   Mk 10.45; 14.22–24.37ff. 66–72.
39.   See Hengel, *Gospels*, pp. 96; 269–70 n. 397. Cf. Mk 13.4; *Apoc.* 1.3; Justin *Apol.* 1.67.3.
40.   Cf. Lk. 1.1–4; Acts 1.1; cf. also 10.24–33; 25.23 and the address κράτιστε to the Procurators Felix and Festus 23.26; 24.3; 26.25. That all demonstrates the milieu of the addressee. We do not know if this Theophilus (his name can be an alias) was a baptized Christian. Cf. Acts 13.7–12.

times.[41] Probably, Matthew's work was put into circulation after 90 CE, under the analogous title εὐαγγέλιον κατὰ Μαθθαῖον, now for the first time under the name of an apostle. So it was able to push its simpler 'precursor', Mark, into second place, indeed almost to displace it.

The situation with Luke-Acts, which was written about ten or fifteen years earlier, is more difficult. In this real 'Jesus biography', the word 'Gospel' does not occur, but the verb εὐαγγελίζεσθαι 'to proclaim the saving message', is used by Luke more frequently than Paul, whose travelling companion he was. Only in Acts does he speak twice at a decisive point of preaching the 'Gospel', once in the mouth of Peter and once in the mouth of Paul.[42] From this I conclude that Luke knew that the term εὐαγγέλιον also played a role in the Petrine preaching as a summary of the saving message. It is no coincidence that the word also appears once in 1 Peter,[43] as well as in all the letters of Paul.

But back to Luke.[44] For him – in a Pauline way – εὐαγγέλιον in the mouth of Peter or Paul means the oral message of salvation after Easter, especially for the Gentiles, and not as in Mark a 'biographical' account of Jesus. Therefore despite his model, Mark, he does not use this word at all in the Gospel and contents himself with the verb εὐαγγελίζεσθαι. Therefore in the preface Lk. 1.1-4, he does not say that the 'many' had composed a 'Gospel' before him; they only had 'compiled a narrative (διήγησις) of the events'. He prefers a neutral term and proves himself to be – far ahead of his time – the first Christian historian and apologist. His brief preface, unique in early Christianity, resembles those in the scientific writings of antiquity, not least those by doctors. Probably he is identical with 'Luke, the beloved physician' of Col. 4. The simple 'Gospel according to Mark' is no longer adequate as reliable instruction for the 'very noble Theophilus', so Luke wants to write a better biography. We find the first quotations in educated Christians like Basilides and Justin. Marcion took it over because it came from a disciple of Paul. All three already knew it with the title εὐαγγέλιον κατὰ Λουκᾶν. In my view Theophilus, who was honoured and instructed by the work, put it into circulation under this title, copying Mark's title and sending it to other communities.

---

41.   It occurs three times with the addition τῆς βασιλείας: 4.23; 9.35; 24.14. Only in 26.13 = Mk 14.9 do we have τὸ εὐαγγέλιον τοῦτο which already presupposes the written Gospel.

42.   Acts 15.7: Peter at the apostolic council: [...] διὰ τοῦ στόματός μου ἀκοῦσαι τὰ ἔθνη τὸν λόγον τοῦ εὐαγγελίου καὶ πιστεῦσαι, 20.24 Paul in the farewell address at Miletus: διαμαρτύρασθαι τὸ εὐαγγέλιον τῆς χάριτος τοῦ θεοῦ: both texts are the last great speeches of the two apostles before a community. They can be considered as their legacy.

43.   4.17: τῶν ἀπειθούντων τῷ τοῦ θεοῦ εὐαγγελίῳ cf. 5.13' Ἀσπάζεται ὑμᾶς ἡ ἐν Βαβυλῶνι συνεκλεκτὴ καὶ Μᾶρκος ὁ υἱός μου. Both the use of the word εὐαγγέλιον and the mention of Mark as the pupil of Peter in Rome connects this pseudepigraphic letter from the end of the first century with the c. 20 years earlier Gospel of Mark and with the later reliable church traditions in Papias, Irenaeus, Clement of Alexandria and the old Gospel prologues. Cf. Hengel, *Gospels*, pp. 99–100.

44.   See the important study of Loveday C.A. Alexander, *The Preface to Luke's Gospel* (SNTSMS, 78; Cambridge: Cambridge University Press,1993); cf. also my review-article about the commentary to Acts of J. Jervell, *Der Jude Paulus und sein Volk: Zu einem neuen Actakommentar*, Theologische Rundschau 66 (2001), pp. 338–68.

Once the works of Mark, Luke and Matthew had been circulated under this form of title, later imitators were compelled to use it. If a new account of Jesus' earthly ministry wanted recognition, it should bear the title 'Gospel'. This was familiar and indicated a unique content, 'the saving message of Jesus' as a story and the authority standing behind it as author. Texts without titles had little chance to find acceptance in the communities of the church. Only esoteric literature like some texts of the Nag Hammadi library, written for small 'enlightened' conventicles made an exception. But even there titles had been later added secondarily. This need must be also applied to the fourth Gospel according to John, edited by the disciples of John the Elder after his death under the title εὐαγγέλιον κατὰ Ἰωάννην, which could be also related to John the son of Zebedee.[45] His gospel distances itself from the account of the Synoptics and goes its own way. Here christological 'dogmatics' have nearly absorbed the story of Jesus and transformed it.

It is almost a miracle that the church preserved the four earliest Gospels that we possess, despite their striking discrepancies, and resisted any attempt at harmonization. In so doing it created for itself a permanent cause of offence. The temptation to expand the series of four partially contradictory Gospels by new narratives about Jesus with additional 'information', like secret revelations of the Risen Christ, was stimulated further by the plurality of those which were already in existence shortly after 100 CE. On the other hand these four Gospels bore witness that the one 'truth of the Gospel' could be seen in a variety of ways and under different aspects.[46] The abundance of early Christian testimony about Jesus of Nazareth could never have developed in this way and borne rich fruit had it been based only on one harmonizing Gospel in the style of Tatian's *Diatessaron*.

10. *The Gospel as a Message of Salvation for the Whole Church*

Contrary to a widespread view, none of the four Gospels was written by and for one particular community. Each primarily gives the views of its author. So we should stop talking automatically about 'the community of Mark', 'Luke', or even worse of 'the Q community'. The Gospel-writers wanted to represent in their quite different forms the one truth for all believers basing themselves upon their own personal authority. Therefore their writings were disseminated relatively quickly in the larger communities of the empire. The exchange between these was lively from the start. The title 'message of salvation', εὐαγγέλιον, to be supplemented by the name of the author was quite appropriate for the new written biographical and kerygmatic 'narratives about Jesus', beginning with Mark's work in Rome. The differences between the four authors were accepted, because it was known that the 'apostolic testimony' had already had a variety of forms, since for a long time there had been 'Petrine', 'Pauline', 'Johannine' and 'Jewish Christian' teaching in the communities. The letters of Paul already indicate this multiplicity (and the tensions

45.   Cf. Jn 21.23-25. The title εὐαγγέλιον κατὰ Ἰωοάννην is already attested by the very early two Bodmer Papyri P[66] and P[75].
46.   For the term ἡ ἀλήθεια τοῦ εὐαγγελίου see already Paul Gal. 2. 5.14.

connected with it). There was dispute in the church from the beginning. That was very human.

It was the lively exchange between the important communities, which made it impossible later to reduce the multiplicity of Gospels to one Gospel. It is also improbable that, as is often claimed, communities as a rule had only a single anonymous Gospel book each. At best they will have preferred one text to others. The bookcases of the large and influential communities like Rome, Ephesus, Antiochia, Caesarea or Alexandria were already well equipped at the end of first century. We see it from the library of Clement in Rome, the Gospel of Matthew and later from Justin Martyr. In the end the church wanted the plurality of the Gospels, just as it also refused to prescribe a stereotyped 'unitary theology'. Despite the strong awareness of the unity of the church, there was an amazing multiplicity of doctrinal views, which constantly led to differences. Between 70 and 140 CE the thought and teaching of the church was almost too lively and there was much 'experimentation', often with vigorous arguments. In his preface Luke clearly refers to the prior work of the 'many'. He wants to improve it; however, he does not reject their work but builds on it. Thus 'plurality' does not necessarily mean chaos nor – as often today – a dismissal of the question of truth.

In the course of the consolidation of the church in the second century, the multiplicity of Gospel-like writings brought with it the danger that the tradition would run wild. This was countered through the adoption of the rule of faith and the monarchical episcopate, and by a concentration on the four earliest Gospels and the letters of Paul, which had been collected about 100 CE. Here it was believed that the 'apostolic testimony' of Jesus had been preserved 'unfalsified'. One essential reason for this 'consolidation' was the excessive religious philosophical speculation of Christian 'Gnostics', who (since the first decades of the second century) denied the reality of the humanity of Jesus, the saving significance of his death and the creation of the world as God's work, in favour of a Platonizing dualistic doctrine of the soul. From a historical perspective the appeal to the apostolic 'deposit of faith', which we already find in the Pastoral Epistles, was certainly open to attack, for there is no chemically pure, 'unfalsified tradition' in human possession. Human tradition is always shaped by those who hand it on and interpret it. Nevertheless, according to all our historical knowledge, theological judgment and a sober comparison between the apocryphal Gospel texts and the four Gospels, the church of the second century could not have made a better choice.

LITERACY, LITURGY, AND THE SHAPING OF THE NEW TESTAMENT CANON

Harry Gamble

Early Christianity presents us with a provocative paradox. On the one hand, it was a religious movement that from the very beginning was deeply invested in books, above all the scriptures of Judaism, but subsequently also Christian texts. On the other hand, it was a religious movement of quite limited literacy: only a very small percentage of Christians could read. On the face of it, this is a puzzling situation. I aim to explore the terms of this paradox, indicate how it was mediated, and finally suggest what this means for our understanding of the history of the biblical canon.

Christianity as a Bookish Religion

As far back as we can see into its history, Christianity depended on texts to warrant its fundamental proclamation that Jesus is the messiah of Israel. If we look to the earliest missionary and confessional statements available to us, we consistently find allusions to and quotations of Jewish scripture adduced in immediate support of Christian claims. According to the very old confessional formula cited by the apostle Paul but fashioned by those before him, 'Christ died for our sins *in accordance with the scriptures,* he was buried, and he was raised on the third day *in accordance with scriptures*' (1 Cor. 15.3b–4). Moreover, if we attend more generally to Paul's letters, which are the earliest extant Christian writings, we find that he himself frequently resorts to Jewish scripture in proof of the gospel. That Paul does this in writing to his predominantly or exclusively Gentile congregations shows that he clearly expected them both to be familiar with Jewish scripture, and to acknowledge its relevance and authority.[1] The same expectations are present in most of the rest of the earliest Christian literature, perhaps most impressively in the Gospel of Matthew, the Gospel of John, and the epistle to the Hebrews. The crucial role that Jewish

---

1.   In Paul's letters the scriptures of Judaism are cited approximately one hundred times, with high concentrations in Gal. and Rom., but a general absence in several other letters (Phil., 1–2 Thess., Phlm). From the latter fact the conclusion has been drawn (*e silentio*) that Jewish scriptures were not commonly used in Paul's churches (Adolf von Harnack, 'Das Alte Testament in den paulinischen Briefen und in den paulinischen Gemeinden', *SBAW* [1928], pp. 124–41), or indeed in Gentile Christianity generally during the apostolic period (W. Bauer, 'Der Wortgottesdienst der ältesten Christen', in G. Strecker [ed.], *Aufsätze und kleine Schriften* [Tübingen: Mohr, 1967], pp. 155–209). To the contrary, see my *Books and Readers in the Early Church* (New Haven and London: Yale University Press, 1995), pp. 211–14.

scripture plays in these writings was not freshly devised by their authors. Rather, they drew upon a tradition of scriptural exegesis and application that was rooted in the very beginnings of Christianity, and was already highly developed by the time it emerges into our field of vision in the Christian literature of the second half of the first century. And indeed it is almost impossible to imagine an early Christianity that was not constructed upon the foundations of Jewish scripture.

Beyond its reliance on the scriptures of Judaism, Christianity soon enough began also to produce its own writings: letters of authoritative teachers, narratives about Jesus, collections of his sayings, apocalypses, narratives about apostolic figures, manuals of community organization and the like. This was not, to be sure, literature of a belletristic sort that might appeal to any person of literary interest and taste. Nor was this literature intended to be, or initially taken to be, scriptural in its own right. Early Christian writings were, rather, a practical sort of literature that aimed to be serviceable to Christian communities, mainly in communication, instruction, documentation, edification, evangelism, and organization.

Early Christianity's heavy dependence on books was something that it had in common with Judaism, but in their bookishness Christianity and Judaism stood apart from all other ancient religious movements. Greek and Roman religions of the period, whether civic and public or private and voluntary, did not typically either produce or use texts on any scale that would enable them to be compared with Christianity and Judaism. Although in connection with those religions we are acquainted with various particular items – such as votive inscriptions, hymns, prayers, magical texts, aretaologies, and ritual manuals – there is nothing in quantity or type that would justify speaking of religious literature, and there is nothing that even begins to resemble the authoritative body of writings treasured by Judaism and adopted by Christianity as scripture, nor to approximate the early and on-going production of texts within Christianity.[2] Indeed, if judged in terms of its commitment to books, Christianity had a much closer resemblance to ancient philosophical movements and schools than to any contemporaneous religious movement.[3]

---

2.   William V. Harris, *Ancient Literacy* (Cambridge, MA: Harvard University Press, 1989), esp. pp. 218–21 and 298–306, and A.K. Bowman and G. Wolf, 'Literacy and Power in the Ancient World', pp. 1–16 (esp. pp. 12–14), and R.L. Fox, 'Literacy and Power in Early Christianity', pp. 126–48, both in A.K. Bowman and G. Wolf (eds.), *Literacy and Power in the Ancient World* (Cambridge: Cambridge University Press, 1994). For a demurer, see M. Beard, 'Writing and Religion: Ancient Literacy and the Function of the Written Word in Roman Religion', in J.H. Humphrey (ed.), *Literacy in the Roman World* (JRASS, 3; Ann Arbor: University of Michigan, 1991), pp. 35–58, who argues that texts played a larger role in pagan religions than allowed by William Harris. Yet Beard characterizes the role of texts in Graeco-Roman religion as 'symbolic rather than utilitarian', and even on her showing the texts in question hardly constitute a religious literature.

3.   On the general resemblances of Christianity to philosophical movements see E.A. Judge, 'The Early Christians as a Scholastic Community', *JRH* 1 (1960–61), pp. 125–37; R.L. Wilken, 'Collegia, Philosophical Schools, and Theology', in S. Benko and J.J. O'Rourke (eds.), *The Catacombs and the Coliseum: The Roman Empire as the Setting of Primitive Christianity* (Valley Forge, PA: Judson, 1971), pp. 268–91; W. Meeks, *The First Urban Christians* (New Haven: Yale, 1983), pp. 81–84, and L.C.A. Alexander, 'Schools, Hellenistic', *ABD* V, pp. 1005–11.

Christianity's orientation to texts was, moreover, something that stood out in the eyes of its ancient critics. When in the middle of the second century Lucian of Samosata satirized the figure of Peregrinus, what especially caught his attention about Christianity was its penchant for writing and interpreting books.[4] When, later in the same century, Celsus undertook his wide-ranging attack on Christianity, he knew he needed to acquaint himself with their books, and he did so.[5] When at the beginning of the fourth century the emperor Diocletian sought to disable and extirpate Christianity, his very first edict mandated that Christian books be confiscated and burned.[6] And when in the fourth century Porphyry sought to discredit Christianity, he did so mainly by criticizing their books.[7]

Thus both the early Christians and their detractors attest for us the particular interest that Christianity had in books and the importance that they attached to them. Early Christianity was manifestly a 'textual community', whose communal life was recognizably oriented around books.

Early Christian Literacy

The remarkably bookish habits of Christianity stand in sharp tension with another unquestionable fact, namely that very few Christians could read. The question of the nature and extent of literacy in the ancient world has only recently been systematically addressed in scholarship.[8] We know classical cultures principally through their literary remains, for which we have a deep appreciation, and so we have been content to assume that literacy was very widespread in the classical epoch. But it was not. In his stimulating book, *Ancient Literacy* William Harris has challenged our sanguine assumptions by arguing that throughout the entire period of classical Greek, Hellenistic and Roman imperial civilization, the rate of literacy in the population as a whole was about 10 percent, although in a few places and periods it may have been a little higher or a little lower.[9] Ordinarily only one in ten people had the capacity to read at any level (and writing, incidentally, was a separate and still rarer skill). Harris's study has provoked a large response, and although many have suggested refinements and qualifications of his view, even his critics agree that his general conclusion is unassailable. There was no mass literacy in the ancient world. The forces and institutions required to foster and to sustain widespread literacy were simply absent. Literacy tended to be the preserve of a small and mostly elite fraction of society as a whole.

But what about Christians in particular? Can we differentiate them from this larger picture and consider them characteristically more literate than their non-

---

4.   *De morte Per.* 11.

5.   Origen, *Contra Cel.* 1.34, 40, 58, 68; 2.24, 27, 32, 34, 36, 55, 59, 52; 6.16; 7.18.

6.   Eusebius, *Hist. Eccles.* 8.2.4–5, *Mart. Pal.* Praef. 1, *Vita Const.* 3.1.4.

7.   See R.L. Wilken, *The Christians as the Romans Saw them* (New Haven: Yale University Press, 1984), pp. 126–63.

8.   Harris, *Ancient Literacy*; for a variety of critical responses see Humphrey (ed.), *Literacy in the Roman World*; and Bowman and Wolf (eds.), *Literacy and Power*.

9.   Harris, *Ancient Literacy*, pp. 323–37.

Christian compatriots? Apparently we cannot. Even if we reject the traditional view that the constituency of Christianity was drawn mainly from the lower and least educated echelons of the population of the Roman Empire, the picture changes little. Modern studies of the social make-up of early Christian groups indicate that, especially in its urban settings, Christianity attracted a socially diverse membership representing a rough cross-section of Roman society, though lacking much representation from both its lowest and the highest strata.[10] Since members of the upper classes were less numerous, high levels of literacy would have been somewhat rarer in Christian circles, but moderate levels of literacy were probably about the same in Christian groups as outside them. Hence we cannot suppose that the extent or type of literacy was any greater among Christians than in society at large. If anything, Christians are likely to have been *less* literate, which is to say, fewer than one in ten could read, and probably fewer still in the small and provincial congregations that were typical of Christianity in its first centuries. We must assume, then, that the vast majority of Christians were illiterate, not because they were unique, but precisely because they were in this respect typical members of ancient society. Except among its political, military and literary elite, ancient society operated mainly through oral communication.

Yet to say only this is to neglect an important dimension of the situation. Although 'mass *ill*-literacy' was undeniably the rule in the ancient world, the literate and oral modes nevertheless intersected and overlapped, frequently and effectively, with the result that the illiterate majority had the opportunity to participate in literacy. And here we need to make several important observations about the relationships between writing and speaking, texts and speech, literacy and orality. While many theorists have proposed that there is a great divide between literacy and orality, and that the social, cognitive, linguistic and hermeneutical dynamics of oral and literate cultures are so distinct as to make them fundamentally incompatible and mutually exclusive, what we know about the societies of the ancient Mediterranean points in a different direction. There the oral and the written modes were certainly not incompatible or mutually exclusive, but co-existed in a complex synergy. This synergy was at work both in the production and in the use of texts.

In the production of texts an author normally dictated (orally) to a scribe, who wrote what he heard and thus produced a text from speech, converting the oral into the written. So common was this practice that the verb *dictare* came to mean 'compose' as well as 'dictate'. Likewise in the reproduction (or copying) of texts, in which the author of a text was not involved, a scribe normally dictated to himself, that is, read aloud the text he was copying, and transcribed into a new copy what he

---

10.   For the modern social description of early Christian communities, see Meeks, *The First Urban Christians*, esp. pp. 72–73 (on Pauline churches); in addition: E.A. Judge, *The Social Pattern of Christian Groups in the First Century* (London: Tyndale, 1960); G. Theissen, *The Social Setting of Pauline Christianity: Essays on Corinth* (trans. John Schutz; Philadelphia: Fortress Press, 1982); A.J. Malherbe, *Social Aspects of Early Christianity* (Philadelphia: Fortress Press, 2nd edn, 1983); P. Lampe, *Die Stat-römischen Christen in den ersten beiden Jahrhunderten: Untersuchungen zur Sozialgeschichte* (WUNT, 18; Tübingen: Mohr, 1987) and, for the second and third centuries, D.J. Kyrtatis, *The Social Structure of the Early Christian Communities* (London: Verso, 1987).

heard himself reading, in the process converting the written into the oral, and then the oral back into the written.[11] (Actually, we today tend to do the same thing when copying out a text.)

In the use of texts also we find a similar synergy between the written and the oral. In the ancient world, silent reading was virtually unknown. All reading, including private reading, was normally reading aloud.[12] The principal reason for this is to be found in the way texts were written, namely in *scriptio continua*, or continuous writing, in which there were no divisions (spaces) between words or paragraphs, nor any punctuation, so that the characters ran uninterruptedly across the lines and down the page, presenting the reader with an undifferentiated mass of text. A special effort is required to read a text written in this way: *scriptio continua* is most easily read phonetically, with the aid of the ear: the sense of the text arises only as the syllables are pronounced and heard. Even the literate commonly preferred not to exert themselves in private reading, but to be read to by a literate household slave or freedman.[13] But beyond these features of private reading, we must also note that ancient texts were very frequently read out in public. The occasions and venues of public reading were many and various, and I mention only a few.[14] When an author had composed a work, it was common practice for him to hold a *recitatio* or public reading, at which it was read out to a gathered company of the author's friends, patrons and admirers, and thus given its premiere.[15] But in many ordinary contexts of public life texts were read out to any and all hearers. Works of poetry and prose were read aloud at dinner parties, in small literary salons, in public

11. On the psychological and physiological aspects of visual copying see Alphonse Dain, *Les manuscrits* (Paris: rev. edn, 1964), pp. 40–46, and K. Junack, 'Abschreibpraktien und Schreibergewohnheiten in ihrer Auswirkung auf die Textuberlieferung', in E.J. Epp and G.D. Fee (eds.), *New Testament Textual Criticism: Its Significance for Exegesis (Essays in Honor of Bruce Metzger)* (Oxford: Clarendon Press, 1981), pp. 277–95.

12. The literature is now extensive: J. Balough, 'Voces Paginarum: Beiträge zur Geschichte des lauten Lesens und Schreibens', *Philologus* 82 (1927), pp. 84–109; L. Wohleb, 'Ein Beitrag zur Geschichte des lauten Lesens', *Philologus* 85 (1929), pp. 111–12; G.L. Hendrickson, 'Ancient Reading', *CJ* 26 (1930–31), pp. 182–96; E.S. McCartney, 'Notes on Reading and Praying Audibly', *CP* 43 (1948), pp. 184–87; F. Di Capua, 'Osservazione sulla lettura e sulla preghiera ad alta voce presso gli antichi', *RAAN* 28 (1953), pp. 59–99; B.M.W. Knox, 'Silent Reading in Antiquity', *GRBS* 9 (1968), pp. 421–35; W. Allen, 'Ovid's *Cantare* and Cicero's *Cantores Euphonionis*', *TAPA* 103 (1972), pp. 1–14; D.M. Schenkeveld, 'Prose Usages of *AKOUEIN* "To Read"', *CQ* 42 (1992), pp. 129–41; M. Schlusser, 'Reading Silently in Antiquity', *JBL* 111 (1992), pp. 499; P. Saenger, 'Silent Reading: Its Impact on Late Medieval Script and Society', *Viator* 13 (1982), pp. 367–414; R.J. Starr, 'Reading Aloud: *Lectores* and Roman Reading', *CJ* 86 (1991), pp. 337–43. The implications of this practice for the study of early Christian texts have been emphasized by T.E. Boomershine, 'Peter's Denial as Polemic or Confession: The Implications of Media Criticism for Biblical Hermeneutics', *Semeia* 39 (1987), pp. 47–68 (esp. 63–66); and P. Achtemeier, '*Omne verbum sonat*: The New Testament and the Oral Environment of Late Western Antiquity', *JBL* 109 (1990), pp. 3–27.

13. Starr, 'Reading Aloud' (n. 12).

14. See J. Carcopino, *Daily Life in Ancient Rome* (New York: Bantam, 1971), pp. 220–29, and E. Rawson, *Intellectual Life in the Late Roman Republic* (London: Duckworth, 1985), pp. 51–53.

15. On the *recitationes* see esp. K. Quinn, 'The Poet and his Audience in the Augustan Age', *ANRW* 30.1, pp. 75–180 (esp. 158–65).

forums and at the baths; but they were also read, and dramatic texts were performed, in theatres and at public festivals; rhetorical declamations by orators were made in public forums and diatribes were openly delivered by sophists and popular philosophers; and official decrees were read out to the general public, and so on. In all such circumstances texts were converted into oral pronouncements accessible to any who would listen. Ancient authors were all well aware that what they wrote would normally be not so much seen as heard in public reading, and hence they wrote more for the ear than for the eye. As a rule, then, no ancient text is encountered as it was intended to be unless it is read aloud.

The ways in which texts were produced and used signify a close interplay between the written and the oral. They also show us that the great illiterate majority were not disenfranchised from literature and literary culture, but had frequent opportunity, by means of public reading, to participate in it, to become acquainted with texts, and to appreciate their value. With this observation we come to a consideration of early Christian liturgy.

Early Christian Liturgy

We have said on the one hand that early Christianity had a heavy investment in books, yet, on the other hand, that the vast majority of Christians were illiterate, and unable to read those books. This paradox found its resolution in the context of early Christian worship, for here Christian texts were read aloud in the gathered assembly, and heard by literate and illiterate alike.

We know far less than we would like about the early Christian service of worship. The first detailed and instructive description of it appears only in the middle of the second century with Justin Martyr, who has this to say (*Apol.* 1.67):

> On the day called the day of the sun there is an assembly of all those who live in the towns or in the country, and the memoirs (*apomnemoneumata*) of the apostles or the writings (*suggraphai*) of the prophets are read for as long as time permits. Then the reader ceases, and the president speaks, admonishing and exhorting us to imitate these excellent examples. Then we all rise together and pray, and…when we have completed our prayer, bread is brought, and wine and water, and the president in like manner offers prayers and thanksgivings according to his ability and the people assent with Amen; and there is a distribution and partaking by all of that over which thanks have been given, and to those who are absent a portion is sent by the deacons.

Here we encounter a two-part service, consisting in the first of the public reading of texts by a reader and a hortatory address by the 'president' (bishop), and, in the second, of the celebration of the eucharist. I am interested here only in the former, the 'service of the word'.[16]

---

16.   On the service of the word, in addition to the older studies of P. Glaue, *Die Vorlesung heiliger Schriften im Gottesdienst* (Berlin: Duncker, 1907) and Bauer, 'Der Wortgottesdienst' (n. 1), see now J.C. Salzmann, *Lehren und Ermahnen: Zur Geschichte des christlichen Wortgottesdienstes in den ersten drei Jahrhunderten* (WUNT, 59; Tübingen: Mohr, 1994).

Justin was writing in Rome, but he described what he took to be the characteristic shape and substance of Christian worship wherever it took place. Although his account comes from about 150 CE, there is every reason to think that this sort of assembly for worship goes back to the very earliest days of the church. The service of the word – the reading and exposition of texts – closely mirrors the Jewish synagogue service, which Christianity, originally a sectarian offshoot of Judaism, must have adopted and adapted to its own use in its earliest days. The public reading of texts in the context of Christian worship is already taken for granted by the apostle Paul, who at the end of his earliest letter says, 'I adjure you by the Lord that this letter be read to all the brothers and sisters' (1 Thess. 5.27). The author of the letter to the Colossians (whether Paul or not) makes a similar request: 'When this letter has been read among you, have it read also in the church of the Laodiceans, and see that you read also the letter from Laodicea' (Col. 4.16). Late in the first century, the author of the Apocalypse clearly anticipated the public reading of his own book by pronouncing a blessing upon 'the one who reads [...] and those who hear' (Rev. 1.3). Somewhat later, near the beginning of the second century, the author of 1 Timothy admonished the church leader, 'Timothy', to 'attend to the reading of scripture, to preaching and to teaching' (1 Tim. 4.13). We must assume that originally and continuously Jewish scriptures were read in Christian assemblies, but it is clear that from a very early time Christian writings began to be read alongside them, and by the time of Justin readings were regularly taken from these two groups of texts, Jewish and Christian.[17]

In all instances there is one who reads. There developed by the end of the second century a minor order of the clergy called 'readers' (*anagnostai, lectores*), persons specifically chosen and formally consecrated for this task in each congregation. But in the earlier period this was not an official responsibility: the task of reading would have fallen to any member of the community who happened to be literate. For access to its books, a congregation was therefore dependent on the one, or on those few, who could read, and who did so in the assembly for worship. In this way the mainly illiterate congregation participated in literacy and became familiar with the texts that were read. The paradox with which we began is thereby resolved: the illiteracy of Christians generally was not a bar to their hearing and understanding of texts, which were routinely read aloud in the service of worship.

But we should ask: what was involved, attitudinally and actively, in the public reading of texts in the setting of Christian worship? Given the religious setting, we might expect that Christians would have taken towards their books attitudes that could be described as esoteric, or cultic, or ritualistic – attitudes that were natural in the larger religious environment of antiquity. For example, because most people were illiterate, texts were frequently viewed as mysterious objects, harbouring secrets difficult to access. Or again, texts might be thought holy, and given special handling that showed deep reverence toward them. Thus in Judaism texts of the

---

17.   Justin refers to the reading of 'the writings of the prophets *or* the memoirs of the apostles', which leaves open the possibility that on a given occasion the reading might be from only one group. But if Christian writings might be read alternately with Jewish scripture, this already implies that scriptural status had accrued to (some) Christian writings.

Torah were most carefully and exactly transcribed according to fixed conventions, and special gestures accompanied their use. Yet again, texts might be thought to have a certain potency that prompted ritualistic regard and use. But in fact we see nothing of such attitudes toward books in early Christianity.

What we see instead is a thoroughly pragmatic attitude. This can be deduced, among other places, from early Christian manuscripts themselves, which, although they are immensely valuable for their contents, are also richly informative as social artefacts that reveal much about their users. Here I wish only to mention a few features characteristic of our very earliest (second and third century) Christian manuscripts that symptomize this textual pragmatism. First, it is well known that virtually all early Christian manuscripts are codices, or leaf-books, whereas the conventional form of proper books was the roll. The codex was ordinarily used only as a mere notebook for recording ephemera, notes, and first drafts.[18] These codices were, accordingly, small and compact, having the appearance not of books but of pamphlets. As books went, Christian ones were unconventional, informal, and undistinguished. This suggests that when Christians began using the codex not merely for notes but as a vehicle of texts, they did so not because those books had a special status as aesthetic or cult objects, but because they meant them to be practical books for everyday use, the handbooks, as it were, of Christian communities.[19] Second, we should attend to the way these earliest Christian manuscripts are written. As a rule, they are written in a single broad column to the page, not in the elegantly tall, narrow columns that characterized literary works inscribed in roll books. Moreover, they were not written in the standard book hand typical of literary texts, characterized by careful script, well formed, separated, upright letters evenly maintained along a line, features that lent it clarity, regularity, beauty and high legibility. Yet neither were they transcribed in the ordinary documentary hand, a more rapidly written, less careful, semi-cursive script that was used to write workaday documents such as contracts, receipts, and letters. The hand in which Christian manuscripts were written lay in between these, and may be called 'reformed documentary'.[20] It has its closest affinities not with literary texts but with the documentary papyri, yet it is written with somewhat greater care, aiming at greater legibility. It is a third and intriguing feature of early Christian manuscripts that they regularly employ the convention of *nomina sacra* (sacred names), whereby certain words, most especially Jesus, Christ, Lord, God, but others besides, were written in a contracted form, usu-

18.   On the emergence of the codex as a book-form see C.H. Roberts and T.C. Skeat, *The Birth of the Codex* (London: Oxford University Press for the British Academy, 1987), and on its technological development see E.G. Turner, *The Typology of the Early Codex* (Philadelphia: University of Pennsylvania Press, 1977). For a survey see Gamble, *Books and Readers*, pp. 49–66.

19.   For artistic representations of codices which seem to indicate the ambiguous status and middle-class associations of the codex, see the remarks of Loveday Alexander, 'Ancient Book Production and the Circulation of the Gospels', in R. Bauckham (ed.), *The Gospels for All Christians: Rethinking the Gospel Audiences* (Edinburgh: T. & T. Clark, 1998), pp. 71–111, esp. pp. 79–82.

20.   C.H. Roberts, *Manuscript, Society and Belief in Early Christian Egypt* (Schweich Lectures, 1977; London: British Academy [Oxford University Press], 1979), pp. 14–23; cf. E.G. Turner, in *Greek Manuscripts of the Ancient World* (ed. P. Parsons; London: University of London Institute of Classical Studies, 2nd edn, 1987), pp. 20–21.

ally the first and last letters with a horizontal stroke over them. However this scribal practice arose, it quickly became standard.[21] This constitutes another affinity with documentary materials, where abbreviations were common, but it also suggests that early Christian manuscripts were intended for in-house use, since these abbreviations would have been readily intelligible only to Christians. Finally, I note that early Christian manuscripts appear to be generally better furnished with reading aids than other manuscripts – punctuation, accents, breathing mark, diareses – and sometimes we find in them fewer letters to the line, and fewer lines to the page than might be expected, all of these contributing to greater ease of reading.[22]

From such features of early Christian books it is a ready inference that they were produced with a view not to beauty but to utility. They do not have the character of literary manuscripts. They are constructed, rather, for practical use in the life of Christian communities, above all serviceability for reading, and more particularly for public reading.

The act of reading aloud publicly required both skill and preparation. It could not be done, and certainly not well, unless the reader closely familiarized himself with the text in advance, learning how to decode *scriptio continua*: what syllables went together to make a word, what groups of words constituted phrases and sentences, where to pause, where the voice should rise or fall, what to emphasize, and so on. Clearly, reading this sort of text was as much an act of interpretation as of merely decoding. Moreover, the reader had to enunciate clearly and project their voice. In sum, the reading was nothing less than an oral performance of the text, and the text served as the 'score'.

But there is a question remaining, namely why books were read at all in Christian worship. One answer, as I have suggested, is the merely historical one: this is what had been done in the synagogues, and it was naturally carried over into Jewish-Christian congregations, and passed from there into general practice also among gentile Christian communities. That historical answer, though probably accurate, does not quite address the question of purpose and effect: what was the reading of books meant to accomplish, and more especially, what did it actually accomplish? Here I find entry to the last element of my topic, the history of the canon.

The History of the Canon

The question of how, when, and why the New Testament came into being – a firmly delimited collection of precisely 27 documents – is still very much in dispute among biblical scholars and church historians. The dominant hypothesis in the twentieth century was that the New Testament canon took shape in consequence of the great theological controversies of the second century – with Marcionism, with gnosticism, and with Montanism – the cumulative effect of which was to require the church to fashion an exclusive collection of authoritative books to which it might appeal for

---

21. Roberts, *Manuscript, Society and Belief*, pp. 26–48.
22. See the comments of Roberts, *Manuscript, Society and Belief*, pp. 9–10, 14, 21–25, and Turner, *The Typology of the Early Codex*, pp. 84–87.

the support and vindication of its convictions.[23] To put this another way, the motive for the formation of the canon, and the actual function of the canon thus formed, have been conceived primarily and indeed almost exclusively in terms of the history of doctrine, so that the canon has been understood as a defensive weapon contrived in the service of orthodoxy. I believe this is a mistaken view, and that we need instead to conceive of the history of the canon *as a function of the history of the public reading and interpretation of scripture*, that is, as a consequence not of the history of doctrine, but of the history of liturgy. There is much to be said in favour of this, though here I can only mention a few salient points.

First, we need to be reminded that in its application to books or texts, the Greek word *kanon* did not have the sense of 'norm' or 'standard' or 'rule' (all of which were, however, common meanings of the word). It had, rather, the simple sense of 'list' or 'catalogue'.[24] The first to apply the term *kanon* to Christian books was Athanasius, bishop of Alexandria, in the middle of the fourth century, and by it he clearly meant 'the list' of books that are acceptable for reading in the church, that is, in the churches' service of worship.[25] When, about a half century earlier, Eusebius, bishop of Caesarea, considered which books were authoritative in the church he did not, like Athanasius, use the term *kanon* or speak of them as *kanonizomenoi* (canonical, or 'in the canon'). He rather spoke of books as 'acknowledged' (*homologoumenoi*) or 'disputed' (*antilegomenoi*) within the church (*Hist. Eccles.* 3.25.1-7). In judging whether a book was 'acknowledged', several criteria were important to him, including genuineness of authorship, but equally important was traditional usage.[26] This meant, on the one hand, books that had been cited and used by the earlier Christian writers with whose works he was familiar. But it also meant something else, and something more important, namely books that had been 'used publicly' (*dedemosieumenai*) in most churches. The verb, *demosieuein*, which Eusebius repeatedly employs, means 'to make public' or 'to make known publicly, and it can only refer to the public reading of such books in the service of worship. So the emphasis is upon the tradition of use, and above all on public (liturgical) use. Consistent, continuous, and widespread liturgical reading qualifies a book as 'acknowledged' or 'accepted', and the absence of such use is an important indication that a book is 'disputed' or 'spurious'. And if we turn to the famous Muratorian fragment,

---

23.   This view was taken by Adolf von Harnack, *The Origin of the New Testament and the Most Important Consequences of the New Creation* (trans. J.R. Wilkinson; London: Williams & Norgate, 1925), and, more fully by Hans von Campenhausen, *The Formation of the Christian Bible* (trans. J.A. Baker; Philadelphia: Fortress Press, 1972), and has been widely echoed in subsequent studies. I have expressed strong reservations about this dogmatic explanation of the history of the canon in *The New Testament Canon: Its Making and Meaning* (Philadelphia: Fortress Press, 1985), pp. 59–65. See now esp. I.P. van Tonder, 'An Assessment of the Impact of Second-Century Heretical Christian Movements on the Formation of the Catholic Christian Canon of Scripture' (dissertation, Cambridge University, 2000).

24.   Th. Zahn, *Grundriss der Geschichte des neutestamentlichen Kanons* (Leipzig: Deichert, 2nd edn, 1904), pp. 1–14; *Geschichte des neutestamentlichen Kanons* (Erlangen: Deichert, 1888–92), I, pp. 122–25.

25.   *De decretis Nicaenae synodi*, 18.3; cf. *Ep. Fest.* 39.

26.   Cf. G. Robbins, 'Eusebius' Lexicon of Canonicity', *StPat* 25 (1993), pp. 134–41.

which has been traditionally dated to the end of the second century, we find the author not only providing information on how various scriptural documents came into being, but also rendering judgments about their authority. Here the question is framed in terms of whether a book is 'received' (*recipere*) in the church, and this question is referred not to a theoretical criterion, but to a practical question, whether a particular book is to be 'publicly read to the people in church'.[27] The author's principal concern was with what may and may not be read *liturgically*, and that depended on what had *customarily* been read liturgically.

In all these instances we have appeals to the actual, long-standing usage of the church. Given the very low level of literacy in Christian communities, we must be careful to understand that usage necessarily refers to the liturgical setting in which these texts came to be read (usually by one) and heard (by all others). Over the years a *tradition of reading* had developed in Christian communities, but that also meant a tradition of hearing and a tradition of interpretation and understanding. It was this tradition that provided the basis, finally, for a determination of the canon, that is, the *catalogue*, of those books that might be read. Although from time to time the church appealed to various criteria of canonicity (e.g. authorship, derivation from the apostolic period, orthodoxy, etc.), the ultimate criterion for the canonical, authoritative status of a book was its reception by the church, and there could be no more certain or compelling indication of reception by the church than that such a book had over long years been publicly read in the service of worship.[28] In this sense we can say with full justice that the formation of the canon of scripture was nothing other than the church's retrospective recognition of its own reading habits, whereby the *de facto* tradition was finally made *de jure*.

We may perhaps judge the effect of the long-standing tradition of the liturgical reading of scripture from an intriguing episode of which we learn from the great bishop and theologian, Augustine, in a letter that he wrote to Jerome, the translator of the Vulgate.[29] In place of the Old Latin version that was in customary use in North Africa, Jerome's new Latin translation of the book of Jonah had been liturgically read to the Christian congregation at Oea (modern Tripoli, in Lybia). Augustine writes to Jerome that:

> In the course of this reading the bishop came upon a word [...] of which you have given a very different rendering from that which had long been familiar to the senses and memory of all the worshippers and had been read for so many generations in the church.[30] Then there arose such a tumult in the congregation, espe-

27. The Muratorian Fragment, Line 78, cf. lines 68-72. See J. Stevensen (ed.), *A New Eusebius* (London: SPCK, 1957), pp. 144–47.

28. On ancient criteria of canonicity, see the thorough discussion of K.-H. Ohlig, *Die theologische Begrundung des neutestamentlichen Kanons in der alten Kirche* (KBANT; Dusseldorf: Patmos, 1972), and, on the question of 'reception' by the church, pp. 269–95. For public reading, pp. 296–309.

29. Augustine, *Ep.* 71A, 3.5, cf. *Ep.* 75.

30. The text was Jon. 4.6, and the issue was the name of the plant that sheltered Jonah. The Hebrew was *qiqiyon*, which was rendered in the LXX as *kolokunthe* (round gourd, pumpkin), and in the Old Latin (to which Augustine's readers were accustomed) as *cucurbita* (gourd). Jerome's Vulgate rendering was *hedera* (ivy).

cially among the Greek-speakers, correcting what had been read and denouncing the translation as false, that the bishop was compelled to ask assistance from Jewish residents.

Finally the bishop buckled under this pressure, and reverted to the accustomed (Old Latin) rendering. As Augustine put it, 'the man was compelled to correct your version in that passage [...] since he desired not to be left without a congregation – a calamity which he narrowly escaped'.

This episode enlightens us about an important aspect of the liturgical reading of scripture. Within the whole range of scriptural literature, the particular text at issue here, the book of the prophet Jonah, was relatively minor. Other texts, certainly the Gospels, were no doubt read far more frequently. Yet the congregational hearers of this text had nevertheless become so familiar with it through public reading that they knew it by heart, and were so committed to it that when an unaccustomed and unexpected word was pronounced, they very nearly broke into a riot![31] Augustine speaks of how the text had managed to impress itself upon 'the senses and the memories of all the worshippers'. The congregation was not listening for new information, but for what they had heard time and time again and already knew, word for word. This incident occurred at the beginning of the fifth century (403 CE), but it gives us an important insight into the role of scripture reading in worship since the early years of the church.

We ordinarily bring a consumer attitude to texts and reading. When we read, we are looking for new information, and once we have extracted that information, we have no further use for the text. But liturgical reading depends upon another attitude, for the same texts are read over and over again, yet lose none of their value in the process, but rather gain in esteem. The worshippers in Tripoli wanted only to hear again what they had heard countless times already. This suggests that the role of liturgical reading lies in its ability to *remind* rather than to instruct. (It is perhaps worth recalling here that the Greek word for reading, *anagnosis*, literally means 'a knowing again', hence a *re*-minding.)

The practical effect of the liturgical reading of scripture in the early church was therefore not, in the first place, to provide information, but to shape and re-enforce the self-understanding of Christian congregations. Such reading invites involvement from the hearers, providing them with an opportunity to find themselves in the scriptural story, to enter the world of the text, and to be identified and socialized within that world.[32] The public reading of scripture is not only about the past, but also and equally about the present, to the extent that the hearers understand

---

31.   It may be that their familiarity with the text was not entirely dependent on public reading since Jonah was a prominent motif in early Christian sarcophagal art. See Y.-M. Duval, *Le livre de Jonas dans la littérature chrétienne greque et latine* (2 vols.; Paris: Etudes Augustiniennes, 1973), esp. I, pp. 19–65, on artistic representations, liturgical use, and early commentaries.

32.   For such a 'process theory' of textuality, writing and reading see, among others, D. Brandt, *Literacy as Involvement: The Acts of Writers, Readers and Texts* (Carbondale, IL: Southern Illinois University Press, 1990). On the nature of reading in religious communities in particular, see also Paul J. Griffiths, *Religious Reading: The Place of Reading in the Practice of Religion* (New York: Oxford University Press, 1999), esp. pp. 40–54.

themselves in terms of the scriptural story.[33] Hence the early Christian communities learned to live within scripture, and to actualize the world of meaning articulated by it.

The history of the canon, at least in its fundamental dynamic, is far better understood as the outgrowth of the liturgical life of early Christianity than as a dogmatic construction. In eventually formalizing the canon of the Christian Bible in the fourth and fifth centuries, Christians were merely stating what they had long been accustomed to read, and who, in consequence, they had become: a people of the book. To borrow a phrase from Jeremiah, the new covenant had come to be 'written upon their hearts'.

As a textual community, early Christianity was defined by its readings through its reading habits. In large measure, early Christian congregations achieved their specifically Christian identity and ethos by means of repeatedly hearing the scriptures read and expounded in the service of worship.[34] Illiterate though most of them were, this hearing enabled them to participate in the text of scripture, and to live in the world that the text constructed.

33.   On the functionality of the scriptural canon in this sense see, for example, Hans Frei, *The Eclipse of Biblical Narrative: A Study in 18th and 19th Century Hermeneutics* (New Haven: Yale University Press, 1974), and C.M. Wood, *The Formation of Christian Understanding: An Essay in Theological Hermeneutics* (Philadelphia: Westminster Press, 1981).

34.   On the phenomenon of 'textual communities' whose life and identity revolve around reading, writing and living in accordance with texts, see B. Stock, *The Implications of Literacy: Written Language and Models of Interpretation in the Eleventh and Twelfth Centuries* (Princeton: Princeton University Press, 1983).

EARLY CHRISTIAN PREFERENCE FOR THE CODEX

Graham Stanton

On 19 November 1931 *The Times* of London announced the acquisition by Mr A. Chester Beatty of 12 manuscripts, 11 of which were fragmentary copies of Biblical writings.[1] Their discovery caused a considerable stir at the time. They were described by their editor, Sir Frederic G. Kenyon, as a 'unique group of early manuscripts'.[2] They included, Kenyon claimed, 'the earliest extant manuscript of any part of the Bible'.[3]

For a decade or so the Chester Beatty Biblical Papyri retained their standing among Biblical scholars as the sensation of the age. Nonetheless in the following decades they were overshadowed somewhat by further dramatic discoveries: the Dead Sea Scrolls and the Nag Hammadi Library in the 1940s, and the Bodmer papyri in the 1950s. I hope that the re-housing and superb display of the Chester Beatty Library in Dublin Castle will encourage renewed scholarly study of the 12 codices, for they continue to raise interesting questions in several areas of Biblical and early Christian studies.

For Biblical scholars, the most important of the 12 Chester Beatty Biblical manuscripts is the papyrus codex of the four Gospels and Acts (P^{45}). This codex is usually dated to the middle of the third century CE. T.C. Skeat, the doyen among papyrologists, did not exaggerate when he noted recently that it is 'a unique monument of early Christian literature and a treasure of the Irish nation'.[4]

All the Chester Beatty papyri were published remarkably quickly by Frederic Kenyon in handsome editions which remain invaluable for specialists 70 years later. Kenyon's comments on the collection as a whole and on the individual codices are astute. Although some of his observations now need modification in the light of further study and further discoveries, they still repay careful consideration. In this article I shall take as my starting-point Kenyon's comments on the codex format of the manuscripts, for they raise a set of fascinating issues, even though Kenyon himself did not seem to appreciate fully the importance of his observations.[5]

1. F.G. Kenyon (ed.), *The Chester Beatty Biblical Payri: Descriptions and Texts of Twelve Manuscripts on Papyrus of the Greek Bible* (16 vols.; London: Emery Walker, 1933–41).
2. Kenyon, I, *Text*, p. 18.
3. Kenyon, V, *Text*, p. ix.
4. T.C. Skeat, 'A Codicological Analysis of the Chester Beatty Papyrus Codex of Gospels and Acts (P45)', *Hermathena* (A Trinity College Dublin Review), 155 (1993), p. 27.
5. Kenyon's textbooks were published in several editions and were widely influential. But neither he nor the later editors of his textbooks (Kenyon died in 1949) developed his comments on

In the *General Introduction* to the Chester Beatty papyri published by Kenyon in 1933, he noted that the 12 manuscripts were all codices: 'it is for the early history of the codex form of book that they are so important'. He went on to observe that until recently the earlier part of the fourth century had been taken as the date of the supersession of the roll by the codex. The Chester Beatty Biblical papyri, however, not only 'confirm the belief that the Christian community was addicted to the codex rather than to the roll, but they carry back the use of the codex to an earlier date than there has hitherto been any good ground to assign to it'.[6]

The Chester Beatty papyri seemed to Kenyon to confirm the use of the codex in the second century, 'and even probably in the earlier part of it'. This suggestion was based on his proposed dating of the Numbers and Deuteronomy codex: 'written in a fine hand, of the second century, perhaps of the first half of it'.[7] Two years later in his edition of this two column codex Kenyon was able to appeal to several of the leading papyrologists of the day for support for his dating, noting, however, A.S. Hunt's 'over-cautious' preferred date, late second or early third century. Kenyon believed that this manuscript was 'not only the earliest manuscript in the Chester Beatty Biblical collection, but also the earliest extant manuscript of any part of the Bible, and the earliest example of the codex form of manuscript'.[8] Although Hunt's more cautious dating has won the day,[9] no one now doubts that Christians used the codex in the first half of the second century, if not even earlier.[10]

Kenyon also drew attention to the striking use of *nomina sacra* in the Numbers and Deuteronomy codex. He noted that as Ἰησοῦς (= Joshua) was regularly abbreviated in the manner used by Christian scribes to abbreviate Ἰησοῦ (=Jesus), this codex was almost certainly produced for a Christian community. Most scholars still accept Kenyon's conclusions: use of abbreviated *nomina sacra* and the codex format is an indication that a copy of an Old Testament writing is Christian rather than Jewish.[11]

Kenyon noted that so long as the roll was the form of book in use, no work of materially greater length than one of the Gospels could be contained in a single roll. So whereas five rolls would have been needed for the four Gospels and Acts, among the Chester Beatty papyri was one codex from the third century which

---

the origin of the codex format; hence his own contribution has not received the recognition it deserves. See, for example, F.G. Kenyon, *The Text of the Greek Bible* (ed. A.W. Adams; London: Duckworth, 3rd edn, 1975), p. 9, and F.G. Kenyon, *Our Bible and the Ancient Manuscripts: Being a History of the Text and its Translations* (London: Eyre & Spottiswoode, 1895), pp. 41–43.

6. Kenyon, I, *Text*, p.12

7. Kenyon, I, *Text*, p. 8.

8. Kenyon, V, *Text*, p.ix.

9. See, for example, Roberts, *Manuscript, Society and Belief*, pp. 78-81.

10. The general acceptance of Roberts's dating of the codex papyrus fragment now known as P[52] to the first half of the second century has been particularly influential. See C.H. Roberts, *An Unpublished Fragment of the Fourth Gospel in the John Rylands Library* (Manchester: Manchester University Press, 1935).

11. For fuller discussion and bibliography, see C.M. Tuckett, ' "Nomina Sacra": Yes and No?', in J.-M. Auwers and H.J. de Jonge (eds.), *The Biblical Canons* (Leuven: University Press, 2003), pp. 431–38.

originally contained all these writings.[12] Kenyon was well aware of the significance of this new evidence for the physical existence of the fourfold Gospel, but he seems not to have appreciated the fact that this codex contains rare and important evidence for the joint circulation of Luke's Gospel and Acts.

In at least one respect Kenyon's comments on the significance of the Chester Beatty papyri were truly prophetic. 'When, therefore, Irenaeus at the end of the second century writes of the four Gospels as the divinely provided evidence of Christianity, and the number four as almost axiomatic, it is now possible to believe that he may have been accustomed to the sight of volumes in which all four (Gospels) were contained'.[13] In 1933 those comments must have seemed to many Biblical scholars to be unduly speculative. For many decades little notice was taken of them. However more recent discoveries have enabled this insight to be placed on a much firmer footing, for we now have almost certain evidence for the existence of two earlier codices which originally contained all four canonical Gospels.[14] The theological case for acceptance of the fourfold Gospel and the availability and pragmatic advantages of a single codex for four Gospel writings did not develop independently. Canon and codex are indeed inter-related.

Kenyon noted correctly that the Chester Beatty papyri confirm that the Christian community was 'addicted to the codex rather than to the roll'.[15] How is that 'addiction' to be explained? This is a question which continues to tease to this very day, for more recent discoveries underline the extent of the 'addiction'. Twelve further early fragmentary papyri of New Testament writings were published between 1997 and 1999.[16] All are in the codex format, not the roll which was still being used almost universally for literary texts.

Why did Christians prefer the codex? In the second part of this paper I shall discuss this fascinating question by working backwards, so to speak, from the point at which scribes copying non-Christian writings began to prefer the codex format. I shall then discuss the reasons why Christian scribes became obsessed with the new format at a much earlier period. Finally, I shall turn to the key question: How are we to explain the *initial* use of the codex by Christian scribes?

* * *

Up until about 300 CE very nearly all literary texts were 'published' or copied in the roll format. But by the fourth century, only about 25 per cent still used the roll, and

---

12.   Kenyon, I, *Text*, p.12.

13.   Kenyon, I, *Text*, p.13.

14.   For full discussion, see Stanton, 'The Fourfold Gospel', *NTS* 43 (1997), pp. 317–46, now included, with light revsion, in Graham Satanton, *Jesus and Gospel* (Cambridge: Cambridge University Press, 2004), pp. 63–91.

15.   Kenyon, I, *Text*, p.12.

16.   P. Oxy 4403 and 4404 = P[104-5], fragments of Matthew; P. Oxy 4445-8 = P[106-8], fragments of John; P. Oxy 4494-4500 = P[110-115], fragments of Matthew, Luke, Acts, Romans, Hebrews, and Revelation – *Oxyrhynchus Papyri*, vols. LIV, LV, LVI.

by the fifth century, the percentage had dropped still lower to around 10 per cent.[17] During these centuries almost all Christian copies of Biblical manuscripts were in the codex format; so too were most non-Biblical Christian manuscripts. On the other hand, Jewish scribes continued to prefer the roll.

Although early Christian use of the codex has attracted lively discussion, less attention has been given to the reasons why non-Christian scribes adopted the codex format. That important transition can be pin-pointed to the decades around 300 CE. Fresh light on that transition has recently been shed by William V. Harris, well-known for his work on levels of literacy in antiquity.[18]

In line with the views of earlier writers, Harris accepts that cost and ease of reference were vital advantages of the codex form, as was its increased capacity. But he suggests that there were further factors at work. It is no coincidence, he argues, that the transition from roll to codex for literary writings took place c. 300 CE 'in a period when the numbers and the respectability of the Christians were strongly increasing'. By the end of the third century 'no simple contrast could be drawn between the culture of the Christians and the pagans. It was now possible to be both a Christian and an ardent lover of the classics without any great strain.'[19]

If Harris is correct, it was Christian preference for the codex for *Christian* writings which provided a major impetus to the use of this format for 'secular' writings c. 300 CE. So why did Christian scribes become obsessed with the new format?

For reasons I shall mention below, I do not think that Christian scribes invented the codex. So why did it become the almost universally accepted format for Christian writings, perhaps from about 100 CE? In a recent publication I discussed the various explanations which have been offered and then set out my own. I noted that early Christian codices, whether Roman or Christian, were quite small in size and therefore much more portable than rolls. Christian scribes preparing writings to be carried by missionaries, messengers, and travellers over long distances would have readily appreciated the advantages of the codex.[20] Their general counter-cultural stance would have made them more willing than their non-Christian counterparts to break with the almost unanimous preference for the roll and experiment with the unfashionable codex.[21] I also noted that copying and using the Old Testament Scriptures and their foundation writings in a new format was one of the ways Christians expressed their sense of 'newness'. Once the new format began to be adopted, its usefulness for collections of writings such as the four gospels and the Pauline corpus would have enhanced its value.

17.   For the details, see Roberts and Skeat, *The Birth of the Codex*, pp. 36–37. More recent discoveries, or alternative datings for some of the papyri, do not alter the general picture.

18.   W.V. Harris, 'Why did the Codex Supplant the Book-Roll?', in J. Monfasani and R.G. Musto (eds.), *Renaissance Society and Culture, Essays in Honor of Eugene F. Rice Jr* (New York: Italica Press, 1991), pp. 71–85.

19.   Harris, 'Why did the Codex Supplant the Book-Roll?', pp. 74 and 84.

20.   Michael McCormick, 'The Birth of the Codex and the Apostolic Lifestyle', *Scriptorium*, 39 (1985), pp. 150–58.

21.   Stanton, 'The Fourfold Gospel', pp. 317–46, esp. 338–39.

Eldon J. Epp has recently added a further important consideration. The likely content of the codices carried by early Christian missionaries and teachers (whether Mark, Old Testament *testimonia*, the Pauline corpus, the four-gospel codex) is less important than the mere presence and use of the codex 'in the highly charged setting of evangelism and edification in pristine Christianity – especially when a respected visitor is present with this new mark (i.e. a codex) of his/her calling'.[22]

All these factors were instrumental in encouraging Christian scribes to use the new codex format. But they all relate to what I would now call stage two: the rapid and almost universal acceptance of the new format by Christian communities. How are we to explain stage one: the initial use of the codex format by Christian scribes at a time when in all probability rolls of Christian writings were in existence, and when the roll was certainly the norm in society at large?

In order to answer this question we must first sketch the origins of the codex. The codex was a development of the earlier use of wooden tablets, several of which could be held together by a cord which passed through holes in the tablets. *Codex* was the Latin word for a set of tablets held together in this way. Tablets were covered in wax which was incised with a stylus and used for notes of various kinds, including school exercises; they could be readily re-used. We now have a number of surviving examples of such stylus tablets from the first and later centuries.[23]

Until recently it was generally assumed that stylus tablets were the standard writing-material for letters and documents in those parts of the Roman Empire where papyrus was not readily available. However the publication in 1983 and 1994 of the very large number of writing tablets from Vindolanda (Northumberland, England) which date from c. 100 CE necessitates a re-appraisal of this view. The Vindolanda discoveries have not yet received the attention from New Testament scholars which they deserve. They came too late for more than passing mention in Joseph van Haelst's major study and in Harry Gamble's fine survey.[24]

The Vindolanda tablets are 'thin slivers of smooth wood which are written with pen and ink', and may conveniently be referred to as 'leaf tablets'.[25] Most were used for official documents, as well as for letters and drafts of letters. However, at least one of the Vindolanda tablets contains a literary text, a line of Virgil; three others may be literary or semi-literary.[26] In the light of their publication, it is

22.   Eldon Jay Epp, 'The Codex and Literacy in Early Christianity and at Oxyrhynchus: Issues Raised by Harry Y. Gamble's *Books and Readers in the Early Church*', *Critical Review of Books in Religion* 10 (1997), p. 21.

23.   For full details and references, see A.K. Bowman, and J.D. Thomas, *Vindolanda: The Latin Writing-Tablets* (Britannia Monograph Series; London: Society for the Promotion of Roman Studies, 1983), IV, pp. 33–35.

24.   Joseph van Haelst, 'Les Origines du Codex', in Alain Blanchard (ed.), *Les Débuts du Codex* (Turnhout: Brepols, 1989), pp. 13–35 esp. 15–16. Van Haelst under-estimates the importance of the Vindolanda tablets for the origin of the codex on the basis of the 'concertina' format and the absence of writing on both sides (p. 15 n. 5). However, as I have noted above, there is now further evidence of diversity in format. Cf. Gamble, *Books and Readers*, p. 268 n. 35.

25.   Bowman and Thomas, *Vindolanda: The Latin Writing-Tablets*, p. 32.

26.   A.K. Bowman, *Life and Letters on the Roman Frontier: Vindolanda and its People* (London: British Museum, 1994), p. 18.

probable that some of the many literary references in first and second century writings to notebooks (*pugillaria*) may be to leaf tablets rather than to stylus tablets.

In 1983, the editors of the Vindolanda tablets accepted that for two reasons they could not be described as a primitive codex: the 'concertina' format of many of the tablets, and the fact that with only a couple of partial exceptions they were not written on both sides of the leaf. However, they also noted that the existence of this wooden notebook in this format at a period which was clearly an important one for the development of the codex may be of some significance for that development.[27]

In 1994 the tablets were re-edited, together with the considerable finds from the 1985–89 excavations. The editors note that there was no standard format for documents, though a diptych format, with the address written on the back of the right-hand half of the diptych is the norm for letters.[28] Somewhat surprisingly, the editors do not comment further on the relationship of the leaf tablets to the origins of the codex. But there can now be little doubt that with the very thin Vindolanda leaf tablets from c. 100 CE, inscribed with pen and ink, we have extant examples of notebooks which were the forerunners of the codex.[29] They are a more direct antecedent than re-usable stylus tablets covered in wax, even though we have more extant examples of the latter.

It has been generally accepted for some time now that parchment or papyrus notebooks (*membranae*) were also the forerunners of the codex, even though the earliest *extant* examples are from the end of the second or the third century CE.[30] There is plenty of literary evidence which confirms that they were well-known and widely used much earlier.[31] Quintilian's comments from about 90 CE are particularly important: 'It is best to write on wax owing to the facility which it offers for erasure, though weak sight may make it desirable to employ parchment by preference [...] But whichever we employ, we must leave blank pages that we may be free to make additions when we will.' The reference here to wax tablets and to pages on the left side being left blank confirms that Quintilian is aware of the advantages of the notebook.

Perhaps it is not surprising that examples of parchment or papyrus notebooks from an earlier period have not survived, and that only recently have excavations at Vindolanda and a few other sites brought to light wooden leaf tablets. These notebooks were used for letters, and for ephemeral notes and documents of various

27.   Bowman and Thomas, *Vindolanda: The Latin Writing-Tablets*, pp. 40–44.

28.   A.K. Bowman, and J. David Thomas, *The Vindolanda Writing-Tablets: Tabulae Vindolandenses II* (London: British Museum, 1994), pp. 40–46.

29.   Bowman, *Life and Letters on the Roman Frontier*, p. 10 notes that with writing-tablets still coming out of the ground in the 1990s, conclusions can only be tentative and provisional.

30.   Cf. J. van Haelst: 'Le carnet de parchemin est une étape intermédiaire indispensable entre la tablette de cire et le codex. Ce sont ses feuillets qui, multipliés selon les besoins, pourront éventuellement contenir une oevre littéraire de quelque étendue', in *idem*, 'Les Origines du Codex', p. 20.

31.   See Roberts and Skeat, *The Birth of the Codex*, pp. 15–23 and van Haelst, 'Les Origines du Codex', p. 18 for details and bibliography.

kinds, but not for writings which might be treasured by a later generation, for which the roll was the norm. The literary evidence for the widespread use of different types of notebooks together with the extant examples from the end of the first century confirm that for some people in the Graeco-Roman world notebooks were part of everyday life.

We are still unable to reconstruct with confidence how, why, and when the more substantial papyrus and parchment codex evolved out of the wooden, parchment or papyrus notebook.[32] But literary evidence confirms that by the end of the first century the codex was being used by a small number of non-Christian writers for more substantial writings than notes, documents, drafts, and letters. As we shall see in a moment, some of these writings were literary: it is a mistake to assume from the origins of the codex that this format was reserved solely for utilitarian writings or handbooks.[33]

At present there are two rivals for the accolade of the earliest *extant* codex: P. Oxy. 30, a parchment codex in Latin from about 100 CE which is usually known as *De Bellis Macedonicis*, and P[52], the well-known papyrus fragment of Jn 18 which probably dates from about 125 CE. Although P. Oxy. 30 is fragmentary, it is clearly a historical writing, and not an ephemeral set of notes.

Was the codex format a Christian invention? The earliest extant examples just noted do not settle the question. Their paleographical dating is not certain, and in any case there is literary evidence for earlier non-Christian use of the codex which must be weighed carefully.

Writing between 84 and 86 CE, the Roman poet Martial refers to the availability of parchment codices for travellers: pocket editions of Homer, Virgil, Cicero, Livy, and Ovid which are referred with the words *in membranis* or *in pugillaribus membraneis* (*Ep.* 1.2, and 14.184–92). Although C.H. Roberts and T.C. Skeat claimed in their influential *The Birth of the Codex*, that Martial's 'experiment was stillborn', their arguments have not carried the day.[34]

We do have a sprinkling of codices of non-Christian writings from the second century. Although they make up only two per cent of the total (the remainder are on rolls) they cannot be dismissed as insignificant. One is a parchment in Latin (P. Oxy. 30, noted above). Three are parchment codices in Greek; fourteen are papyrus codices in Greek. Many are literary writings.[35]

The evidence of P. Petaus 30 (first published in 1969) is particularly important. This letter in Greek, which can be dated confidently to the second century, but not more precisely, refers to eight parchment codices (*membranae*), which were purchased, and six more which were not. P. Petaus 30 'implies a touring book-seller

---

32. Roberts and Skeat, *The Birth of the Codex*, correctly note that the transition from papyrus to parchment was of an entirely different character from, and quite unconnected with, the transition from roll to codex (p. 10). They allow the possibility that the papyrus codex and the parchment codex may have developed in parallel (p. 29).

33. Roberts and Skeat, *The Birth of the Codex*, p. 5 n. 1, note that it is quite wrong to describe the papyrus codex as a 'bastard form'.

34. Roberts and Skeat, *The Birth of the Codex*, p. 29.

35. See the slightly different lists with full details in Roberts and Skeat, *The Birth of the Codex*, p. 71 and in van Haelst, 'Les Origines du Codex', pp. 23–25.

offering literary *membranae* in the second century'.[36] The social setting is im-portant: these codices were part of a *mobile* bookshop. Martial, it will be recalled, refers to pocket editions of literary codices (*membranae*) which *travellers* would find useful. The earliest non-Christian codices seem to have been used for a variety of writings, including literary writings in the 'classical canon' of the day. As far as we can judge, they first became popular with travellers.[37]

Is it more likely that non-Christian scribes were influenced by Christian scribes in the initial development of the codex, or vice versa? Neither the earliest extant codices nor the literary evidence is absolutely decisive.[38] However, in my view the literary evidence from Martial and the evidence of P. Petaus 30 strongly suggest that codices were not unknown in non-Christian circles in the latter half of the first century, that is at the time of the composition of the New Testament writings. At this time it is most unlikely that the invention of the codex format by Christian scribes would have been imitated and developed by non-Christian scribes, albeit in a limited way. So in all probability the roll was used for the original copies of the New Testament writings. Luke-Acts offers some support: like many writers of his day, Luke designed his two volumes to fit onto a standard-sized roll apiece. Within a couple of generations of their composition, the earliest Christian writings began to circulate in codices.

I am now convinced that the use of papyri codices for Gospels, for Pauline epis-tles, and for Christian copies of the Septuagint, was preceded by the Christian use of parchment or papyrus notebooks. As we have seen above, several types of note-books were widely used in the Graeco-Roman world in the first century. The first followers of Jesus (pre-Easter, as well as post-Easter) will have been familiar with them.[39] So it is natural to suppose that notebooks will have been used for collec-tions of Scriptural passages, for collections of sayings of Jesus, and for drafts of letters.[40] It would not have been easy for Christian missionaries or teachers to carry

36. E.G. Turner, *Greek Papyri* (Oxford: Clarendon Press, 2nd edn, 1980), p. 204.

37. Michael McCormick, 'Typology, Codicology and Papyrology', *Scriptorium* 35 (1981), pp. 331–34. 157 suggests that the literary as well as the grammatical fragments may have been used by travelling teachers.

38. Several more recent writers have been reluctant to accept the view of Roberts and Skeat (*The Birth of the Codex*) that Christians invented the codex. See, for example, R. Lane Fox, 'Literacy and Power in Early Christianity', in Alan K. Bowman and Greg Woolf (eds.), *Literacy and Power in the Ancient World* (Cambridge: Cambridge University Press, 1994), pp. 126–48 (p. 140); also Epp, 'The Codex and Literacy in Early Christianity and at Oxyrhynchus', pp. 15–16, who is now more hesitant than in some of his earlier publications.

39. Ulrich Luz, *Matthew 1–7* (Edinburgh: T. & T. Clark, 1989), pp. 46–47, suggests that Q traditions may have been collected in a rather large notebook 'bound together with strings on the margin. It permitted an insertion of new leaves at any time.' See also Migaku Sato, *Q und Prophetie: Studien zur Gattungs- und Traditionsgeschichte der Quelle Q* (WUNT, 2.29; Tübingen: Mohr, 1988). A. Millard, *Reading and Writing at the Time of Jesus* (Sheffield: Sheffield Academic Press, 2000), draws attention to the extensive archaeological evidence for the amount of writing being done in first century Palestine and suggests that reports of Jesus sayings and actions may have been recorded in notebooks.

40. E.R. Richards, *The Secretary in the Letters of Paul* (WUNT, 42;Tübingen: Mohr, 1991), pp. 164–65, and p. 191 suggests that Paul kept notes for his letters in notebooks.

a handful of rolls of favourite Christian Scriptures such as the Psalms and Isaiah on their often arduous journeys. So we can readily understand why notebooks may have been used.

In words attributed to Paul, 2 Tim. 4.13 provides important support for this suggestion: 'When you come, bring the (traveller's) cloak I left with Carpus at Troas, and the books (in roll format), particularly my notebooks (μαλιστα τας μεμ-βρανας)' (or, possibly, 'my books in codex form').[41] What were the contents of the notebooks of a writer of a later generation who was associated with Paul the traveller? Perhaps a collection of 'faithful sayings', or favourite Old Testament passages, or even Jesus traditions!

I do not think that any of the 'big bang' theories which have been advanced for the adoption of the codex by Christian scribes is convincing.[42] Once they discovered how useful the codex format was, it very quickly became the norm for copies of the gospels, of Paul's letters, and for Christian copies of the Scriptures. I have set out above the reasons why I think this happened.

The speed with which the new format was adopted universally within early Christianity is astonishing, as is the rapid deployment and development of *nomina sacra*, the method of abbreviation used for 'God', 'Jesus', and other related terms. Both factors are directly relevant to any inquiry into the early reception of the Gospels. At first sight they seem to offer support for the claim that the Gospels were written for all Christians, rather than for a set of individual Christian communities.[43] However, in my judgment the codex became the norm for copies of the Gospels only a couple of generations after they were first written.

There is a further consideration which has an even more direct bearing on the early reception of the Gospels. We need not suppose that once the codex began to be used, notebooks with Jesus traditions (or with favourite passages of Scripture) immediately ceased to be used. Quintilian speaks of seeing Cicero's own notes for some of his speeches, which were still in circulation more than a century after the author's death.[44] So why should we not suppose that notebooks with Jesus traditions, continued to be used even after copies of individual Gospels began to circulate? Christian communities which did not have a copy of a full Gospel may have had to make do with parchment or papyrus notebooks for some time. If Christian missionaries and teachers continued to use parchment or papyrus notebooks with Jesus traditions (and Old Testament passages) *alongside* copies of the Gospels and oral traditions, we should not be surprised at the varied ways Old Testament and Jesus traditions are cited or alluded to in the Apostolic Fathers and in the writings of Justin Martyr.[45]

41.   See McCormick, 'Typology, Codicology and Papyrology', pp. 331–34. 155.

42.   See Stanton, 'The Fourfold Gospel', pp. 336–39 for details.

43.   R.J. Bauckham (ed.), *The Gospels for all Christians: Rethinking the Gospel Audiences* (Grand Rapids: Eerdmans, 1998).

44.   Quintilian, *Inst. Or.* 10.7.30-31. I owe this reference to Loveday Alexander, 'Ancient Book Production', p. 93.

45.   For further discussion, see G.N. Stanton, 'Jesus Traditions and Gospels in Justin Martyr

Perhaps we may dare to hope that further discoveries of manuscripts as important as the Chester Beatty Biblical papyri will extend our knowledge of one of the most momentous developments in the history of writings and of books, the transition from the roll to the codex-book format, and in particular the reasons why Christian scribes were the first to have a clear preference for the codex.[46]

and Irenaeus', in J.-M. Auwers and H.J. de Jonge (eds.), *The Biblical Canons* (Leuven: University Press, 2003), pp. 351–68.

46.   A fuller version of this chapter is included in Stanton, *Jesus and Gospel*, pp. 165–91.

THE DIATESSARON AND THE FOURFOLD GOSPEL

William L. Petersen

The word *Diatessaron* is Greek. 'Dia' (διά) means 'through' and 'tessaron' (τεσσάρων) means 'four'. The word means 'through [the] four' – referring to the four
gospels: Matthew, Mark, Luke and John. The *Diatessaron* was a gospel harmony –
that is, a single account of Jesus' life, from birth to death, which drew bits and
pieces of its narrative from each of the gospels: 'out of many gospels, one gospel'.

Before delving into the subject of gospel harmonies in general – and the *Diatessaron* in particular – a few words are necessary about the *Diatessaron*'s com-
piler. Reports from early Christianity tell us it was assembled by a man named
Tatian. He was born in Assyria – a rather large and vaguely defined area in the
Middle East which, in popular usage of the time, indicated a region stretching from
Media in the east to the Tigris River in the west, and from the Armenian mountains
in the north to Ctesiphon in the south; it could also refer to Syria in general.

Like many young people, both ancient and modern, Tatian sought to discover a
'true' philosophy upon which to ground his life. He wandered through the ancient
world in search of a system of thought that would satisfy this hunger. At some point
in his wanderings through various philosophical schools, he came into contact with
Christianity and was converted. Eventually he ended up in Rome, where he studied
with the early Christian teacher and philosopher Justin Martyr. After Justin's death
(he was martyred sometime between 163 and 167 CE), Tatian founded his own
philosophic school there, but soon ran into problems. He was accused of being
'puffed up with pride' at being a teacher, and of propounding heretical ideas.
Because of this he was expelled from the primitive Roman congregation about 172
CE. He left Rome and returned to the East, presumably to his homeland, where his
teachings supposedly had great influence.[1] It is presumed that he composed the
Diatessaron – this gospel harmony – sometime after his departure from Rome. If
one were to select 175 CE as the date of its composition, one would probably be
quite close.

With this sketch of Tatian's life out of the way, let us now consider the rather
obvious question: Why would someone want to create a gospel harmony? The concept of a gospel harmony seems – at least at first sight – rather foreign to us.

To answer the question – why a harmony – we need to familiarize ourselves with
the situation that prevailed from the beginning of Christian literature (which is

---

1.   For a full biography of Tatian (and for greater detail on other points mentioned in this
chapter in passing), see W.L. Petersen, *Tatian's Diatessaron: Its Creation, Dissemination, Significance and History in Scholarship* (VCSup, 25; Leiden: Brill, 1994), pp. 35–83, esp. 67–72.

usually placed at about 50 CE, the approximate date of the oldest letters of St Paul) down to about 175 CE, the date of the *Diatessaron*.

Christianity was a new sectarian movement. As is normal in such new religious movements, chaos reigned supreme. Leadership was contested and lines of authority were unclear; beliefs were poorly defined and doctrines were still developing; problems were solved on the spur of the moment and misunderstandings were common.[2]

Without any central authority, but beset with competing theological camps, early Christian literature developed in an uncontrolled, spontaneous fashion. Whoever wanted to write a gospel could – and often did. Whoever wanted to advocate a particular theological viewpoint could – either under his or her own name, or pseudonymously, under the name of an apostle or other biblical character.[3] Restricting one's self to gospels written before the date of the *Diatessaron* – that is, before 175 CE or so – a *partial* list would include the following.[4]

Table 1. *A Partial List of Gospels Composed before 175 CE.*

Gospel of Mark (c. 70 CE?)[5]
Gospel of Matthew (c. 85 CE?)
Gospel of Luke (c. 90 CE?)
Gospel of John (c. 100 CE?)
Gospel of the Ebionites (c. 125 CE?)
Gospel of the Egyptians (c. 125 CE?)
Gospel of the Hebrews (c. 125 CE?)
Gospel of the Nazoraeans (c. 125 CE?)
Gospel of Thomas (c. 140 CE?)[6]
Gospel of Peter (c. 150 CE?)
'Unknown Gospel' [P. Eg. 2] (c. 150 CE?)
Gospel of Judas (c. 170 CE?)
Infancy Gospel of James (c. 170 CE?)

2. Leadership was disputed: James, 'the brother of Jesus', appears to have led the Jerusalem Christians after Jesus' death (Acts 15.13–20), but later in the tradition, Peter emerges as the principal figure; Paul, meanwhile, displays open contempt for the 'pillars' leading the Jerusalem church, including James and Peter (Gal. 2.1–14). Beliefs were often poorly defined: observe Jesus' own inconsistent teachings on divorce (see the last item in Table 3, below). Spur of the moment solutions were common: see Paul's remark that, 'The rest is from me, not the Lord' (1 Cor. 7.12).

3. This phenomenon has been widely studied; see J.H. Charlesworth, 'Pseudonymity and Pseudepigraphy', in *ABD* V, pp. 540–41 (with bibliography).

4. The dates are those of J.K. Elliott, *The Apocryphal New Testament* (Oxford: Oxford University Press, 1992), or other standard works.

5. While these first four titles are well-known to us today as the four 'canonical' gospels, we must be careful about equating the *textual form* they had in the first and second centuries with the textual form they have today. Manuscript evidence and quotations in early Christian literature make it clear that the form of even these gospels was rather different from the form in which they circulated in the fourth century and later. Numerous studies have repeatedly come to this conclusion; see, e.g., H. Koester, *Ancient Christian Gospels* (London: SCM Press; Valley Forge, PA: Trinity International, 1990).

6. Two early gospels circulated under the name of Thomas; here we mean the 'Coptic' *Gospel of Thomas*, found at Nag Hammadi in 1945, not the *(Infancy) Gospel of Thomas*.

Our point is rather simple: gospels were breeding like rabbits, and a multiplication of *gospels* invariably meant a multiplication of *theologies*.

Many of these documents contain words of Jesus not found in the canonical gospels;[7] they tell of otherwise unknown episodes from his life.[8] The theologies they contain are occasionally rather close to – but usually rather distant from – the theologies we find in our present canonical text.[9]

It is in this sea of multiple gospels that we find the first answer to our question, 'Why a gospel harmony?' A harmony *selects* from among these gospels, and creates – in a very subtle and covert manner – a canon.[10] The 'approved' version of events is included in the harmony, while the 'rejected' versions are omitted. In this way, a harmony steered its readers among the rocky shoals of multiplying gospels. Additionally, a harmony did not require a church council or ecclesiastical approval: the composer simply compiled it, and 'put it on the market'. The harmony, itself, was a *de facto* 'canon'.

Another problem early Christianity faced can be summed up in a single name: Celsus. A pagan philosopher who wrote about 180 CE, Celsus was a sharp critic of Christianity.[11] He (like others both before and after him) used inconsistencies among the gospels to cast doubt upon Christianity and ridicule it.[12] If these Christians really had the 'word of God', said Celsus, then why was 'God's word' so inconsistent and contradictory?

An example of such an inconsistency is the number and description of the creatures that the women encounter at Jesus' empty tomb.[13]

---

7. The best-known example of this is the famous *Gospel of Thomas* (a translation is available in J.M. Robinson [ed.], *The Nag Hammadi Library in English* [Leiden: Brill, 1977], pp. 117–30).

8. The *Infancy Gospel of James* (also known as the *Protevangelium Iacobi*) and *the Gospel of Peter* are excellent examples; see their texts in Elliott, *Apocryphal*, pp. 48–67 and 150–58, respectively.

9. See, for example, the brief introductions provided by Elliott, *Apocryphal*; the *Gospel of Peter*, for example, has an 'adoptionist' and/or 'Docetist' theology (for definitions of terms with which the lay reader may not be familiar, see F.L. Cross and E.A. Livingstone [eds.], *The Oxford Dictionary of the Christian Church* [Oxford: Oxford University Press, 3rd edn, 1997]).

10. 'Canon' is a technical term designating those writings that are determined by a particular group to be authoritative.

11. On Celsus, see H. Chadwick, *Origen: Contra Celsum* (Cambridge: Cambridge University Press, 1953).

12. We lack specific names of critics before him, but it is reasonable to assume that they existed, given his rather late date; after him, we may point to the writings of the last pagan – but Christian educated – emperor, Julian the Apostate. On Julian see, for example, Tj. Baarda, 'Luke 22.42–27a. The Emperor Julian as a Witness to the Text of Luke', in *NovT* 30 (1988), pp. 289–96.

13. This is, in fact, one of the examples cited by Celsus: Origen, *Contra Celsum*, 5.52 (Chadwick, p. 305).

Table 2. *Who Greets the Women at the Empty Tomb.*

Mt. 28.2–5	Mk 16.5–6	Lk. 24.4–5	Jn 20.11–13
And suddenly there was a great earthquake; for an angel of the Lord, descending from the heaven, came and roll back the stone and sat on it…	As they entered the tomb, they saw a young man, dressed in a white robe,…	While they were perplexed about this, suddenly two men in dazzling clothes stood beside them…	Then, still weeping, she stooped to look inside, and saw two angels in white sitting where the body of Jesus had been…
But the angel said to the women, 'Do not be afraid…'	But he said to them, 'Do not be alarmed…'	But the men said to them, 'Why do you seek…'	They said, 'Women, why are you weeping…'

As the foregoing synopsis makes clear, among the many differences among the accounts is the *number* and *identification* of the creatures that greet the women. In Matthew it is 'an angel' (in Greek: ἄγγελος); in Mark it is 'a young man' (Greek: νεανίσκον); in Luke it is '*two* men' (in Greek: ἄνδρες δύο); while in John it is 'two angels' (Greek: δύο ἀγγέλους). So not only does the number vary among the gospels, but the designation of the creature[s] varies, as well.

There are many other inconsistencies among the gospels, as the next table shows.

Table 3. *Inconsistencies among the Gospels.*

Matthew	Mark	Luke	John
26.19 Jesus dies on Passover	14.16 Jesus dies on Passover	22.13 Jesus dies on Passover	19.14 Jesus dies one day before Passover
21.12–13 He cleanses the Temple just before his death (at the final Passover)	11.15–19 He cleanses the Temple just before his death (at the final Passover)	19.45–48 He cleanses the Temple just before his death (at the final Passover)	2.13–25 He cleanses the Temple two years (two Passovers) before his death
5.32 and 19.9 Exception to condemnation of remarriage after divorce	10.11–12 No exception to condemnation of remarriage after divorce	16.18 No exception to condemnation of remarriage after divorce	[no parallel]

This list could be multiplied several hundred-fold.

It is here, then, in the attack of critics – who cited such contradictions and inconsistencies as evidence that Christianity was a fraud – that we find the second answer to our question 'Why a gospel harmony?' A harmony, by its very nature, combines parallel texts into a single account. Inconsistencies are reconciled; contradictions are removed. Whether the harmonist chooses to omit inconsistent material, or edits it so as to reconcile it, the end result is always the same: a single account, which a critic cannot play off against itself.

Another answer – the third – to our question 'Why a harmony?' is precedent. The idea of harmonizing gospel accounts was not invented by Tatian. We can say this because we know of *other* gospel harmonies *earlier* than Tatian's *Diatessaron*. In fact, Tatian's teacher, Justin Martyr, apparently used a harmony of Matthew, Mark and Luke; John, interestingly enough, does not seem to have been part of his harmony. Reports also survive of other early harmonies: one is attributed to a certain Ammonius of Alexandria – but we know nothing of Ammonius or his harmony; we are also told that Theophilus, bishop of Antioch, who died near the end of the second century, created a gospel harmony.

Perhaps the most surprising realization is that the canonical gospels themselves are harmonies of earlier material. It has long been known that some sort of a relationship exists among the gospels. The vast majority of scholars presume that Matthew combined Mark with other materials to create his gospel of Matthew – an example is found in the following table.

Table 4. *Harmonization in the Canonical Gospels*

Matthew 9.11–13		Mark 2.16–17
When the	1	When the scribes of the
Pharisees saw this,	2	Pharisees saw that he was eating
	3	with sinners and tax collectors,
They said to his disciples,	4	they said to his disciples,
'Why does your teacher eat	5	'Why does he eat
with tax collectors and sinners?'	6	with tax collectors and sinners?'
But when he heard this, he said,	7	When Jesus heard this, he said
	8	to them,
'Those who are well have no	9	'Those who are well have no
need of a physician, but those who	10	need of a physician, but those who
are sick.	11	are sick;
Go and learn what this means, 'I	12	
desire mercy, not sacrifice'.	13	
For I have come to call not the	14	I have come to call not the
righteous but sinners'.	15	righteous but sinners'.

As you can see, Mark's text has been taken over word for word by Matthew in the portions marked with single straight underlining; however, Matthew must have acquired the text underlined with broken underlining (lines 12 and 13) from some source other than Mark, for Mark lacks lines 12 and 13.[14] Matthew is *harmonizing* – combining – at least two sources into his single gospel. So our evidence shows

14. Should one wish to invert the dependence – and argue that Mark is borrowing the text from Matthew, then one must acknowledge that Mark has deliberately omitted the words found in Matthew in lines 12 and 13.

that the technique of gospel harmonization was already employed by the composers of the oldest gospels known to us.

This should not be surprising, for we presume that behind the written gospels lie oral traditions – that is, cycles of stories handed down, developed, and eventually joined into longer narratives – which finally were written down. Such a scenario (which is presumed to apply not just to Christian texts, but also to other ancient secular and non-Christian religious texts) mandates the assumption of harmonization.

Our fourth and final answer to the question 'Why a gospel harmony?' is self-evident from the foregoing. Given the problems that arose naturally from the inconsistencies and contradictions among the gospels, a harmonized text is preferable to any other form of the text for *teaching children*, for *evangelization and missionary work* – in short, *for introducing the novice to the story of Jesus' life*. Perhaps this is why the *Diatessaron* was – to the best of our knowledge – the form in which the gospel first appeared in many languages, and why, during the Middle Ages, when missionary activity was accelerating, there was a flourishing of vernacular harmonies based on the *Diatessaron* in Europe.[15] Why confuse a child or 'babe in the faith' with four or more accounts of Jesus' life? Why open the door to all the messy questions that a careful perusal of the individual gospels always elicits? Simply harmonize the story, and it all goes down smooth as honey.

We have reached the conclusion of our search for answers to the question 'Why a harmony?' We have found four: first, the creation of a harmony performed the necessary task of selecting among the many gospel accounts and theologies circulating in early Christianity. Second, a harmony was a clever means of disarming learned critics of Christianity, for a harmony removed the very inconsistencies and contradictions they used against the new religion. Third, harmonization was simply 'in the air' in the early church, and had been used from the very beginning of Christian tellings of Jesus' life and death. Fourth and finally, harmonization was – and remains – the easiest way to introduce a child or a prospective convert to the life of Jesus.

We discover, then, that harmonization is a very ancient Christian activity, which continues even today. The motives behind harmonization are complex and diverse. Because of these multiple, mixed motives, we cannot single out *one* as being responsible for the creation of the *Diatessaron* – or even for the early church's affinity for harmonization. The most one can do is to suggest the *matrix* of motives out of which harmonies seem to have arisen in the early church.

***

With this examination of harmonization behind us, let us now turn to the *Diatessaron* itself.

15. The majority of the European vernacular harmonies related to the *Diatessaron* appear to have been translated in the period 1150–1300, which, in the words of D. Plooij, *A Primitive Text of the Diatessaron* (Leyden: Sijthoff, 1923), p. 66, was a period that saw a 'great revival [of] preaching of the Gospel to the people, for which purpose a harmonised Text of the Gospels was most convenient'.

As you recall, Tatian created his gospel harmony about 175 CE. It appears that he copied from his teacher's harmony: Justin Martyr apparently had a harmony compiled of material from Matthew, Mark and Luke. Tatian seems to have taken this pre-existing harmony and revised it. He added material from the Gospel of John, and expanded Justin's rather brief harmony. Justin's harmony was in Greek, the original language of the canonical gospels. Tatian knew Greek, so he would have had no trouble working from the Greek text of Justin's harmony. But it seems that Tatian's *Diatessaron* was first issued in Syriac. This Semitic language is closely related to Hebrew, but written with a different alphabet. So it seems that Tatian and his harmony were a bridge between the Greek and the Syrian Christian worlds.

In the Christian East, the *Diatessaron* seems to have been wildly popular. We know that it was the standard gospel text of the Syrian church until about 425 CE, when steps were taken to suppress it. Theodoret, bishop of Cyrrhus from 423 to 457 CE, was a Greek sent to this provincial Syrian city two days' journey from Antioch. Theodoret tells us that his diocese consisted of about 800 Syriac-speaking parishes. Early in his bishopric, he made an inspection trip through his diocese. He reports: 'I myself found *more* than *two hundred copies* of [the *Diatessaron* gospel] in *reverential* use *in the churches* of our diocese, and all of them I collected and *removed*, and instead of them *I introduced* the gospels of the four evangelists'.[16] Theodoret's report means that in 425 CE or so, more than a quarter of the Syriac-speaking churches in his diocese were still using the *Diatessaron* – apparently in a liturgical setting. The fact that many distinctive Diatessaronic variant readings are found in the oldest Syriac version of the four separate gospels has convinced scholars that the *Diatessaron* was the oldest gospel text in Syriac. In short, Syrian Christians first encountered the story of Jesus' life in the form of the *Diatessaron*. It remained in 'reverential use' in the churches there well into the fifth century, until it was finally suppressed by orthodox reformers imported from the Greek world, such as Theodoret, who 'introduced' the four separate gospels.

Probably because of actions such as those by Theodoret, no copy of the *Diatessaron* survives today. Apparently, at one time, Theodoret had 'more than' 200 copies in his hands – yet today we have not a single one. This is demonstrates a valuable corollary of our study: the early Church was *very* efficient at suppressing and destroying literature of which it disapproved. We have a very long list of documents we know existed in the first two Christian centuries, but which now are known only by title or through quotations; the documents themselves have vanished.[17]

In the case of the *Diatessaron*, we are forced to reconstruct its text from various secondary sources. These consist of, first, translations of the *Diatessaron* into languages other than Syriac; second, quotations from the *Diatessaron*; and, third, the text of the separate gospels which have been influenced by the *Diatessaron*.

---

16.   Theodoret, *Haer. Fab. Comp.*, I.20 (*PG*, vol. 83, col. 372).

17.   Among the many examples are: the Judaic-Christian gospels, whose names we know (*The Hebrew Gospel*; *The Gospel of the Ebionites*), but which have vanished; the numerous gnostic texts cited by Fathers (*The Gospel of Truth*, etc.), which were known only by title until the discovery of the Coptic library at Nag Hammadi in Egypt in 1945; Celsus' critique of Christianity, titled *On the True Word*, which has vanished.

While reconstructing the *Diatessaron*'s text is not easy, we are fortunate in having a wide variety of sources, in a multitude of languages from which to work. For example, translations of the *Diatessaron* survive in Arabic, Latin, Old High German, and Persian. Quotations from the *Diatessaron* survive principally in Syriac and Armenian, but also in Parthian and other languages.[18] As these languages suggest, the *Diatessaron* spread widely throughout ancient Christendom: its readings turn up as far east as at the fabled city of Turfan, in the middle of the Gobi Desert, in China, and as far west as England; as far south as Arabia, and as far north as Germany. In fact, I think it is correct to say that no other document of early Christianity – except for the canonical gospels themselves – saw wider dissemination than the *Diatessaron*.

Let us now look at some passages from the *Diatessaron*, in order to see precisely what its text looked like. Our first example concerns 'Peter's Denial'. We begin our examination with a synopsis of the synoptic gospels, Matthew, Mark and Luke, followed by the text of the *Diatessaron*.

Tables 5a & 5b *Peter's Denial.*

Matthew 26.33–34	Mark 14.29–30	Luke 22.33
And answering Peter said to him: 'If all are scandalised in you, I will never be scandalised'.	And Peter said to him: 'Even if all are scandalised, I will not'.	And he said to him:
		'Lord, with you I am ready to go to prison and to death'.
Jesus said to him, 'Truly I say to you…'	Jesus said to him, 'Truly I say to you…'	Jesus said, 'I tell you, Peter…'

	The Text of the Diatessaron
1	[And] Peter answered
2	and said:
3	'If all
4	are scandalised in you,
5	I will never
6	be scandalised, for with you
7	I am ready
8	to go to prison and
9	to death'.

18.   For a comprehensive listing of these sources and a description of them, see Petersen, *Tatian's Diatessaron*, pp. 445–89; a stemma of the Diatessaronic tradition is found on p. 490.

The first table (5a) gives the text in Matthew, Mark, and Luke. The corresponding text of the *Diatessaron* is presented in the second table (5b). No fewer than 6 of our Diatessaronic witnesses – in languages ranging from Arabic to Middle High German – conflate the Matthean and the Lucan form of Peter's answer in exactly the same way, creating a new saying of Jesus, found in no canonical gospel.[19]

Our second example offers a fascinating insight into the process of harmonization and how Tatian sometimes employed translation techniques to achieve his goals.[20]

Tables 6a and 6b. *A 'Staff' or a 'Stick'? (Solved Like 'Shoes' or 'Sandals'?)*

Matthew 10.9–10	Mark 6.8–9	Luke [10.4] and 9.3
Take no gold or silver or copper in your belts, no bag for your journey, or two tunics, or shoes		['no shoes': 10.4]
	He ordered them to take nothing for their journey	He said to them: 'Take nothing for your journey,
or a staff,	except a staff; no bread, no bag, no money in their belts; but to wear sandals and not to put on two tunics.	no staff, nor bag, nor bread, nor money – not even an extra tunic.
for labourers deserve their food.		
'shoes' (ὑποδήματα) NO 'staff' (ῥάβδον)	'sandals' (σανδάλια) TAKE 'staff' (ῥάβδον)	'shoes' (ὑποδήματα) NO 'staff' (ῥάβδον)

	The Text of the Diatessaron *(reconstructed from the Ephrem Commentary)*
1	Take no gold nor silver,
2	or copper in your belts,
3	no bag for your journey
4	or two tunics,

19.   They are the Arabic, Persian, Latin, Middle Dutch, Middle Italian, and Middle High German Harmonies; the only variation consists of minor differences (conjunctions, pronouns or proper names) in the introduction to the passage. See W.L. Petersen, *The Diatessaron and Ephrem Syrus as Sources of Romanos the Melodist* (CSCO 475 [Subsidia 74]; Louvain: Peeters, 1985), pp. 88–92.

20.   The great German New Testament scholar Theodore Zahn was the first (1894) to notice this variant; Tj. Baarda examined it in 'A Staff Only, Not a Stick: Disharmony of the Gospels and the Harmony of Tatian (Matthew 10.9f.; Mark 6.8f.; Luke 9.3 & 10.4)', in J.-M. Sevrin (ed.), *The New Testament in Early Christianity* (BETL, 86; Louvain: Peeters, 1989), pp. 311–34. See also Petersen, *Tatian's Diatessaron*, pp. 165–66.

5	but a <u>staff</u> (***shabta***) only, (= Mark's positive)
6	<u>not a stick</u> (***hutra***), (= Matt & Luke's negative)
7	and <u>not shoes</u> (= ὑποδήματα [Matt & Luke])
8	<u>but sandals</u> (= σανδάλια [Mark]).

While all the Greek gospels use the identical word for 'staff' – the common, standard Greek word ῥάβδον – Tatian, in the *Diatessaron*, uses two different Syriac words. Noting this contradiction (apparently Tatian had a sharper eye than modern exponents of Biblical inerrancy, who maintain there are no contradictions in the Bible), Tatian had to find some method for resolving it, for the statements of Matthew and Luke ('do *not* take a staff'), directly contradict Mark ('*take* a staff'). How was he to achieve this? It seems likely that Tatian found his answer in another part of this same passage where *synonyms* had been employed to solve what, originally, may have been the same problem, this time relating to what sort of foot wear was permitted. Note that there is *almost* a contradiction in our present text regarding whether or not to wear foot coverings: Matthew and Mark have Jesus forbid 'shoes' (ὑποδήματα) while Mark imposes the requirement to wear 'sandals' (σανδάλια).[21] In normal Greek usage, these two words have virtually identical meanings; however, since two of the gospels (Matthew and Luke) forbid the things, and the third gospel (Mark) requires them, the identical word could not be read across all three gospels, lest a contradiction arise.[22]

It seems that Tatian – perhaps using this example of 'sandals/shoes' for a model – employed the same technique when he noticed that all three gospels read 'staff' (ῥάβδον), but in two of them (Matthew and Luke) Jesus *forbade* the thing, while the third gospel (Mark) Jesus *permitted* the identical object. Selecting two *Syriac* synonyms, Tatian translated the Greek word ῥάβδον by the Syriac word *shabta*, or 'staff' in the Marcan parallel (line 5), but used a different Syriac word (*hutra*, or 'stick') for the Matthean and Lucan parallel in line 6. Later Syriac commentators on the *Diatessaron* comment upon the difference and even suggest what lay behind Jesus' reasoning: Jesus permitted the *shabta* (the word Tatian used to translate Mark's ῥάβδον: 'take a staff') because this was interpreted as a walking stick, useful in rocky terrain or for fending off snakes and wild animals. In Matthew and Luke, however, where Tatian chose to translate the Greek ῥάβδον by the Syriac *hutra*, or 'stick' ('do not take a *stick*'), the *hutra* was interpreted as a symbol of worldly authority and power, rather like a sceptre or a mace – possibly a military implement; therefore Jesus forbade it. Thus, in contrast to the entire Greek – and, for that matter, Latin – gospel tradition, Tatian's Syriac *Diatessaron* contained no

21. The use of identical vocabulary across all three gospels elsewhere in this passage (for example, all three use the same word for 'bag' [πήραν] and 'tunic/s' [χιτῶνας]), leads one to suspect that, in an earlier version of the gospels than that preserved in our manuscripts today, *all three* gospels read 'shoes' (or, possibly, 'sandals'), and that some early scribe detected the problem and substituted the synonym 'sandals' for the 'odd man out' – the only gospel which *requires* wearing a certain foot covering – namely, the Gospel of Mark.

22. Indeed, the standard Greek lexicon of the New Testament (*A Greek-English Lexicon of the New Testament and other Early Christian Literature* [ed. and rev. F.W. Danker; University of Chicago Press, 3rd edn, 2000]) gives 'sandal' as the definition for both terms (s.v., pp. 913, 1037).

contradiction here – and yet it presented *both* of Jesus' instructions – which in Greek read, 'take nothing *except* a staff' (so Mark) and 'take *no* staff (so Matthew and Luke).

Let us conclude this series of examples with a passage from the end of the gospels – from the crucifixion account. In Matthew, Mark and John, when Jesus dies, we find the 'Centurion's Confession'. But in Luke, we find a unique detail, stating that the crowds 'returned home, beating their breasts':

Tables 7a, 7b, and 7c *The Reaction of the Crowds to Jesus' Death.*

Luke 23.43

And when all the crowds
who had gathered there
for this spectacle saw what had taken place,
they returned home, beating their breasts.

The Text of the Diatessaron

---
1   And when all the crowds
2   who had gathered there
3   for this spectacle saw what had taken place,
4   they returned home, beating their breasts
5   and saying 'Woe to us! What has befallen us?
6   Behold, the judgment of the destruction
7   of Jerusalem has come and arrived'.

The Gospel of Peter

Then the Jews and the elders and the priests,
when they perceived how great the evil they
had done to themselves, began to lament
and say: 'Woe unto our sins;
the judgment and the end
of Jerusalem has drawn near'.

Tatian includes the Lucan reading in the *Diatessaron* (lines 1–4) – but he also includes a new feature, found in none of the canonical gospels: the direct speech of the crowd: 'Woe to us! What has befallen us? Behold, the judgment of the destruction of Jerusalem has come and arrived' (lines 5–7). No fewer than five Diatessaronic witnesses – including witnesses as ancient as the third and fourth century – present this reading.[23] More important for us is the fact that this same variant reading is also found in an apocryphal gospel, the *Gospel of Peter*, which is roughly contemporary with the *Diatessaron* (see Table 1).

---
23.   They are the *Doctrina Addai*, Aphrahat, Ephrem Syrus, and the Vetus Syra in the East, and a single Vetus Latina manuscript (MS g[1]: *Codex Sangermanensis* [VII cent.]) in the West. For a full discussion of the evidence for this reading, see Petersen, *Tatian's Diatessaron*, pp. 414–20.

This curious reading, today found in no canonical gospel, leads one to wonder: 'Are there other extra-canonical (sometimes called 'non-canonical') variants in the *Diatessaron*, and, if so, what do they mean?'

To answer this question, let us focus our attention on a single person and his witness to the text of the *Diatessaron*, Ephrem the Syrian, or Ephrem Syrus.

Without dispute, Ephrem is one of the giants of early Christianity. In the Roman tradition, Ephrem is a Doctor of the Church and a saint, whose feast day is 9 June. He was born about 306 CE and lived most of his life in the frontier Syrian city of Nisibis. He has been described as 'a theological star of the first magnitude'. A monk and an enormously gifted poet, he wrote hundreds of metrically-complex hymns and poetic sermons. His poetry is unquestionably the acme of Classical Syriac literature.[24]

Near the end of his life, as the Persians advanced on Nisibis, he fled to Edessa, the center of Syrian Christianity. We presume it was here that he composed a commentary on the *Diatessaron*.[25] He died in Edessa in 373 CE – about fifty years before the imported Greek bishop Theodoret of Cyrrhus would begin his round-up of copies of the *Diatessaron*, removing them from 'reverential usage' in 'more than' two hundred churches in his diocese.[26]

Since we are always dependent upon secondary sources for reconstructing the text of the *Diatessaron*, Ephrem's commentary was eagerly sought. It had two advantages over all other sources: first, its language was the same as that of the original *Diatessaron*, and, second, we could be certain that Ephrem had a *Diatessaron* before him as he quoted its text, and then set down his comments upon that passage.

No copy, however, of Ephrem's *Commentary on the Diatessaron* was known to exist. Finally, in 1836, a single manuscript, dated 1195, was identified. It was, indeed, the Ephrem *Commentary on the Diatessaron* – but it was an Armenian translation of the original Syriac version. Discovered in the library of the St. Lazarus monastery of the Mechitarist monks in Venice, it was published by the monks that same year, 1836. Perhaps assuming that it would be of interest only to Armenians, no translation was provided; even the title was completely in Armenian. The result was predictable and: to paraphrase David Hume, the work 'fell still-born from the press'.[27]

Later, around 1850, a second Armenian manuscript was discovered in the same Mechitarist library in Venice. A Latin translation was prepared on the basis of these two Armenian manuscripts, and published in 1876, by Professor Georg Moesinger of Salzburg.[28] As might be expected, this Latin translation reached a wider audience,

---

24. On Ephrem's biography, see the Introduction of C. McCarthy, *Saint Ephrem's Commentary on Tatian's Diatessaron* (Journal of Semitic Studies, Supplements, 2; Oxford: Oxford University Press, 1993), pp. 9–14.

25. An English translation is available; see the previous note for the reference

26. See n. 16, above.

27. Hume's remark on the poor reception accorded his *Treatise of Human Nature*, published anonymously in 1739 (the original quote reads 'dead-born', and occurs in chapter 1 of Hume's *My Own Life* [London: W. Strahan and T. Cadell, 1777; usually published as: *The Life of David Hume, Esq., Written by Himself*]).

28. I.B. Aucher and G. Moesinger (eds.), *Evangelii concordantis expositio* (Venetiis: Libraria PP. Mechitaristarum, 1876).

and soon it was being used by scholars throughout Europe. But scholarship still lacked a copy of the commentary in the original Syriac.

All that changed in 1957. In that year, a Syriac manuscript was sent to the Department of Printed Books and Oriental Manuscripts of the British Museum for evaluation by the Keeper, Mr. Cyril Moss. He dated the manuscript to the late fifth century, or about 490 CE. The 75 folios of the manuscript fell into two parts: the first 10 folios consisted of theological correspondence between two early church writers. The remaining 65 folios consisted of Ephrem's *Commentary on the Diatessaron* – in the original Syriac. Although the text was not continuous – there were several large gaps – it nevertheless contained about 60 percent of the Commentary previously known only through the two Armenian manuscripts in Venice.[29]

The folios had been sent to the British Museum for evaluation by none other than Alfred Chester Beatty, the founder and benefactor of the Chester Beatty Library in Dublin, who had acquired the manuscript for his collection.[30] The story does not end there, however, for in 1984, five of the missing folios of the manuscript came on the market, and were purchased by the Trustees of the Library; a further 36 of the missing folios were purchased in 1986.

Figure 2. *The Syriac Commentary on the Diatessaron by St. Ephrem the Syrian Dublin, CBL Syr 709 ff. 45r–44v* (© The Trustees of the Chester Beatty Library, Dublin.)

29.   For a fuller description of these events and the manuscript, see L. Leloir, *Saint Éphrem, Commentaire de l'Évangile concordant, texte syriaque* (Chester Beatty Monographs 8; Dublin: Hodges & Figgis, 1963).

30.   It is thanks to Beatty that the only known Syriac copy of Ephrem's *Commentary on the Diatessaron* resides in Dublin, where it rests catalogued as Chester Beatty Library, Syr Ms 709.

In connection with this great discovery and its publication, it is fitting to pause for a moment to pay tribute to the scholar-monk, Dom Louis Leloir, of the Abbey of Clervaux in Luxemburg. For more than 50 years, Dom Louis laboured on Ephrem, especially on the *Commentary on the Diatessaron*. In 1953 and 1954, prior to the discovery of the Beatty manuscript, Leloir completely re-edited the two Armenian manuscripts in the Mechitarist library in Venice, providing scholarship with not just a fine critical edition done to the very highest modern standards, but also with a very reliable, quite literal Latin translation. It was only natural that, when the Syriac manuscript came to light, the Library should turn to Dom Louis to prepare the *editio princeps*. Under the Dublin imprint of the firm Hodges and Figgis, the Library itself published this edition of the Syriac text and a Latin translation in 1963, shortly before Chester Beatty died in 1968. The discovery of the two additional sets of 'missing' folios, purchased in 1984 and 1986, led Dom Louis to devote the last years of his life to preparing these for publication; this edition appeared in 1990, two years before Dom Louis' death on 15 August, 1992, at the age of 80.[31]

Everyone who works on the Syriac Ephrem *Commentary* owes Dom Louis an enormous debt of gratitude. His editions are models of accuracy and clarity, and his numerous ancillary 'tool' publications on Ephrem, on the *Commentary*, on Ephrem's Bible text, and on Ephrem's theology are indispensable.[32]

Let us now return to the matter raised by our discovery (see Tables 7a, 7b, 7c) that the *Diatessaron*'s version of the reaction of the crowds to Jesus' death included a fragment of text not found in any canonical gospel today, but found, in antiquity, in the *Gospel of Peter*. This discovery caused us to wonder whether there were other extra-canonical materials in the *Diatessaron* and, if there were, what might account for their presence.

In order to answer these questions, let us consider two passages from the *Diatessaron*, both pertinent to this issue of extra-canonical readings. Both of the passages occur in Ephrem's *Commentary*.

We begin with Jesus' baptism. The text of the synoptic gospels is followed by the *Diatessaron*'s reconstructed text.[33]

---

31. *Saint Éphrem, Commentaire de l'Évangile concordant, texte syriaque (Manuscrit Chester Beatty 709). Folios Additionnels* (Chester Beatty Monographs 8(b); Louvain: Peeters, 1990).

32. Among these are: a French translation of the *Commentary*, based on both the Syriac and the Armenian texts: *Ephrem de Nisibe, Commentaire de l'Évangile concordant ou Diatessaron* (Sources chrétiennes 121; Paris: Editions du Cerf, 1966); a synopsis of gospel citations from the *Commentary*, with parallels in other early Christian writings: *Le témoignage d'Éphrem sur le Diatessaron* (CSCO, 227 [Subsidia 19]; Louvain: Peeters, 1962); and a study of Ephrem's theology and exegetical method: *Doctrines et methods d'Éphrem d'après les oeuvres éditées* (CSCO, 200 [Subsidia 18]; Louvain: Peeters, 1961).

33. While the pertinent variant reading is found in Ephrem's *Commentary*, and there is no doubt but that it was part of the text of the *Diatessaron* (see note 34, below), the quotations from the *Diatessaron* found at this point in Ephrem's *Commentary* are not substantial enough to give us certainty about the precise text of the entire passage (paralleling Mt. 3.16–17) as he found it in the *Diatessaron*. This presents a problem for the scrupulous scholar who wishes to present the information to the general public. In order to avoid getting bogged down in the details of reconstructing

Tables 8a and 8b *Jesus' Baptism.*

Matthew 3.16–17	Mark 1.10–11	Luke 3.21 22
And when Jesus had been baptised,	and	and when Jesus also had been baptised, and was praying,
just as he came up from the water,	just as he was coming up out of the water,	
suddenly the heavens were opened to him	he saw the heavens torn apart	the heaven was opened,
and he saw	and	and
the Spirit of God descending	the Spirit descending	the Holy Spirit descended upon him in bodily form
like a dove and alighting on him.	like a dove on him.	like a dove.
And a voice from heaven said,	And a voice came from heaven,	And a voice came from heaven,
'This is my Son,	'You are my Son,	'You are my Son,
the Beloved, with whom I am well pleased'.	the Beloved; with you I am well pleased'.	the Beloved; with you I am well pleased'.

The Text of the Diatessaron

Key: Matthew Mark Luke Non-Canonical

1	and when Jesus also
2	had been baptised
3	and was praying
4	just as he was coming up
5	out of the water,
6	a great light shone from the water, and
7	he saw the heavens
8	torn apart
9	and he saw
10	the Spirit of God
11	descending
12	in bodily form
13	like a dove
14	and alighting on him.
15	And a voice
16	from heaven said,
17	'You are my Beloved Son,
18	with whom I am well pleased'.

the *Diatessaron*'s text for a lay audience, a conservative approach was adopted: the text presented as the *Diatessaron*'s is that of Codex Fuldensis, a sixth-century Latin gospel harmony related to the *Diatessaron*; at the appropriate point in its text, the variant from Ephrem's *Commentary* has been inserted, resulting in a reconstructed text intended only for purposes of illustration to a lay audience. This reconstruction should *not* be cited for scholarly purposes.

Once again, as we have come to expect, we note that the *Diatessaron* presents a rather subtle harmony of the gospels. Matthew is the source for lines 1–2, 9–11, and 14–16; Mark provides lines 4–5, 7–8, and 17–18; Luke is used the least, being the source for only lines 3 and 12–13. But what catches our eye is a reading found in none of our gospels today: 'a great light shone from the water, and' (line 6). This is a *locus classicus* of Diatessaronic studies, for this variant is found in a wide variety of Diatessaronic witnesses – including Ephrem's *Commentary* on the *Diatessaron*.[34] An early church Father, (St) Epiphanius, bishop of Salamis, writing about 375 CE, knows this reading, and states that it is part of a gospel used by a very early Judaic-Christian sect known as the Ebionites.[35]

So we are faced with a reading in the *Diatessaron* which either (1) comes from what we today regard as an 'extra-canonical' source (perhaps the Judaic-Christian gospel 'used by the Ebionites'?), or – if it comes from one of the 'canonical' gospels – (2) demonstrates that the *textual shape* of the canonical gospels in the late second century – when Tatian composed the *Diatessaron* – was *different* from the form they have today.

Let us now look at our second example, which is found in the Chester Beatty manuscript of the Ephrem *Commentary* in Syriac. The so-called 'Rejection at Nazareth' – when Jesus preaches in the synagogue in Nazareth, but is rejected by his native village – has a coda in the Gospel of Luke, lacking in the other canonical gospels. Only Luke tells us that the villagers drove Jesus out of the village, took him to the top of a hill, and prepared to throw him off the precipice – but Jesus mysteriously slipped through the crowd. It is here that the world's greatest living expert on the *Diatessaron*, Professor Tjitze Baarda, of Amsterdam, discovered a remarkable variant. Compare the standard text of Luke (in the left column) with that of the *Diatessaron* (in the right column).

Table 9 *The Rejection at Nazareth.*

Luke 4.28–31		The Diatessaron
When they heard this,	1	When they heard this,
all in the synagogue	2	all in the synagogue
were filled with rage.	3	were filled with rage.
They got up,	4	They got up,
drove him out of the town,	5	drove him out of the town,
and led him to the brow of the hill	6	and led him to the brow of the hill
on which their town was built,	7	on which their town was built,
so that they might hurl him off the cliff.	8	so that they might hurl him off the cliff.
	9	And when they cast him down
	10	from the height into the depth
	11	he did not fall and was not hurt.

34. For a review of the evidence (at least eight Diatessaronic witnesses give the reading), see Petersen, *Tatian's Diatessaron*, pp. 14–20. This reading is found only in the Armenian version of the Ephrem *Commentary*; the Syriac manuscript of the *Commentary* in the Chester Beatty Library has a gap at this point in the text, where some folios are missing.

35. The reference is from Epiphanius' *Panarion* 30.13; on the Ebionites, see the article by S. Goranson, 'Ebionites' in *ABD*, II, pp. 260–61.

Luke 4.28–31		*The* Diatessaron
But he passed	12	
through the midst of them	13	Through the midst of them
	14	he flew.
and went on his way.	15	and
He descended to Capernaum,	16	descended to Capernaum,
a city in Galilee and was teaching them	17	a city in Galilee and was teaching them
on the Sabbath.	18	on the Sabbath.

The *Diatessaron*'s text is virtually identical with the Lucan text – until we reach line 9.[36] Here the *Diatessaron* departs from the text of Luke; it goes its own way through line 15. In line 16, the *Diatessaron* rejoins the Lucan text. According to the *Diatessaron*'s remarkable text, Jesus *is* physically *thrown from the cliff* (lines 9–11 and 14), and then *'flies' down to Capernaum* (lines 14–16). This remarkable variant occurs not just in Ephrem's Syriac *Commentary*, but four other texts – including one from St Augustine of Hippo.[37]

This reading is certainly not that of the Gospel of Luke today, and it stands in no known manuscript of Luke, in any language. Nevertheless, it was, apparently, a reading current in the time of Tatian, and he apparently considered worthy of inclusion in the *Diatessaron*; later – presumably due at least in part to its presence in the *Diatessaron* – it was reproduced without remark by leading early Christians such as Ephrem and Augustine.

With this example, we have come to the point where we may attempt to answer the two questions posed earlier. The first question was, 'Are there other extra-canonical variants in the Diatessaron?' Our answer must be 'yes indeed, there are other extra-canonical variants in the Diatessaron'. This is clear from the two examples we have just considered: first, the 'light' at Jesus' baptism (a variant reported to have stood in the *Gospel of the Ebionites*; see Table 8); second, the 'flying' Jesus at Nazareth, who 'comes down' to Capernaum (see Table 9).

If the answer to this first question were 'yes', then a second question naturally arises: 'What does the presence of such extra-canonical variants in the *Diatessaron* mean?' Well, their meaning depends on how we explain their *arrival* in the *Diatessaron*. There are only two possible explanations:

Option 1. If Tatian used only the canonical gospels when he composed the *Diatessaron* about 175 CE, then these readings – by definition – had to have been part of the text of the canonical gospels at that time.[38] This would mean that the text of

36. The text is the reconstruction of Tj. Baarda, '"The Flying Jesus", Luke 4.29–30 in the Syriac Diatessaron', *VC*, 40 (1986), pp. 313–41. It is also discussed in Petersen, *Tatian's Diatessaron*, pp. 312–14.

37. In Augustine, it occurs in *Contra Faustum*, 26.2.

38. The option that these extra-canonical readings crept into the *Diatessaron* itself, later in its transmission history (say, in the fourth or fifth century), must be considered, but it can be rejected immediately. The reason for the quick rejection is three-fold. (1) The identical, non-standard variant occurs in multiple Diatessaronic witnesses, which are geographically and linguistically diverse (this suggests that the variant is not some external tradition which has later interpolated

the canonical gospels in the year 175 CE was significantly different from the text we have before us today. Put differently, the text of the canonical gospels in the year 175 CE had not yet finished evolving, and had not yet reached its final form.

If we reject this first option, and wish, instead, to maintain that the raw materials from which Tatian worked had a text similar to the text of our gospels today, then the only other viable explanation is equally striking:

Option 2. When compiling his *Diatessaron*, Tatian – in addition to the four canonical gospels we have today (whose form was also like that known to us today) – also used extra- or non-canonical traditions, either oral or (more likely)[39] written. This eclectic use of sources means that some Christians – including, apparently, Syrians, Armenians, and others – had no problem conflating what we regard as extra-canonical traditions with what we today regard as canonical traditions. Indeed, Tatian tossed them all in a single pot, and came up with a stew that proved popular from the Gobi to the Cotswalds, from the Schwartzwald to the Rub al Khali.

The Diatessaron has sometimes been used as evidence of the de facto existence of a four-gospel canon by the late second century, when Tatian created his harmony. As we have seen, however, the reality is more complex.

In conclusion, there are four lessons to be drawn from our study of the *Diatessaron* for the 'beginning of the book' and the fourfold gospel.

First, *the Diatessaron was an attempt to create a single, definitive gospel – a 'super-gospel' – superseding all other gospels. It was, in that sense, a frontal assault on the four-gospel canon.*

Tatian probably created his harmony to be exactly what it was in the early Syrian church: the *single*, the *definitive* gospel. The four gospels we call canonical were expected to fade into the mists of time, just as the sources of Matthew or Mark or Luke or John have faded into the mists of time. A harmony is not just an acknowledgement of the fourfold gospel: it is, rather, a rejection of a multiple-gospel canon, and a battle-call to a single-gospel canon.

Second, *the very act of harmonization demonstrates that the traditions being harmonized – the traditions being dissected, revised and rearranged – were not regarded as sacrosanct.*

itself into a Diatessaronic witness; the geographic and linguistic diversity point to its presence in the most ancient strata of the Diatessaronic tradition, from which all these various later witnesses derive). (2) Sometimes, these extra-canonical variants are known *only* from Diatessaronic witnesses (this suggests that their genesis lies within the Diatessaronic circle of texts, and against the possibility that these variants originated elsewhere, and were imported into the Diatessaronic tradition at a later date). (3) Where non-Diatessaronic texts have these same extra-canonical variants, they tend – generally speaking – to be contemporaneous with the composition of the *Diatessaron*, namely mid-to-late second century (this suggests that 'the' gospel text known to Tatian at the time he composed the *Diatessaron* contained these variants).

39. Recall that two (the 'woes' at Jesus' crucifixion [Table 7], and the 'light' at his baptism [Table 8]) of our three non-canonical variants occur in non-canonical gospels; this is persuasive evidence for their circulation in a written source, not just in oral tradition.

Rather than being sacrosanct, the traditions were viewed as simply 'raw materials', out of which a more fitting edifice was being constructed in the harmony. Put differently, the sources Tatian used were *not* endowed with such a sacrosanct status for him or his audience that he could not rip the sources apart, rearrange them, and then present his new construction to an appreciative Christian audience.

Third, *if Tatian used the canonical gospels as his only source, then the Diatessaron proves that their form in the late-second century was different from the form they now have.*

This is 'Option 1', above. It means the form of the gospels in 175 CE was very different from what it is today. Rather than being 'stable', with a firmly-fixed form, the 'canonical' (or, more accurately, 'proto-canonical') gospels in 175 CE would have been 'unstable', works in progress, with traditions still being added to and excised from them.[40]

Fourth, *if Tatian used other, extra-canonical sources in addition to the four canonical gospels, then the warm reception accorded the Diatessaron demonstrates that early Christians had 'ecumenical' tastes when it came to traditions about Jesus; they did not object to Tatian interleaving canonical and extra-canonical material.*

This is 'Option 2', above, the only other alternative. The fact that Tatian's *Diatessaron* placed canonical and extra-canonical material side-by-side, intertwining sources so that it was virtually impossible to tell where the text of the Gospel of Luke ended and the text of the *Gospel of Peter* began (see Table 7), and the fact that the *Diatessaron* received such wide dissemination and popular acclaim, means that such juxtapositions were not just accepted, but embraced.

The consequences of these conclusions for canonicity, for the integrity of the text of the canonical gospels, for the fourfold gospel, and for the Word, and its beginning, are, I think, quite clear.

---

40. As surprising as this may sound to the lay reader, it has long been recognized by scholarship; see the footnotes in almost any Bible concerning the text of the Gospel of Mark, post Mark 16.8 (i.e. 16.9–20; there are four different endings to the Gospel of Mark in the manuscripts; the oldest ends at 16.8), or concerning the well-known story of the 'Woman Caught in Adultery' (John 7.53–8.11; no manuscript of John before about 400 CE. contains this famous story). For additional information, consult any standard introduction to the text of the New Testament e.g. F.G. Kenyon, *The Text of the Greek Bible* (ed. A.W. Adams; London: Duckworth, 3rd edn, 1975); B.M. Metzger, *The Text of the New Testament* (Oxford: Clarendon Press, 2nd edn, 1968); or K. Aland and B. Aland, *The Text of the New Testament: An Introduction to the Critical Editions and to the Theory and Practice of Modern Textual Criticism* (trans. Erroll F. Rhodes; Grand Rapids, MI: Eerdmans; Leiden: Brill, 2nd edn, 1989).

THE NAG HAMMADI GOSPELS AND THE FOURFOLD GOSPEL

James Robinson

The Nag Hammadi Codices are a collection of 13 books no longer in the form of scrolls, but rather in the form of a book with pages, that is in the form of a codex, discovered near Nag Hammadi in Upper Egypt in 1945. The editing and publication was first monopolized by the French and then by the Germans. Finally, with the help of UNESCO's International Committee for the Nag Hammadi Codices, of which I was Permanent Secretary responsible for preparing the volumes, it was possible to break the monopoly, by publishing a facsimile edition in 12 volumes (1972–84),[1] plus a single volume English translation, *The Nag Hammadi Library: In English* (1977),[2] plus a critical edition, *The Coptic Gnostic Library,* in 14 volumes (1975–86),[3] which is now available in a 5 volume paperback reprint.[4]

There are 48 different tractates in the 13 Nag Hammadi Codices, four of which are called 'Gospels': *The Gospel of Truth, The Gospel of Philip, The Gospel of the Egyptians*, and *The Gospel of Thomas*. Like all of the Nag Hammadi tractates, these four 'Gospels' are translations from Greek originals. Thus we have four Greek Gospels in the New Testament, and four Greek 'Gospels' in the Nag Hammadi Codices.

---

1. *The Facsimile Edition of the Nag Hammadi Codices* (Leiden: Brill, 1972–84): *Codex VI* (1972), *Codex VII* (1972), *Codices XI, XII* and *XIII* (1973), *Codex II* (1974), *Codex V* (1974), *Codex IV* (1975), *Codex III* (1976), *Codex VIII* (1976), Codex I (1977), *Codices IX* and *X* (1977), *Cartonnage* (1979), *Introduction* (1985).

2. *The Nag Hammadi Library: In English*, translated by members of the Coptic Gnostic Library Project of the Institute for Antiquity and Christianity, James M. Robinson, Director (ed. James M. Robinson and Marvin W. Meyer; Leiden: Brill, 1977, pb edn 1984); San Francisco: Harper & Row, 1977, pb edn 1981; 3rd rev edn, ed. James M. Robinson and Richard Smith; Harper & Row and Brill, 1988; first HarperCollins pb edn, 1990). Greek edition abridged, adapted and translated by S. Agourides from the first edition, CRISTIANIKOS GNWSTIKISMOS: TA KOPTIKA KEIMENA TOU NAG HAMMADI STHN AIGUPTO (Athens: KENTRO BIBLIKWN MEGETWN 'ARTOS ZWHS', 1989).

3. The sub-series The Coptic Gnostic Library appeared in the series Nag Hammadi [and Manichaean] Studies (Leiden: Brill), as vols. 4 (1975), 11 (1979), 15 (1981), 16 (1981), 20 (1989), 21 (1989), 22 (1985), 23 (1985), 26 (1984), 27 (1991), 28 (1990), 30 (1996), 31 (1991), 33 (1995).

4. *The Coptic Gnostic Library: A Complete Edition of the Nag Hammadi Codices* (Leiden, Boston, Cologne: Brill, 2000): Vol. 1 = Nag Hammadi Studies, 22, 23. Vol. 2 = Nag Hammadi and Manichaean Studies, 33; Nag Hammadi Studies, 20, 21, 4. Vol. 3 = Nag Hammadi Studies, 27, 26, 11. Vol. 4 = Nag Hammadi and Manichaean Studies, 30; Nag Hammadi Studies, 31, 16. Vol. 5 = Nag Hammadi Studies, 15, 28.

The claim that there are four Gospels among the 13 Nag Hammadi Codices is rather misleading. In early Christianity, the title 'Gospel' was freely assigned to texts, to accredit them as authoritative, in order to compete with the Gospels that were in the process of gaining canonicity. In the case of the Nag Hammadi 'Gospels', this seems to be part of a much broader tendency, which can be traced in the emergence of titles for various tractates. This calls for some explanation:

It was common in antiquity to choose, as an opening line for a text, a phrase which the author expected the public to use as a nickname for the text, a broad hint as to what the contents would bring, since titles themselves were often not used. This common practice of antiquity still survives today in Papal encyclicals, whose opening phrase becomes in practice the title by which that encyclical is known, for which reason an appropriate opening phrase is always chosen.

Thus Irenaeus, Bishop of Lyon late in the second century, when he criticized Valentinians for entitling the gospel written only recently by themselves as the 'Gospel of Truth', was probably referring to an untitled Nag Hammadi tractate, which we, like Irenaeus, call *The Gospel of Truth*, precisely because the opening line read: 'The gospel of truth is joy for those who have received from the Father of truth the grace of knowing him […]'. This was no doubt heard by Irenaeus as a title, which was in fact precisely what the Valentinian author had intended.

In other instances, such an appropriate phrase at the beginning of the text, what is technically called the *incipit*, has been lifted out and repeated, separated as a title from the body of the text by a blank line above and below and surrounded by dashes as decoration. Let me illustrate:

A text which begins: 'Concerning the hypostasis of the Authorities (ἐξουσία) in the Spirit of the Father of Truth […]' (NHC II, 4: 86,20–21), has as its subscript title at the end (NHC II: 97,22–23), set off by blank space with two decorated lines, the summary of that beginning as its title: '*The Hypostasis of the Rulers* (ἀρχῶν)'. A text which begins: 'The revelation (ἀποκάλυψις) which Adam taught his son Seth in the seven hundredth year' (NHC V, 5: 64,2–4), has as its superscript title (64,1) and its subscript title (85,32), both set off by blank space and decoration, the title '*The Apocalypse of Adam*'.

A text which begins: 'The paraphrase which was about the unbegotten Spirit' (NHC VII, 1: 1,2–3), has as its superscript title (1,1), set off by blank space and decoration, the title '*The Paraphrase of Shem*'.

A text which begins: 'The revelation of Dositheos about the three steles of Seth, the Father of the living and unshakable race' (NHC VII, 5: 118,10–13), has as its subscript title (127,22), set off by blank space and decoration, the title '*The Three Steles of Seth*'.

A text which begins: 'The teaching of the savior and the revelation of the mysteries and the things hidden in silence, even these things which he taught John, his disciple' (NHC II, 1: 1,1–5), has on the front flyleaf facing the beginning of the text the title: '*The Apocryphon of John*' (NHC III), and again as a subscript title (NHC II, 1: 32,8–10; III, 1: 40,10–11; IV, 1: 49,27–28; P. Berol. 77,6–7) the title '*The Apocryphon of John*'.

A text which begins: 'These are the secret sayings which the living Jesus spoke and which Didymus Judas Thomas wrote' (NHC II, 2: 32,10–12), has as its subscript title, set off by blank space with two decorated lines at the end (NHC II, 1: 51,26–27), the title: '*The Gospel according to Thomas*'.

A text which begins: 'The secret words that the Savior spoke to Judas Thomas which I, even I Mathaias, wrote down, while I was walking, listening to them speak with one another' (NHC II, 7: 138,1–4), has as its subscript title, set off by blank space and decorated lines at the end (145,18), the title: '*The Book of Thomas*'.

A text which begins: 'Eugnostos the Blessed, to those who are his' (NHC III, 2 [and V, 1]: 70,1–2), has as its subscript title, set off by blank space and two decorated lines at the end (90,12–13), the title: '*Eugnostos the Blessed*'.

A text which begins: 'It is the Lord who spoke with me: 'See now the completion of my redemption. I have given you a sign of these things, James, my brother'' (NHC V, 3: 24,11–13), has as its superscript title, crowded between the preceding tractate and the first line of the text, where there is hardly room for it, as if it were an afterthought (24,10), the title '*The Apocalypse of James*', but again as a subscript title set off appropriately on two lines with decoration (44,9–10), the title '*The Apocalypse of James*'.

An immediately following text which begins: 'This is the discourse that James the Just spoke in Jerusalem, which Mareim, one of the priests, wrote down' (NHC V, 4: 44,13–17), has as its superscript title on two lines (44,11–12), the title: '*The Apocalypse of James*'.

A text which begins: 'Peter the apostle of Jesus Christ, to Philip our beloved brother and our fellow apostle and to the brethren who are with you: greetings!' (NHC VIII, 2: 132,12–15), has as its superscript title on two lines, set off by blank space and decoration (132,10–11), the title: '*The Letter of Peter Which He Sent to Philip*'.

The editors of *The Gospel of the Egyptians* first collected this data and made the important observation.[5]

> A closer look at these titles reveals that there was more involved than the need for a short and memorable phrase. What stands out is that the canonical terms 'gospel', 'letter' and 'apocalypse' have been introduced even though these designations were not used in the tractate itself. These secondary titles betray a Christianisation process.

It is almost as if the Nag Hammadi Codices were prepared as a kind of counter-canon, an alternative to the New Testament, or at least claiming equal status.

Thus, as we turn to the four 'Gospels' among the Nag Hammadi Codices, we must keep in mind this proclivity to use the names of literary genres given authority by their prominence in the emerging canon of the New Testament. In each such

---

5. *Nag Hammadi Codices III, 2 and IV, 2: The Gospel of the Egyptians (The Holy Book of the Great Invisible Spirit)* (edited with translation and commentary by Alexander Böhlig and Frederik Wisse in cooperation with Pahor Labib; The Coptic Gnostic Library; NHS, 4; Leiden: Brill, 1975), 'The Title', pp. 18–23, esp. 19–20.

case, one must ask to what extent such a title is appropriate to the text itself, apart from its tendentious and secondary use in the Nag Hammadi Codices.

This approach then represents a middle ground between those, such as J.-M. Sevrin, who argue that the revered title 'Gospel' should be reserved for the canonical Gospels,[6] and, on the other hand, Elaine Pagels, who has entitled her best-selling book *The Gnostic Gospels*, which is not a study of the four Nag Hammadi tractates called 'Gospels', but rather her appeal to Gnosticism in general to support the kind of inward religiosity she advocates as her overall 'gospel'.[7]

I turn, then, to the four Nag Hammadi tractates that are called 'Gospels': *The Gospel of Truth*, *The Gospel of Philip*, *The Gospel of the Egyptians*, and *The Gospel of Thomas*.

1. *The Gospel of Truth*

The Gospel of Truth is from Nag Hammadi Codex I, which is also known as the Jung Codex, so some of you may know *The Gospel of Truth* as the first tractate of

---

6.   In a discussion at the Society of Biblical Literature (on 19 xi 95), on the occasion of the fiftieth anniversary of the Nag Hammadi discovery, following my plenary address entitled 'Nag Hammadi: The First Fifty Years'.

7.   Elaine Pagels, *The Gnostic Gospels* (New York: Random House, 1979). What she means by *The Gnostic Gospels* is not really the same thing as I have been asked to address here in terms of 'the Nag Hammadi Gospels'. Her interest is not the gnostic Gospels, but the gnostic gospel, the gospel of Gnosticism, as she understands it in Jungian terms (132–33):

Whoever follows the direction of his own mind need not accept anyone else's advice [...] those gnostics who conceived of *gnosis* as a subjective, immediate experience, concerned themselves above all with the internal signifiance of events. Here again they diverged from orthodox tradition, which maintained that human destiny depends upon the events of 'salvation history'—the history of Israel, especially the prophets' predictions of Christ and then his actual coming, his life, and his death and resurrection. All of the New Testament gospels, whatever their differences, concern themselves with Jesus as a historical person. And all of them rely on the prophets' predictions to provide the validity of the Christian message. [...] But according to the *Gospel of Thomas*, Jesus dismisses as irrelevant the prophets' predictions. [...] Such gnostic Christians saw actual events as secondary to their perceived meaning.

For this reason, this type of gnosticism shares with psychotherapy a fascination with the nonliteral significance of language, as both attempt to understand the internal quality of experience. The psychoanalyst C. G. Jung has interpreted Valentinus' creation myth as a description of the psychological processes. Valentinus tells how all things originate from 'the depth', the 'abyss'—in psychoanalytic terms, from the unconscious. From that 'depth' emerge Mind and Truth, and from them, in turn, the Word (Logos) and Life. And it was the word that brought humanity into being. Jung read this as a mythical account of the origin of human consciousness. [...]

A follower of Valentinus, the author of the *Gospel of Philip*, explores the relationship of experiential truth to verbal description. [...] This gnostic teacher criticizes those who mistake religious language for a literal language, professing faith in God, in Christ, in the resurrection or the church, as if these were all 'things' external to themselves.

the Jung Codex, published with great fanfare in 1956, and with less fanfare published again as Nag Hammadi Codex I in 1977. Actually, as already mentioned, *The Gospel of Truth* has no title at all, comparable to titles of Nag Hammadi tractates set off by space and decorations at the beginning or end. Rather, the word 'gospel' appears only in the opening line of the text, which reads: 'The gospel of truth is joy for those who have received from the Father of truth the grace of knowing him [...]'. Here the word 'gospel' refers to the message, the good news, not to a book or a genre of books, such as we are using the term here in referring to 'the Fourfold Gospel'. In this regard the opening line of *The Gospel of Truth* is more like the opening verse of the Gospel of Mark, which reads: 'The beginning of the gospel of Jesus Christ, the Son of God'. Mark did not begin his Gospel by saying what is obvious, that this is the beginning of his book, his Gospel, but rather with the emphasis that this is the beginning of the Christian message, 'the beginning of the good news of Jesus Christ, the Son of God'. At the beginning of *The Gospel of Truth*, just as at the beginning of Mark, 'gospel' does not mean a book, a biography of Jesus, but refers to the message itself, the good news.

In the phrase 'gospel of truth', 'of truth' is an adjectival phrase in the genitive, a cumbersome circumlocution for a simple adjective, and really means no more than the adjective 'true', 'the true gospel', much as in the case of the Dead Sea Scrolls the founder's title, 'the teacher of righteousness', really means only 'the righteous teacher'. In both cases the expression is meant invidiously: 'The righteous teacher' in an oblique reference to Jerusalem's unrighteous teachers, from whom the Essenes have withdrawn to the area of the Dead Sea so as to maintain their purity until the time comes when they can return vindicated and uncontaminated to Jerusalem. Similarly 'the true gospel' hints broadly that there is an untrue gospel, a false Christian message that is perhaps all that the common mass of Christians would be able to understand, 'tell me the stories of Jesus'. For since *The Gospel of Truth* was composed in the second century, the term 'gospel' was already being attached to biographies of Jesus such as the four canonical Gospels. So when Irenaeus picked up the invidious smear implicit in referring to the 'true' gospel, he sensed it as a put-down of other Gospels such as those that were becoming the Fourfold Gospel.[8]

> Those who are from Valentinus, setting themselves outside of any fear and producing their own compositions, take pride in the fact that they have more gospels than there really are. For, they even have advanced to such a degree of audacity that they entitle the gospel written not long ago by themselves as the 'Gospel of Truth', although it does not at all conform to the gospels of the apostles, so that not even the gospel exists among them without blasphemy. For, if what is produced by them is the 'Gospel of Truth', and if it is dissimilar to those which have been transmitted to us by the apostles, those who wish to do so can learn—as is shown by the scriptures themselves— that what has been transmitted by the apostles is not the Gospel of truth.

---

8. Irenaeus, *Ad. Haer.* 3.11.9, cited by Harold W. Attridge, *Nag Hammadi Codex I (The Jung Codex)*. I. *Introduction, Texts and Translation* (ed. Harold Attridge; The Coptic Gnostic Library; NHS, 22; Leiden: Brill, 1985), p. 65.

The Gospel of Truth from Nag Hammadi is however not a biography of Jesus, but rather a homily, a meditation about Christianity from a Valentinian point of view, and hence really has practically nothing to do with the focus of the present conference on 'the Fourfold Gospel'. The invidious opening comment against the Gospels that at that time were becoming canonical is the only reason it has ever been referred to as itself a 'gospel'. Hence it calls for no further discussion in a conference devoted to 'Gospels', since it is itself not a 'Gospel', if by that one means, as one does, a text primarily recording traditions about Jesus.

2. *The Gospel of the Egyptians*

Two copies of *The Gospel of the Egyptians* are in the Nag Hammadi Codices III and IV, which attests to its popularity in early Christianity. There is also a completely different *Gospel of the Egyptians* mentioned by Origen, Hippolytus and Epiphanius, and quoted by Clement of Alexandria.[9] It is these quotations that make it clear that *The Gospel of the Egyptians* in Nag Hammadi Codices is not what the church fathers referred to as *The Gospel of the Egyptians*. Rather the Nag Hammadi tractate actually has a quite different title, set off by empty space and decorations at the conclusion (NHC III: 69,18–20), as is typical in the Nag Hammadi Codices: 'The holy book of the great, invisible Spirit'.

This title echoes the opening lines, the *incipit*, for, as we have seen, a formal title set off at the beginning or end of a tractate would appropriately grow out of the *incipit*. The text itself actually began (NHC III: 40,12–13; IV: 50,1–3): 'The holy book of the Egyptians of the great invisible Spirit [...] 'Here 'holy book' in Coptic is apparently not a translation of the Greek εὐαγγέλιον, since in the *incipit*, in the colophon, and in the subscript title (NHC III: 40,12; 69,16.18), ἱερός, the Greek word for 'holy', is used as a loan word. Furthermore, in the *incipit* of both codices, the standard Coptic word for book is used, whereas in the colophon and the subscript title at the end (III: 69, 16.18), the Greek word βίβλος is used as a loan word. So the text itself did not use the word 'Gospel'. Of course, the *incipit* 'holy book' was enough to suggest 'Gospel', so it was easy to imagine 'The holy book of the Egyptians [...]' in the *incipit* becoming 'The Gospel of the Egyptians'. Actually, this step did take place in the colophon, which reads (III: 69, 6–17):

> The gospel (εὐαγγέλιον) of the Egyptians. The God-written, holy, secret book. Grace, understanding, perception, prudence be with him who has written it, Eugnostos the beloved in the Spirit – in the flesh my name is Gongessos – and my fellow lights in incorruptibility, Jesus Christ, Son of God, Savior, ΙΧΘΥΣ. God-written is the holy book of the great, invisible Spirit. Amen.

Yet the substantive inappropriateness of the designation 'Gospel' is clear from the comment, only a few lines below the *incipit*, that the great invisible Spirit, 'the Father whose name cannot be uttered', is hence 'unevangelizable' – εὐαγγελίζεσ-

---

9.   *Fragmente apokryph gewordener Evangelien in griechischer und lateinischer Sprache* (herausgegeben, übersetzt und eingeleitet in Zusammenarbeit mit Egbert Schlarb by Dieter Lührmann; MThSt, 59; Marburg: Elwert, 2000), pp. 26–31.

θαι). The designation 'Gospel' is clearly secondary, part of the Christianizing of what was perhaps originally only a Jewish gnostic text, of the Jewish sect of Sethians.

The editors conclude: 'The title "The Holy Book of the Great Invisible Spirit" should have been preferred but Doresse's title is now too well established to change it'.[10] Jean Doresse, the French graduate student and adventurer, was the first to prepare an inventory of the Nag Hammadi Codices. Hence our first information, and first dis-information, stems from him. His reason for preferring the title *'The Gospel of the Egyptians'* is obvious, when one recalls that the leaf from the Nag Hammadi Codices that always hung in public display at the Coptic Museum in Old Cairo was Codex III, p. 69, with the reading *'The Gospel of the Egyptians'* in full view, as a vindication of Egypt's claim to have had a Gospel of its own. Doresse really knew how to endear himself to the staff of the Coptic Museum, and we have to live with the consequences.

The Gospel of the Egyptians hence does not classify as a 'Gospel', if by that one means, as one does, a text primarily recording traditions about Jesus. Rather it is a Sethian gnostic tractate, in which Seth is identified with Christ.

3. *The Gospel of Philip*

The gnostic *Pistis Sophia*, dating from the last half of the third century, preserves a tradition of three apostles especially entrusted with the sayings of Jesus.[11]

> And when Jesus finished saying these words, Philip sprang up, he took his stand, he laid down the book which was in his hand—for he is the scribe of all the words which Jesus said, and of all the things which he did [...].
>
> It happened now, when Jesus heard Philip, he said to him: 'Hear, Philip, thou blessed one, with whom I spoke; for thou and Thomas and Matthew are those to whom was given, through the First Mystery, to write all the words which I will say, and those things which I will do, and everything which you will see'.

It may be that this tradition, singling out Philip, Thomas and Matthew as the designated scribes of what Jesus said, explains, in part at least, the composition of Nag Hammadi Codex II. For it contains, in second, third, and seventh position, *The Gospel of Thomas*, *The Gospel of Philip*, and *The Book of Thomas*. Of course one would expect to find, instead of *The Book of Thomas*, *The Gospel of Matthew*, for this really to fit. Yet this gnostic tradition found in *Pistis Sophia* probably did not

---

10. Böhlig and Wisse, *Nag Hammadi Codices III, 2 and IV, 2*, p. 18. Jean Doresse proposed his title first in 'Trois livres gnostiques inédits: Évangile des Égyptiens, Épître d'Eugnoste, Sagesse de Jésus Christ', *VC* 2 (1948), pp. 137–43. In his own edition Doresse modified the title to be more inclusive, 'Le Livre sacré du grand Esprit invisible ou L'Évangile des Égyptiens', *JA* 254 (1966), pp. 317–435 (appeared early 1968), see Böhlig and Wisse, p. 18, n. 1 and n. 3.

11. *Pistis Sophia* (text Carl Schmidt, translation and notes Violet MacDermot; The Coptic Gnostic Library; NHS, 9; Leiden: Brill, 1978), pp. 71–72. *Die Pistis Sophia; Die beiden Bücher des Jeû; Unbekanntes altgnostisches Werk* (GCS; Koptisch-gnostische Schriften 1; ed. Carl Schmidt, 4., um das Vorwort erweiterte Auflage ed. Hans-Martin Schenke; Berlin: Akademie-Verlag, 1981), p. 45.

have in view the canonical Gospel of Matthew. It may well have meant *The Book of Thomas*, or, conversely, *The Book of Thomas* may have adjusted its *incipit* to fit: 'The secret words that the Savior spoke to Judas Thomas which I, even I Mathaias,[12] wrote down, while I was walking, listening to them speak with one another'. So Matthias (or Matthew) is indeed the scribe. In this sense, Nag Hammadi Codex II does have 'Gospels' ascribed to Thomas, Philip and Matthew (or Mathaias).

The Gospel of Philip has no superscript title, and the *incipit* does not refer to Philip. But there is a subscript title, not set off as it should be, but crammed into the empty space between this tractate and the next. 'The Gospel' is written in the empty space left at the end of the last line of the text itself, and then 'according to Philip' is in the single blank line between tractates, though not correctly centered in the space—all of which suggests that this title was put here as an afterthought.

This then poses the question as to why this tractate was ascribed to Philip at all. This may be because he is the only apostle mentioned in the tractate by name (NHC II. 3: 73, 8–15):

> Philip the apostle said, 'Joseph the carpenter planted a garden because he needed wood for his trade. It was he who made the cross from the trees which he planted. His own offspring hung on that which he planted. His offspring was Jesus and the planting was the cross.'

One may compare this playing up of Philip to the priority given to Jesus' brothers, James and even more Thomas, in *The Gospel of Thomas*, who are clearly put above Simon Peter and Matthew, also named there (the women Mary in Sayings 21 and 114 and Salome in Saying 61 apparently did not come in question). Thus Sayings 12 and 13 may have been decisive for the title *of The Gospel of Thomas*:

> [12] The disciples said to Jesus, 'We know that you will depart from us. Who is to be our leader?' Jesus said to them, 'Wherever you are, you are to go to James the righteous, for whose sake heaven and earth came into being.'
> [13] Jesus said to his disciples, 'Compare me to someone and tell me whom I am like'. Simon Peter said to him, 'You are like a righteous angel'. Matthew said to him, 'You are like a wise philosopher'. Thomas said to him, 'Master, my mouth is wholly incapable of saying whom you are like'. Jesus said, 'I am not your master. Because you have drunk, you have become intoxicated from the bubbling spring which I have measured out'. And he took him and withdrew and told him three things. When Thomas returned to his companions, they asked him, 'What did Jesus say to you?' Thomas said to them, 'If I tell you one of the things which he

---

12.   There is a slight divergence in the spelling, which makes it unclear whether it is Matthew the disciple, or Matthias, the person elected to replace Judas (Acts 1.23–26). Matthew is spelled Ματθαῖας, whereas Matthias is spelled Μαθθίας. The spelling in NHC II, 7: 138,2–3 is Μαθαίας, which agrees and disagrees with both spellings. Perhaps it is an instance of both figures having been merged into one, as may have been the case with the apostle Philip (Mt. 10.3; Mk 3.18; Lk. 6.14; Jn 1.43–46, 48; 6.5, 7; 12.21, 22; 14.8, 9; Acts 1.13) and the evangelist Philip (Acts 6.5; 8.5, 6, 12, 13, 26–40; 21.8). Hans-Martin Schenke, *Das Philippus-Evangelium (Nag-Hammadi-Codex II,3)* (TU, 143; Berlin: Akademie Verlag, 1997), pp. 7–8, speculates that in the case of Philip it could have been only one person, who in the canonical tradition was split into two.

told me, you will pick up stones and throw them at me; a fire will come out of the stones and burn you up'.

This correlation between a prominent figure in the text, and the title of the text, is similar to the canonical Gospel of Matthew, where in Mt. 9.9 one reads that Jesus called the tax collector Matthew and then dined with him. This would of course not be unusual in Matthew, since many disciples are mentioned there, and Matthew is of course listed as one of the Twelve (Mt. 10.3). But when one consults Matthew's source, Mk 2.14, one sees that the Gospel of Matthew has a very special interest in the apostle Matthew. For Mark had told the story of Jesus calling a tax collector and then dining with him, but Mark had named the tax collector Levi, whereas the Gospel of Matthew renamed him Matthew.

In Mark's list of the Twelve, Levi is not included, though he had just been called, and conversely Matthew is named (Mk 3.18), though he had not been explicitly called. So it is understandable that Matthew smoothes out this inconsistency by changing the calling of Levi to the calling of Matthew, and in his list of the Twelve underlines this point by identifying Matthew as 'the tax collector' (Mt. 10.3).

In all three of these instances, Philip, Thomas, and Matthew, one rightly assumes that the pre-eminence of one apostle mentioned by name above the others has to do with that apostle being listed as the author of the Gospel in question, irrespective of whether one has in mind the traditional explanation that the author of the Gospel thus quietly planted his own name in a text which on the surface remains anonymous, or whether one thinks that the name of the Gospel is derived from finding in it one apostle ranked as pre-eminent.

In the case of *The Gospel of Philip*, it must be the name of Philip in the text that leads to designating him as the evangelist, since actual apostolic authorship is impossible. For *The Gospel of Philip* presupposes Valentinianism, and hence is probably to be dated to the second half of the second century.[13]

There is no reason to think that *The Gospel of Philip* was intended as a Gospel.[14] The term εὐαγγέλιον nowhere occurs in the text, and the text does not consist

---

13. Schenke, *Das Philippus-Evangelium*, p. 5.

14. Martha Lee Turner, *The Gospel according to Philip: The Sources and Coherence of an Early Christian Collection* (NHMS, 38; Leiden: Brill, 1996), p. 8:

A number of senses of the word 'gospel' (εὐαγγέλιον) were current in the Gospel according to Philip's time, but the Nag Hammadi document entitled at its end (as was the practice) ΠΕΥΑΓΓΕΛΙΟΝ ΠΚΑΤΑ ΦΙΛΙΠΠΟΣ ('the Gospel according to Philip') corresponds to none of them. It is clearly not a gospel in the sense(s) of the synoptic gospels or John, regardless of whether these are best seen as narrative expansions of kerygma, or as a type of historiography, or as a development of biography. Nor is it a collection of Jesus' sayings, whether wise or apocalyptic or of whatever kind, as were the synoptics' Sayings Source ('Q') and the Nag Hammadi *Gospel according to Thomas*. Neither is it a collection or catena of Jesus' miracles, as seems to have lain behind canonical Mark and John. Nor yet is it a proclamation of the news of salvation—the sense in which Paul used the word, and the sense in which it is used at the beginning of the untitled document known to modern scholarship as the *Gospel of Truth*. Whatever the *Gospel according to Philip* is, it is none of these.

primarily of material having to do with Jesus. Rather it would seem to consist of excerpts from some Valentinian catechism or the like, as has been argued from very early on.[13] The naming of the text a 'Gospel' may have taken place later than its composition as a collection of excerpts, perhaps first in connec-tion with circulating it, what we would call its 'publication' for a wider audience.[16] It is at least possible that the association with Philip is even older.[17] However one cannot classify it as a 'Gospel', if by that one means, as one does, a text primarily recording traditions about Jesus.

4. *The Gospel of Thomas*

The title is written on two lines as the subscript title, set off by a blank line above and below (NHC II, 1: 51,26–27): '*The Gospel according to Thomas*'. It has been shown that the reference to Thomas is supported by Saying 13 and the *incipit*, with its reference to Didymus Judas Thomas. Didymus is the Greek word and Thomas the Aramaic word for 'twin'. So the work is ascribed to Jesus' brother Jude, just as is a minor epistle in the New Testament, but now nicknamed 'Twin', to highlight his claim to preeminence. We have already seen how, in Saying 13, Thomas is the disciple who, speechless, is unable to say who Jesus is, which is in fact the right answer, whereupon Jesus tells him three things that Thomas is afraid to repeat to the others less they stone him. This makes it clear that Thomas has the secret sayings, an idea which was then simply lifted up into the *incipit*.

With regard to the term 'Gospel', present both in the title and in patristic and Manichaean references to this work,[18] the *incipit* suggests another designation: 'These are the secret sayings which the living Jesus spoke and which Didymus Judas Thomas wrote' (NHC II, 2: 32,10–12). Actually, this opening of the text is also extant in one of the three fragmentary Greek copies of *The Gospel of Thomas* (P. Oxy. 1, 655, and, here, 654): οὗτοι οἱ {οι} λόγοι οἱ [ἀπόκρυφοι οὓς ἐλά−] λησεν Ἰη(σοῦ)ς ὁ ζῶν. So the text itself thought of itself as 'secret sayings'. The title 'Gospel' may indeed be secondary, to compete with other works being called 'Gospels' in early Christianity.

15. See Schenke, *Das Philippus-Evangelium*, pp. 5–6, and Turner, *The Gospel according to Philip*, *passim*, for the relevant literature and discussion.

16. Schenke, *Das Philippus-Evangelium*, 7:

> Bei solcher Betrachtung dürfte es dann die nächstgelegene Annahme sein, daß das Neu-Verständnis des Textes unmittelbar mit seiner 'Veröffentlichung' und all-gemeinen Verbreitung zusammenhängt, so daß man sagen könnte: Was immer er vorher gewesen ist, verbreitet wurde er als 'Evangelium nach Philippus'.

17. Schenke, *Das Philippus-Evangelium*, pp. 7–8, gives as his 'Arbeitshypothese': '... die als Quelle des EvPhil (in bloßer Konkretisierung der Vorstellung Isenbergs von den Taufkatechesen) mit "imaginären" (nämlich alten und *verlorengegangenen*) Philippus-Akten rechnet, deren *Missionsreden* der "Autor" des EvPhil exzerpiert hätte'.

18. Wilhelm Schneemelcher (ed.), *Neutestamentliche Apokryphen in deutscher Übersetzung* (1. Band, *Evangelien*, 6. Aufl; Tübingen: Mohr–Siebeck, 1999), pp. 93–94 ('Einleitung' to *The Gospel of Thomas* by Beate Blatz).

In distinction from the three other Nag Hammadi 'Gospels', which really should not be classified as 'Gospels', since they do not consist primarily of traditions about Jesus, *The Gospel of Thomas*, consisting of 114 sayings attributed to Jesus, does in this sense qualify as a 'Gospel', in consisting primarily of traditions about Jesus.

Yet *The Gospel of Thomas* is a Sayings Gospel, not a Narrative Gospel, and hence some have reasoned it should not be considered a 'Gospel' at all, but only a sayings collection. For by the time the canonizing process was underway, the baptismal confession of Rome had become what we know as the Apostles' Creed, in which the public ministry of Jesus is completely skipped, and the crucial information about Jesus is focused on his virgin birth and the cross and resurrection, all of which are missing in *The Gospel of Thomas*. This was no doubt a primary reason for its exclusion from the canon then, and for many still today as reason to look upon it as deficient, not deserving the title 'Gospel'.[19] But since there are by now more than one such sayings collection containing traditions about Jesus, there has instead emerged a trend to distinguish between Narrative Gospels and Sayings Gospel, thereby according both *genres* the title 'Gospel' in modern discussion.[20]

When *The Gospel of Thomas* was first published, its importance was often played down on the basis of its inclusion in the gnostic Codex II of Nag Hammadi. One assumed that sayings shared with the New Testament were simply secondary extracts from the canonical Gospels, once the narrative ingredients had been removed by the gnostics as irrelevant, on the grounds that the gnostic redeemer saves not by what he does, but only by teaching *gnosis*. It was also assumed that sayings not in the New Testament were largely gnostic fabrications. Both of these arguments have lost their force over the intervening half-century. For other Nag Hammadi tractates that are clearly gnostic do use Jesus traditions that are not just his sayings, such as his death and resurrection. And the sayings found in *The Gospel of Thomas*, but not in the canonical Gospels, cannot in most cases be derived from Gnosticism by any stretch of the imagination. *The Gospel of Thomas* clearly stands in the still-living oral tradition of the transmission of sayings of Jesus.

The Coptic translation does indeed survive in a gnostic codex, Nag Hammadi Codex II. But the three Greek fragmentary copies from Oxyrhynchus, P. Oxy. 1, 654, and 655, have no gnostic associations, and hence *The Gospel of Thomas* must be assessed on its own terms. And in fact there are other instances of gnostic and

19.   François Bovon and Pierre Geoltrain (eds.), *Écrits apocryphe chrétiens*, I (Bibliothèque de la Pléiade; Paris: Gallimard, 1997), p. 26 ('Introduction' to *The Gospel of Thomas* by Claudio Gianotto):

> Bien que le terme 'Évangile' figure dans le titre, ainsi que l'attestent le manuscrit copte et la tradition patristique, l'apocryphe n'appartient pas proprement dit à cette catégorie, du moins au sens où on l'entend pour les textes canoniques. Nous n'y trouvons pas de structure narrative; les éléments biographiques concernant Jésus sont pratiquement absent: aucune mention n'est faite de sa mort et de sa résurrection; cet écrit ne constitue qu'un recueil de *logia*, introduits pour la plupart par la formule: 'Jésus a dit', ou bien par une question généralement posée par les disciples. Il est en cela analogue à l'une des sources communes à Matthieu et à Luc, la source Q…'

20.   Frans Neirynck, 'Q: From Source to Gospel', *ETL* 71 (1995), pp. 421–30.

non-gnostic texts being together in the same codex. The discovery of the *Acts of Peter* in the gnostic codex P. Berol. 8502 has not led scholarship to consider the *Acts of Peter* to be gnostic, especially since the polemic of the text is directed against the gnostic master Simon Magus. Similarly, the excerpt from Plato's *Republic* (588B–589B) in Nag Hammadi Codex VI, as tractate 5, does not make Plato into a gnostic. And there are other non-gnostic tractates in the Nag Hammadi Codices, such as the sapiential text *The Teachings of Silvanus* (NHC VII, 4). So, again, *The Gospel of Thomas* must be assessed in its own right.

About the nearest that *The Gospel of Thomas* comes to having a gnostic saying is Saying 50:

> Jesus says:
> 1 If they say to you: 'Where do you come from?' (then) say to them: 'We have come from the light, the place where the light has come into being by itself, has established [itself] and has appeared in their image.'
> 2 If they say to you: 'Is it you?' (then) say: 'We are his children, and we are the elect of the living Father.'
> 3 If they ask you: 'What is the sign of your Father among you?' (then) say to them: 'It is movement and repose.'

But what is completely missing from *The Gospel of Thomas* is the elaborate gnostic mythology that characterizes the gnostic texts that we have known thus far. *The Gospel of Thomas* developed in an environment in which Gnosticism could emerge, but was itself not yet gnostic.

What is perhaps most relevant for 'placing' *The Gospel of Thomas* in relation to Gnosticism is that Christian gnostic texts have normally taken the form of appearances of the resurrected Christ to his disciples, to divulge gnostic mythology. In this way the gnostics could explain the absence of gnostic mythology from mainline Christianity by claiming that gnostic mythology was an esoteric teaching first revealed by the resurrected Christ to the select few. This dominant *genre* of Christian Gnosticism, 'Appearances of the Resurrected to His Disciples', were not called 'Gospels' in the ancient sources themselves. Yet, for all practical purposes, they are for Gnosticism what 'Gospels' are for orthodox Christianity. Hence, let me give you a taste of such gnostic 'Gospels'.

Such gnostic 'Appearances of the Resurrected to His Disciples' do occur in the Nag Hammadi Codices. In early Christian times, the most popular Nag Hammadi tractate of all (to judge by the fact that four copies are extant) was *The Apocryphon of John*, which begins (NHC II, 1:1, 1–3,10).[21]

> And I grieved [greatly in my heart, saying], 'How [was] the savior [appointed], and why was he sent [into the world] by [his Father, and who is his] Father, who [sent him, and of what sort] is [that] aeon [to which we shall go?] For what did he [mean (when) he said to us], 'That aeon to [which you shall go is of the] type of the [imperishable] aeon', [but he did not] teach us concerning [the latter of what

21.   Michael Waldstein and Frederik Wisse (eds.), *The Apocryphon of John: Synopsis of Nag Hammadi Codices II,1; III,1 and IV,1, with BG 8502,2* (The Coptic Gnostic Library; NHMS, 33; Leiden: Brill, 1995), pp. 12–21.

sort it is'.] Straightway, [while I was contemplating these things,] behold, the [heavens opened, and] the [whole] creation [which is] below heaven shone, and [the world] was shaken. [I was afraid, and behold, I] saw in the [light a child who stood] by me. While I looked [at it, it became] like an old man. And he [changed his] likeness (again), becoming like a servant. There [was not a plurality] before me, but there was a [likeness] with multiple forms in the [light,] and [the resemblances] appeared through each other, [and] the [likeness] had three forms. He said to me, 'John, John, why do you wonder, and why [are you] afraid? You are not unfamiliar with this likeness, are you?—that is, do not [be] faint-hearted!— I am the one who [is with you] always. I [am the Father], I am the Mother, I am the Son. I am the undefiled and uncontaminated One. [Now I have come to teach you] what is, [and what was,] and what will come to [pass], that [you may know the things] which are not manifest [and those which are manifest, and to teach you] concerning the [immovable race of] the [perfect Man].

This goes on for several pages (ending NHC II, 1: 32,10). But rather than going on, let me turn to another Nag Hammadi 'Dialogue of the Resurrected with his Disciples', *The Letter of Peter to Philip* (NHC VIII, 2), which begins (132,10–135,14):

They went upon the mountain which is called 'the (mount) of olives', the place where they used to gather with the blessed Christ when he was in the body. Then, when the apostles had come together, and had thrown themselves upon their knees, they prayed thus saying, 'Father, Father, Father of the Light, who possesses the incorruptions, hear us just as [thou hast] [taken pleasure] in thy holy child Jesus Christ. For he became for us an illuminator in the darkness. Yea hear us'. And they prayed again another time saying, 'Son of Life, Son of Immortality, who is in the light, Son, Christ of Immortality, our Redeemer, give us power, for they seek to kill us'. Then a great Light appeared so that the mountain shone from the light of him who had appeared. And a voice called out to them saying, 'Listen to my words that I may speak to you. Why are you asking me? I am Jesus Christ who am with you forever'. Then the apostles answered and said, 'Lord, we would like to know the deficiency of the aeons and their pleroma'. And: 'How are we detained in this dwelling place?' Further: 'How did we come to this place?' And: 'In what manner shall we depart?' Again: 'How do we have [the] authority of boldness?' [And]: 'Why do the powers fight against us?' Then a voice came to them out of the light saying, 'It is you yourselves who are witnesses that I spoke all these things to you. But because of your unbelief I shall speak again. First of all concerning [the deficiency] of the Aeons, this [is] the deficiency, when the disobedience and the foolishness of the mother appeared without the commandment of the majesty of the Father [...]'

Thereupon Jesus gives the gnostic answer to each of the leading gnostic questions that had been posed by the disciples.

This then is what one would expect of a gnostic 'Gospel'. But *The Gospel of Thomas*, instead, opens:

These are the hidden words that the living Jesus spoke. And Didymos Judas Thomas wrote them down. And he said: 'Whoever finds the meaning of these words will not taste death.'

People have of course tried to bring this into line with the expected gnostic 'Gospel' *genre* of a 'Dialogue of the Resurrected with His Disciples', by taking the reference to 'the living Jesus' to mean the resurrected Christ. But nowhere in *The Gospel of Thomas* does 'living' mean 'resurrected'. Rather, it is a participle attached to 'Father' (Sayings 3 and 50), to the 'place' of salvation (Saying 4), to those 'who will not die' (Saying 11), to God in the expression 'the son of the living one' (Saying 37), to Jesus as 'the one living in your presence' (Sayings 52 and 59), to persons in this life ('the living', Saying 59), to one who does not die ('one will die and the other will live', Saying 61), to Jesus' followers in this life ('the one who lives from the living one will not see death', Saying 111), and to a saved person ('a living spirit resembling you males', Saying 114). Hence it would never occur to anyone to take the opening reference to 'the living Jesus' to be a reference to Jesus in a resurrection appearance, if one did not already begin with the assumption that it is a gnostic 'Dialogue of the Resurrected with His Disciples'. That is to say, only a circular argument can lead to such a conclusion.

Actually, what 'the living Jesus' says are mostly sayings the canonical Gospels place during Jesus' 'public ministry' before the resurrection. For example, one would not ascribe to the Resurrected such sayings as:

> Whatever your right hand does, your left hand should not know what it is doing. (Saying 62,2).
> Blessed are you when(ever) they hate you (and) persecute you. (Saying 68,1).
> The harvest is plentiful but there are few workers. But beg the Lord that he may send workers into the harvest'. (Saying 73).
> The kingdom of the Father is like a merchant who had merchandise and found a pearl. That merchant is prudent. He sold the goods (and) bought for himself the pearl alone. (Saying 76).
> [Foxes have] their holes and birds have their nest. But the son of man has no place to lay his head down (and) to rest. (Saying 86).

There is no more reason to ascribe such sayings to the Resurrected than there is to shift them in the canonical Gospels from the Public Ministry to Resurrection Appearances.

Indeed, there are even instances where *The Gospel of Thomas* presents an older version of a saying located during the public ministry in the canonical Gospels. An instance is the 'Parable of the Sower', which in the New Testament (Mk 4.1–9 par. Mt. 13.1–9 par. Lk. 8.4–8) has an allegorical interpretation appended to it on how the word preached by the early church succeeds in the world (Mk 4.13–20 par. Mt. 13.18–23 par. Lk. 8.11–15). For over a century it has been generally agreed that this allegory has been added not by Jesus but by Mark. But this conspicuously secondary allegory is completely absent from *The Gospel of Thomas*, though the parable without the allegory is in fact present (Saying 9).

Another Markan parable is so shot through with allegory in the story line itself that scholars have despaired of being able to peel off the secondary allegorization and reconstruct a parable that one could ascribe to Jesus, namely the 'Parable of the Wicked Husbandmen' (Mk 12.1–12 par. Mt. 21.33–46 par. Lk. 20.9–19), which is actually an allegory sketching the whole of saving history from the Old Testament prophets to the cross and resurrection and destruction of Jerusalem as God's punishment:

A man planted a vineyard, and set a hedge around it, and dug a pit for the wine press, and built a tower, and let it out to tenants, and went into another country. When the time came, he sent a servant to the tenants, to get from them some of the fruit of the vineyard. And they took him and beat him, and sent him away emptyhanded. Again he sent to them another servant, and they wounded him in the head, and treated him shamefully. And he sent another, and him they killed, and so with many others, some they beat and some they killed. He had still one other, a beloved son; finally he sent him to them, saying, 'They will respect my son'. But those tenants said to one another, 'This is the heir; come, let us kill him, and the inheritance will be ours'. And they took him and killed him, and cast him out of the vineyard. What will the owner of the vineyard do? He will come and destroy the tenants, and give the vineyard to others. Have you not read this scripture: 'The very stone which the builders rejected has become the head of the corner; this was the Lord's doing, and it is marvelous in our eyes'?

But *The Gospel of Thomas* (Saying 65) produces the pre-allegorical parable that scholars had thought could not be reconstructed:

A [userer] owned a vineyard. He gave it to some farmers so that they would work it (and) he might receive its fruit from them. He sent his servant so that the farmers might give him the fruit of the vineyard. They seized his servant, beat him, (and) almost killed him. The servant went (back and) told his master. His master said: 'Perhaps <they> did not recognise <him>'. He sent another servant, (and) the farmers beat that other one as well. Then the master sent his son (and) said: 'Perhaps they will show respect for my son'. (But) those farmers, since the knew that he was the heir of the vineyard, seized him (and) killed him. Whoever has ears should hear.

Then the next saying of *The Gospel of Thomas* reads: Jesus says, 'Show me the stone that the builders have rejected. It is the cornerstone.' This quotation from the Old Testament became a prooftext of the resurrection in the primitive church, and so was elevated in the New Testament allegory to the concluding punch line of the allegory itself.

It is of course not the case that each time that a saying or parable is both in the canonical Gospels and in *The Gospel of Thomas*, *The Gospel of Thomas* preserves the older reading, just as it is not the case that the canonical Gospels always preserve the older reading. The evidence simply does not fit a one-sided solution, which was the somewhat doctrinaire thesis of a generation ago. But this has now given way to the recognition that the relative age of readings in *The Gospel of Thomas* and the canonical Gospels must be examined on a case-by-case basis, with sometimes diverging results.

Let me give an instance where the canonical text seems to have the older reading: Saying 16 of *The Gospel of Thomas* reads:

Jesus says:
1 Perhaps people think that I have come to cast peace upon the earth.
2 But they do not know that I have come to cast dissention upon the earth: fire, sword, war.
3 For there will be five in one house: there will be three against two and two against three, father against son and son against father!
4 And they will stand as solitary ones.

This saying does not make sense out of the statistics: five in one house, three against two and two against three. For only father against son and son against father are mentioned. But in Lk. 12.49–53, the same material is given in a way that provides what must be presupposed in *The Gospel of Thomas*, if one wants to make sense of its statistics:

> I came to cast fire upon the earth; and would that it were already kindled! … Do you think that I have come to give peace on earth? No, I tell you, but rather division; for henceforth in one house there will be five divided, three against two and two against three; they will be divided, father against son and son against father, mother against daughter and daughter against her mother, mother-in-law against her daughter-in-law and daughter-in-law against her mother-in-law.

It is only this Lukan text that makes sense of Saying 16 of *The Gospel of Thomas*, with the fifth person being the daughter-in-law who lives in the family home with the parents, the married son, and an unmarried daughter. Hence the Lukan text preserves the older tradition.[22]

Conversely, there has recently come to my attention a striking instance of *The Gospel of Thomas* preserving the older reading, for it even contains a reading so old that it does not yet contain a scribal error present in the canonical Gospels![23] The archaic sayings cluster 'Free from Anxiety like (Ravens and) Lilies' (Mt. 6.25–33 par. Lk. 12.22b–31) is nearly identical in Matthew and Luke. One explains this, as one does in many other such instances, by postulating that they had, along-side their first shared source, the Gospel of Mark, a second shared source, con-sisting of a collection of sayings that scholars have called Q (for the German word *Quelle*, source).

In this archaic sayings collection quoted by Matthew and Luke, the descriptions of the carefree ravens and lilies is presented in strikingly parallel form, in that three verbs describe the practice that humans should emulate, if they are free from anxiety: Ravens 'neither sow nor reap nor gather into barns', whereas lilies 'grow,

---

22. See my detailed presentation in 'Q 12.49-59: Children against Parents—Judging the Time—Settling out of Court', in S. Carruth (ed.), *Documenta Q: Reconstructions of Q Through Two Cen-turies of Gospel Research Excerpted, Sorted, and Evaluated* (Leuven: Peeters, 1997), pp. 119–21.

23. James M. Robinson and Christoph Heil, 'Zeugnisse eines schriftlichen, griechischen vorkanonischen Textes: Mt 6,28b a*, P.Oxy. 655 I,1–17 (EvTh 36) und Q 12,27', *ZNW* 89 (1998), pp. 30–44; J.M. Robinson, 'The Pre-Q Text of the (Ravens and) Lilies: Q 12.22–34 and P. Oxy. 655 (Gos. Thom. 36)', in S. Maser (ed.), *Text und Geschichte: Facetten theologischen Arbeitens aus dem Freundes- und Schülerkreis. Dieter Lührmann zum 60. Geburtstag* (MThSt 50; Marburg: Elwert, 1999), pp. 143–80; J.M. Robinson, 'A Written Greek Sayings Cluster Older than Q: A Vestige', *HThR* 92 (1999), pp. 61–77; J.M. Robinson and Christoph Heil, 'Noch einmal: Der Schreibfehler in Q 12,27', *ZNW* 92 (2001) xxx–xx; *idem*, 'The Lilies of the Field: Sayings 36 of the Gospel of Thomas and Secondary Accretions in Q 12.22b–31', *NTS* 47 (2001), pp. 1–25; J.M. Robinson, 'Excursus on the Scribal Error in Q 12.27', in J.M. Robinson, Paul Hoffmann, and John S. Kloppenborg (eds.), *The Critical Edition of Q: Synopsis including the Gospels of Matthew and Luke, Mark and Thomas with English, German, and French translations of Q and Thomas* (Minne-apolis: Fortress Press; Leuven: Peeters, 2000), pp. xcix–ci. See also the photographs of the relevant texts from a*and P. Oxy. 655 used as endpapers in the *Critical Edition of Q*. This discovery goes back to T.C. Skeat, 'The Lilies of the Field', *ZNW* 37 (1938), pp. 211–14.

they do not work nor do they spin'. But the symmetry is broken in one glaring way: The first thing that lilies do not do, which documents their freedom from anxiety, is neither a negative statement nor is it a chore, but is the comment that lilies grow. This positive statement does not list some task they avoid at all. It does not fit the argument!

T.C. Skeat of the British Museum already solved the problem in 1938, by noting an erased reading in *Codex Sinaiticus*, whose erasures he was studying for the first time with the help of ultraviolet light. There he found that the original scribe had written not at all 'they grow', but rather 'they do not card', the first chore a house-wife performed in making clothing out of wool, and hence exactly what should be listed as the first chore to avoid! The difference is not great in Greek: αὐξάνουσι for 'they grow', οὐ ξαίνουσι for 'they do not card'. Skeat confirmed his ultraviolet reading of the erased text by finding the same reading in Saying 36 of *The Gospel of Thomas*, in one of the early Greek fragments, P. Oxy. 655.

I have followed up on his discovery by locating four places in this archaic sayings collection of Q which have been recognized by scholars over the past cen-tury as secondary intrusions, for purely stylistic and editorial reasons, without com-paring Saying 36 of *The Gospel of Thomas*. However, they turn out to be absent from *The Gospel of Thomas*, thus in effect confirming the scholarly conjecture, but also confirming that *The Gospel of Thomas* has here the older reading.

Thus we have a striking instance of *The Gospel of Thomas* having a correct read-ing that is already corrupted by a scribal error in Q. Indeed the error was already in the archetype of Q from which were made the two copies of Q used one by Mat-thew and one by Luke. The result is that behind those two copies of Q there was a master copy of Q, in which the scribal error was already present, and, even further back, there was a written sayings collection with the originally correct reading, from which the scribal error was made. That is the furthest back, as near to Jesus himself, as anyone has been able to get, in terms of written Greek texts. It is simply not possible to explain away the importance of *The Gospel of Thomas* in this case as being only a belated second century excerpt from the canonical Gospels. In this particular instance it represents a tradition much older and more accurate that the Gospels of Matthew and Luke themselves. Here, if nowhere else, scholars and lay-persons alike can convince themselves that *The Gospel of Thomas* must be included in the study of Jesus and of primitive Christianity, and not simply be relegated to later times and so put aside as of lesser importance.

5. *The Fourfold Gospel*

The prominence of *The Gospel of Thomas* in recent times as *The Fifth Gospel*[24] poses anew the central topic of our conference, the Fourfold Gospel. Enthusiasts for *The Gospel of Thomas* might want to suggest that it should after all be given

---

24. Steven J. Patterson and James M. Robinson, *The Fifth Gospel: The Gospel of Thomas Comes of Age*, with a new English Translation by Hans-Gebhard Bethge *et al.* (Harrisburg, PA: Trinity Press International, 1998).

canonical status and included in the New Testament, while opponents of according it status as a 'Gospel' in its own right could well point to that canonizing zeal as what is to be avoided at all costs. But such rhetoric for and against is really beside the point, since the canon is long since a historical reality that cannot be changed. Matthew, Mark, Luke, and John were included in the canon, for whatever reasons, valid (e.g. their contents) and invalid (e.g. their apostolicity), and have down through the centuries, ever since, played a very important role in history as the Bible's Gospels. *The Gospel of Thomas*, not included in the canon of the New Testament, but buried in the sands of Egypt for 1600 years, has been absent from history all these centuries during which the Bible has played its most decisive rôle. This cannot be changed—one cannot retroactively canonize something that has not shared in this history of the Bible as canon.

On the other hand, the historical importance of *The Gospel of Thomas* for understanding Jesus and the beginnings of Christianity should not be played down by the invidious declassification of it as apocryphal. It would be more accurate to say merely that it ultimately became non-canonical. When Matthew, Mark, Luke, John, and Thomas were written, there was no New Testament canon, and hence no distinction between canonical and non-canonical. They stood on equal footing, and it was only gradually that some were elevated into canonical status, others not.

Perhaps this is clearest when one considers the survival of Gospel manuscripts from the earliest centuries.[25] No manuscript at all has survived from the first century, and very little, and even then only small fragments, from the second century. Here one can list two fragments of the Gospel of John (P^{52} and P^{90}), one of the Gospel of Matthew (P^{104}), one of *The Gospel of Peter* (P. Oxy. 4009), and two of the so-called *Unknown Gospel* (P. Egerton 2 and P. Köln 2255). That is to say, in the second century, Gospels that were later to lose out, as non-canonical, were about as common as Gospels that were later to win out, as canonical. Around 200 CE this began to shift, as the concept of canonicity began to take over, with three copies of Matthew ($P^{(4+)64+67}$, P^{77}, and P^{103}), one of Luke $P^{4(+64+67)}$), one of John (P^{66}), and one of *The Gospel of Peter* (P. Oxy. 2949).

With regard to *The Gospel of Thomas*, there is not only the relatively complete Coptic translation in Nag Hammadi Codex II, from the first half of the fourth century.[26] There are also three very fragmentary copies of the Greek original (P. Oxy. 1, 654, and 655) usually ascribed to the third century. This compares fairly well with the third century statistics for canonical Gospels: five copies of Matthew (P^1,

---

25. This is conveniently laid out in tabular form by Lührmann with Schlarb, *Fragmente apokryph gewordener Evangelien in griechischer und lateinischer Sprache*, pp. 22–23.

26. Søren Giversen, *Apocryphon Johannis: The Coptic Text of the Apocryphon Johannis in the Nag Hammadi Codex II with Translation, Introduction and Commentary* (ATDan, 5; Kopenhagen: Munksgaard, 1963), pp. 34–40, esp. 40: 'In conclusion we can therefore reach this thesis that a relative dating of Codex II will place it after Ecclesiasticus (Louvain) and before Br. M. Ms. Or. 7594. An absolute dating places it as contemporary with Br. M. Pap. 1920 and therefore from 330–40, or more loosely from the first half of the fourth century.' This agrees with the dating of the caronnage that was subsequently found in the covers of Codices I, IV, V and VII. See J.W.B. Barns, G.M. Browne, and K.C. Shelton (eds.), *Nag Hammadi Codices: Greek and Coptic Papyri from the Cartonnage of the Covers* (The Coptic Gnostic Library; NHS, 16; Leiden: Brill, 1981), pp. 3–4, 11.

P^{45}, P^{53}, P^{70}, P^{101}), one of Mark (P^{45}), four of Luke (P^{45},P^{69},P^{75},P^{111}), and twelve of John (P^{5}, P^{22}, P^{28}, P^{39}, P^{45}, P^{75}, P^{80}, P^{95}, P^{106}, P^{107}, P^{108}, P^{109}). Furthermore, it has recently been argued by Søren Giversen, that the three Greek copies of *The Gospel of Thomas* should actually be dated back to the second century.[27] This would put *The Gospel of Thomas* in first place in terms of fragments of copies surviving from that century! It is in any case clear that our modern situation, with the canonical Gospels well known and treasured, but the apocryphal Gospels unknown and looked down on, is very misleading, if we seek to understand the earliest centuries of Christianity, when 'canonical' and 'apocryphal' are largely anachronisms, and popularity was rather evenly distributed.

What is perhaps most striking about the list of surviving papyrus fragments down to the beginning of the third century is what is completely missing: Not only are there no copies of Q, which has ceased to be copied after having been published in enlarged, improved editions known as the Gospels of Matthew and Luke. Also there are no copies of Mark, which had also been published in enlarged, improved editions known as the Gospels of Matthew and Luke, and which also might never have been copied again. But then, in the third century, Mark was apparently gaining in canonicity, for one copy has survived, and indeed not just a tiny fragment, but a relatively complete papyrus copy, located in the Chester Beatty Library in Dublin (P^{45}). In fact, this simply priceless papyrus codex contains all four canonical Gospel and the book of Acts, the only extant book this close to being a complete New Testament prior to the conversion of the Roman Empire, which of course gave Christianity access to deluxe book production. Indeed, in the immediate post-Constantine era huge elegant parchment Bibles were commissioned for the large churches that were built, two of which have survived, the *Codex Sinaiticus*, now in the British Library, and the *Codex Vaticanus*, now in the Vatican Library. But just prior to the conversion of the Roman Empire, the Diocletian persecution at the end of the third century had included in the imperial decree the phrase *traditio codicum*, the handing over and turning in of Christian books for burning. This meant for Christian literature much what the destruction of the library of Alexandria meant for classical literature, the annihilation of our cultural roots. A century ago, one never expected to find whole Christian books that had survived the Diocletian persecution. By far the most important one to have survived is in Dublin. Let your pilgrimage commemorating the year 2000 begin right here!

---

27. S. Giversen, in a lecture entitled 'The Palaeography of Oxyrhynchus Papyri 1 and 654–655', presented at the annual meeting of the Society of Biblical Literature in Boston on 21 November 1999.

THE LATIN GOSPELS, WITH SPECIAL REFERENCE TO IRISH TRADITION

Martin McNamara

Part 1

1. *Early Christianity in the West: Early Latin Christianity*

All four of our canonical Gospels were written in Greek, even though at least one of them (Mark) may have been written in Rome, the centre of the Latin world, and intended primarily for the Roman Christian community. Paul's letter to this same Roman Christian community was also in Greek. Greek was the language of the Christian community in Rome and in the West until the late second century or so. No need was felt for a Latin translation of the Gospels. The earliest Latin citations of the Bible are found in Tertullian (c. 160–c. 225 CE), writing toward the end of the second century.[1]

The *Acts of the Scillitan Martyrs*, drawn up in Latin, on the martyrdom of Christians in the town of Scillium (in modern Tunisia) in the year 180 CE, state that in answer to a question as to what he had in the box or receptacle (*capsa*) he carried, Speratus replied: 'Books and letters of a just man, one Paul'. The reference seems to be to the Epistles of the apostle Paul, which can be presumed to have been in Latin. And if the Pauline epistles were already translated into Latin we can presume that the Gospels also were. About this same year 180 CE the Church in the West (as indeed also in the Syriac- and Coptic-speaking areas) was changing over to the use of the vernacular.

The African Church Father Cyprian (writing c. 250 CE) was clearly using an established Latin translation of the Gospels. In his work *De doctrina christiana*, (composed about 396–97 CE) Augustine speaks of the confusing abundance of Latin translations, and in the letter to Pope Damasus accompanying his revision of the Latin Gospels (c. 384 CE) Jerome speaks in like terms.

These early Gospel texts from c. 250 CE onwards are called the 'Old Latin' (*Vetus Latina*). With Jerome's revision, completed c. 384 CE, a new text came on the scene, one that was later to be known as the Vulgate. These Latin translations were central to Western Latin Church life until the Renaissance and modern times.

2. *Number and Study of the Latin Gospels*

From the third century or so onwards the number of Latin Gospels in circulation at any one time must have been beyond counting. Only a small portion of these are

---

1.   See B.M. Metzger, *The Early Versions of the New Testament: Their Origin, Transmission and Limitations* (Oxford: Clarendon Press, 1977), pp. 285–293.

now extant. To keep an examination of the field within proportions a cut-off point must be introduced. In his classic *Latin Gospel Books from A.D. 400 to A.D. 800,* Patrick McGurk examines 138 texts.[2] This, by reason of definition, excludes full Bibles such as the Codex Amiatinus, and New Testament texts with other material (*Patriciana, Martiniana*) such as the Book of Armagh, and fragments of texts besides. In his groundbreaking four volumes on the Latin Gospels before 900 CE, Bonifatius Fischer deals with 464 manuscripts (even though one or other are later than 900). The 26th edition of the Nestle-Aland Greek and Latin New Testament lists 28 Old Latin texts (including fragments).[3]

Today we are in a very favourable position with regard to the study of the Latin Bible, thanks to the devoted work of many scholars over the past century and a half. There have been editions of Old-Latin biblical texts by British, German and Irish scholars: the *Codex Palatinus* by C. Tischendorf in 1847; others in the Oxford series *Old-Latin Biblical Texts* (seven volumes between 1883 and 1923, containing editions of major Old Latin Gospel texts). A number of studies on the Latin Bible Versions prepared the way for the critical edition of the Vulgate Gospels by John Wordsworth and Henry Julian White (1889–98).[4] They made use of 29 manuscripts for this edition. The critical edition of the Old Latin versions was begun by Adolf Jülicher, and completed by Walter Matzkow and Kurt Aland between 1938 and 1963 (Matthew 1938; John 1963).[5] A new and critical edition of the Vulgate Gospels was published in 1969, under the editorship of R. Weber, with the assistance of B. Fischer, J. Gribomont, H.F.D. Sparks and W. Thiele.[6]

---

2.   P. McGurk, *Latin Gospel Books from A.D. 400 to A.D. 800*, Les Publications de Scriptorium, 5 (Paris and Brussels: Éditions 'Érasme'; Antwerp-Amsterdam: Standaard, 1961).

3.   See [E.] Nestle-[K] Aland, *Novum Testamentum Graece et latine*, 26th edn (Stuttgart: Deutsche Bibelgesellschaft, 1984), pp. 712–13. Basic studies in the field: B. Fischer, 'Das Neue Testament in lateinischer Sprache: Der gegenwärtige Stand seiner Erforschung und seine Bedeutung für die griechische Textgeschichte', in K. Aland (ed.), *Die alten Übersetzungen des Neuen Testaments, die Kirchenväterzitate und Lektionare* (Arbeiten zur neutestamentlichen Bibel, 11; Berlin: de Gruyter, 1972), pp. 1–92; reproduced in Fischer's collected essays: *Beiträge zur Geschichte der lateinischen Bibeltexte* (Aus der Geschichte der lateinischen Bibel, 12; Freiburg: Herder, 1986), pp. 156–274; K. and B. Aland, *Der Text des Neuen Testaments: Einführung in die wissenschaftlichen Ausgaben und in Theorie wie Praxis der modernen Textkritik* (Stuttgart: Deutsche Bibelgesellschaft, 1982), pp. 192–96 (Vetus Latina), pp. 196–97 (Vulgate) [ET *The Text of the New Testament: An Introduction to the Critical Editions and to the Theory and Practice of Modern Textual Criticism* (trans. Erroll F. Rhodes; Grand Rapids, MI: Eerdmans, 2nd edn, 1989)]; B.M. Metzger, *The Text of the New Testament: Its Transmission, Corruption and Restoration* (Oxford: Clarendon Press, 2nd edn, 1968), pp. 72–75 (Old Latin); pp. 75–79 (Vulgate); Metzger, *The Early Versions of the New Testament*, pp. 285–330.

4.   J. Wordsworth and F.J. White, *Nouum Testamentum Domini Nostri Iesu Christi latine secundum editionem Sancti Hieronymi. Pars Prior – Quattuor euangelia* (Oxford; Clarendon Press, 1889–98).

5.   A. Jülicher, W. Matzkow and K. Aland, *Itala. Das Neue Testament in Altlateinischer Überlieferung* (Berlin: de Gruyter, 1938–63).

6.   R. Weber *et al.*, *Biblia Sacra iuxta Vulgatam Versionem* (Stuttgart: Württembergischer Bibelanstalt, 1969).

Bonifatius Fischer has devoted a life's study to the Latin Bible, and in particular to the Gospels. Among his more notable studies on the matter we may mention his authoritative treatment of the Latin Gospels in an essay in 1972 on the New Testament in Latin: the present position of research on the matter and its significance for the history of the Greek text. This was reproduced in a volume of his collected essays in 1986.[7] By then Fischer had perceived that a new approach was needed if we are to understand the transmission of the text of the Latin Gospels.[8] Jerome's Vulgate revision as published in the 1969 Stuttgart edition he regards as resting on sure foundations. And with this, for him, certainty ends. In that same year he announced his major project for the study of the Latin Gospels, which consisted in an exhaustive collation of 16 Gospel pericopes – four for each Gospel – from 464 (mainly) pre-900 CE manuscripts, that is full collation of about one tenth of the whole Gospel material. In each of these 16 pericopes there are about 300 places in which manuscripts differ, for all four Gospels 5690 places. The 464 manuscripts he divides in 29 groups according to the Old Latin text and the geographical origin of the manuscripts. He published the results of his collation in four yearly volumes (one for each Gospel) between 1988 and 1991.[9] Bonifatius Fischer had planned a fifth volume, which would give the principles for the use of the material presented in these four volumes. He died before he could produce this.

Fischer's four volumes are indispensable in any serious study of the complicated transmission history of the Latin Gospels.

3. *Early Latin Gospels*
THE OLD LATIN, *VETUS LATINA. African Type (Afra).*
Manuscripts
k Codex Bobiensis (Turin Biblioteca Nazionale G.VII.15 [1163]). s. IV. Africa. From the Columban monastery of Bobbio. According to Bobbio tradition, preserved in a seventeenth-century note on the fly-leaf of the manuscript, the blessed Abbot Columbanus used to carry this book around with him in his satchel (*pera*). The Codex Bobiensis was written in the fourth century, and apparently in Africa itself. Its biblical text, however, is much older and represents the textual situation of c. 230 CE; this early text form has been retained unchanged in the Bobiensis. The

---

7.   B. Fischer, 'Das Neue Testament in lateinischer Sprache', pp. 1–92; reproduced in Fischer's collected essays: *Beiträge zur Geschichte der lateinischen Bibeltexte* , pp. 156–274.
8.   B. Fischer's new insight was put forward in a paper read at a colloquium in Louvain-la-Neuve in 1986 and published in 1987: B. Fischer, 'Zur Überlieferung des lateinischen Textes der Evangelien', in R. Gryson and P.-M. Bogaert (eds.), *Recherches sur l'histoire de la Bible latine* (Colloque organisé à Louvain-la-Neuve pour la promotion de H. J. Frede au doctorat *honoris causa* en théologie le 18 avril 1986; Cahiers de la Revue théologique de Louvain 19; Louvain-la-Neuve: Publications de la Faculté de Théologie, 1987), pp. 51–104.
9.   B. Fischer, *Die lateinischen Evangelien bis zum 10 Jahrhundert* (Aus der Geschichte der lateinischen Bibel; Freiburg: Herder): *Varianten zu Matthäus*, 1988; *Varianten zu Markus*, 1989; *Varianten zu Lukas*, 1990; *Varianten zu Johannes*, 1991, with the main part of his 1986 lecture reproduced in the introduction to each of the four volumes.

African Church Father Cyprian (died 258 CE) uses an African biblical text, but one more recent than that of *k,* a revised form of *k.* This African text developed rapidly, and there appears to have been a new edition towards the end of the third or in the fourth century. This led to the e, Codex Palatinus, *Afra* text-form. This new form represents a Europeanization, and came about either through revision from Greek Gospel texts or the influence of European Old Latin texts. Its text is nearer to Cyprian than to k.

e Codex Palatinus, Trent, Museo Nazionale (Castel del Buonconsiglio), s. n.; + Dublin, Trinity College, 1709 (N.IV.18) (1 leaf)+ London, British Library additional 40107 (1 leaf). s. V; probably Trent, Italy.
The Dublin fragment was purchased by J. H. Todd in the early 1840s; he dated it to the fourth or early fifth century, and read a study of it to the Royal Irish Academy in 1847,[10] the very year Tischendorf's edition of the *Codex Palatinus* appeared in Leipzig.[11] The text of *e* was written not in Africa, but in upper Italy (Trent?), in the fifth century. It has a lengthy history behind it which it is no longer possible to decipher. Rather than speak simply of it as an African text, it should be regarded as having a fundamental African layer, over which other layers have been laid.

THE OLD LATIN, *VETUS LATINA. European Type.*
For this there are about 18 manuscripts. The core group is represented by the manuscripts b (Veronensis; end of fifth century; probably Verona), ff$_2$ (Corbeiensis; fifth century; Italy); i (Vindobonensis; end of fifth century; Italy), all representing a 'progressive' Italian text from about 350–80 CE. It is related to the Gospel texts used by the fourth century writers Ambrose (c. 339–97 CE), Ambrosiaster (c. 380 CE), and especially in Luke to Lucifer Bishop of Cagliari (died 370–71 CE). It probably was the model that lay behind Jerome in his revision for Pope Damasus (the Vulgate Gospels, completed 384 CE). The Bern fragment t belongs to the same group, and a diluted form of it was still in use in Verona in the eighth century, as is evidenced in the text b$_2$ (Verona, Biblioteca Capitolare). Attached to this core group is the Gallic-Irish group, a group best represented by the Irish text r (Codex Usserianus Primus). We shall consider this group in greater detail below.

10.   Todd's description and examination of the text was published in the *Proceedings of the Royal Irish Academy* 3 (1845–47), pp. 374–81.
11.   C. Tischendorf, *Evangelium Palatinum* (Leipzig: Brockhaus, 1847). Todd compared the text of his fragment with that of the Old Latin *Codex Vercellensis* (*a*; 2nd half of 4th cent.), the *Codex Veronensis* (*b*; end of 5th cent.) and the Vulgate text accepted in his day. His supposition was that the text was written in the fourth or early fifth century. (It is now dated to the fifth century.) In 1879 this leaf was recognized by T.G. Law as belonging to the *Codex Palatinus* (*Academy,* March 1, 1879) and its text was later re-edited in a beautiful facsimile together with the Greek *Codex Rescriptus* (*Z*) by T.K. Abbott *The Codex Rescriptus Dublinensis of St. Matthew's Gospel (Z); also a new edition, revised and augmented; also fragments of the Book of Isaiah, in the LXX version … together with a newly discovered fragment of the Codex Palatinus* by T.K. Abbott (Dublin: Hodges, Foster and Figgis; London: Longmans Green, 1880).

Bilingual Codex Bezae: Latin column (d). MS: Cambridge, University Library, Nn. II.41; s. IV-V

In any study of the Latin Gospels mention must be made of the Latin right-hand side of the bilingual Greek and Latin Codex Bezae. The date and place of origin of this bilingual codex have been much debated. One view is that it originated in Berytus (Beyrouth, the Lebanon). Opinion has been sharply divided as to the nature and independent authority of its Latin text. It would appear that there are three major positions on the matter, not necessarily mutually exclusive:[12] (1) it preserves an ancient form of the Old Latin text, a text that was current no later than the first half of the third century, and may be earlier still; (2) it falls outside the normal framework of the Latin Bible, even though points of contact with the African and European texts cannot be denied;[13] (3) it is basically an Old Latin text, but differing from one Gospel to another. In Matthew, the Latin text presents affinities which are altogether characteristic of the Bobienis (k; VL 1) and to a lesser degree the Palatinus (e) (both of the *Afra* form). For John and Luke (the next Gospels in order in the codex) the text shows signs of revision and here holds a middle position between *e* (of the Afra) and *a* (of the European text), and consequently is closer to the type called 'European'. Mark in the Codex Bezae is much more Europeanized than that of the other three Gospels, with a text which represents an already advanced stage in the evolutionary road of the Vetus Latina.[14]

4. *Jerome's Latin Revision of the Gospels*

In his work *On Christian Doctrine* (*De Doctrina Christiana*; written 396/397 CE) Augustine (354–430 CE) writes as if there was a proliferation of Latin translations of the Bible (including the Gospels?) in the fourth century. In book 2, xi (16), when speaking of the need of Greek and Hebrew as well as Latin to understand the biblical texts, he says:

> The great remedy for ignorance of proper signs [=written words, terms] is the knowledge of languages. And people who speak the Latin tongue need two other languages for the knowledge of Scripture, Hebrew and Greek, that they may have recourse to the original texts if the endless diversity of the Latin translators throw them into doubt. [...] For the translations of the Scriptures from Hebrew into Greek can be counted, but the Latin translators are out of all number. For in the early days of the faith every person who happened to get his hands upon a Greek manuscript, and who thought he had any knowledge, were it ever so little, of the two languages, ventured upon the work of translation.

Similarly in his letter to Damasus, *Novum opus* (384 CE), on his new revision of the Latin Gospels, forestalling objections that Latin texts (*exemplaria*) (rather than

---

12. See Metzger, *The Text of the New Testament*, p. 74.
13. See Fischer, 'Das Neue Testament', in *Beiträge*, pp. 210–11; a similar view in Metzger, *The Early Versions of the New Testament*, p. 318.
14. Thus J.M. Auwers, 'Le texte latin des Évangiles dans le Codex de Bèze', in P.C. Parker and C.-B. Amphoux (eds.), *Codex Bezae: Studies from the Lunel Colloquium, June 1994* (NTTS, 22; Leiden: Brill, 1966), pp. 183–216.

revision from the Greek) should be followed, Jerome can retort (with some exaggeration): 'If we are to pin our faith on the Latin texts, it is for our opponents to tell us *which*; for there are almost as many forms of texts as there are manuscripts' (*Si enim latinis exemplaribus fides est adhibenda, respondeant quibus; tot sunt paene quot codices*).

The model that lay behind Jerome's revision of the Latin Gospels for Pope Damasus (the Vulgate Gospels) seems to have been that, or akin to that, found in the core Latin group. The Greek text against which he revised the Latin seems to have been one or more manuscripts of the *koine* type.

The best authority for the true Vulgate text of the Gospels is Codex Amiatinus (A), copied at Wearmouth-Jarrow c. 700 CE. Another important text is that of the Lindisfarne Gospels (Y) and Codex Fuldensis (F), written by Victor, Bishop of Capua in 546 CE.

5. *Later History of the Vulgate: Mixed Gospel (Vulgate) Texts*

Jerome's revision, later known as the Vulgate Gospels, gradually became accepted. The Old Latin text also continued to be used. Soon, the transmission of both forms of text gave rise to what is known as mixed texts of manuscripts with Vulgate and Old Latin readings. Sometimes it was a question of the Vulgate text with Old Latin readings; at other times an Old Latin text with Vulgate readings. A view put forward by Samuel Berger in his work *L'Histoire de la Vulgate*,[15] and adopted by Wordsworth and White, was that the mixed text of the Gospel in Europe came from Ireland. The editors of the first critical edition of the Vulgate had identified the Irish/Celtic mixed text in the manuscripts DELQR. Bonifatius Fischer has made clear that this is no explanation. Already in the mid-sixth century we have a mixed text in the British Library manuscript, Harley 1775 (written in Upper Italy, and given the Vulgate siglum Z); from Italy again we have Split, Chapter Archives, MS 621 (earlier Chapter Library, s.n.), from the sixth-seventh century, given the symbol P; from Brittany we have *gat* (Gatianum*)* from about 800 CE. In his 1972 essay, reprinted in 1986, Fischer expressed his opinion that the Split MS (P) might well be a bridge between Z (BL Harley 1775) and E (BL Egerton 609) of the DELQR group – and thus we might say a contact point between a Continental exemplar and the Irish/Celtic text. By 1986, however, as already noted, Fischer had come to the conclusion that classification of the Gospel manuscripts of the mixed group required deep collation over the range of the pre-900 CE manuscripts, a collation he set himself to achieve in his four-volume major work. Almost all over Europe, he reminds us, from the sixth to the tenth century there were rich variations of a mixed text formed from the Vulgate and Old Latin of the European type. He further notes that the Old Latin component of such texts will be hard to define since the Old-Latin groups b, ff$_2$, i, h, r, p (Veronensis, Corbeiensis, Claromontanus, Usserianus Primus,

---

15. S. Berger, *Histoire de la Vulgate pendant les premiers siècles du Moyen Age* (Paris, 1893; reprint New York: B. Franklin, 1961). See also M. McNamara, 'The Celtic-Irish Mixed Gospel Text: Some Recent Contributions and Centennial Reflections', *Filologia mediolatina* 2 (1995), pp. 69–108, at 71–72.

Milan, Amb M. 12 sup) and so on plus q, l (Monacensis or Frisingensis, Rehdigeranus) from which texts could arise are already related among themselves.[16]

In its long history through the earlier and later Middle Ages, together with major groups of mixed texts such as the Irish, French and Spanish, the Vulgate has had special recensions known as the Alcuinian and that of Theodulph (both ninth century), and later there were thirteenth-century emendations referred to as correctories (*correctoria*): of Paris; Correctorium *Sorbonicum; Correctorium* of the Domenicans (about 1240); *Correctorium Vaticanum.*

Part II

Irish Gospel Texts

It has been traditionally believed that Christianity, the Gospel, came to Ireland with St Patrick in 432 CE. It is probable, however, that there were Christian communities in Ireland before that time. With the Gospel and the Christian missionaries came the four Gospels, in the Latin form (most probably the *Vetus Latina*) used in the parts of Christian Europe from which the missionaries came. This holds good for the text form and for the other elements that by then had been traditionally connected with the Gospel texts, for instance the Evangelist symbols, the introductory material, the Eusebian canons and such like.

From the time of St Irenaeus onwards the four living creatures of the Apocalypse of John (Rev. 4.6–7) and Ezekiel (Ezek. 1.10–11; 10.12, 14) have been taken as symbols of the four evangelists, generally (following Jerome) in the order Matthew, Mark, Luke and John, represented respectively by a man, lion, calf (or ox) and eagle, although Irenaeus connected Mark with the eagle and John with the lion. The evangelists are represented iconographically in this manner in Gospel books and in other media from c. 400 CE onwards. Notable examples of these four symbols are found in the Book of Armagh, the Books of Durrow and Kells, the Lichfield Gospels, the Mac Durnan Gospels and the book shrine of the Gospels of Molaise (Devenish Island, Co. Fermanagh). The Book of Durrow follows the Iraenaean order: man, eagle (Mark), calf and lion (John).

For our study of the Gospels and the Gospel text in Ireland, first and foremost we have the direct transmission in manuscripts.[17] For the period 600–1200 CE we know of 27 Gospel texts or fragments of texts written in Ireland or by Irish scribes abroad in Irish centres.[18] Together with these we have seven others closely related with Irish Gospel tradition. For a knowledge of the form of Gospel text used we can also make use of the indirect transmission in the form of citations or allusions in

16. B. Fischer, 'Das Neue Testament', in *Beiträge*, p. 207.
17. For the text of the Latin Bible in Ireland see M. McNamara, *Studies on texts of Early Irish Latin Gospels (A. D. 600-1200)* (Instrumenta Patristica, 20; Steenbrugge and Dordrecht, 1990); 'The Celtic-Irish Mixed Gospel Text: Some Recent Contributions and Centennial Reflections', *Filologia mediolatina*, 2 (1995), pp. 69–108.
18. These texts are listed in M. McNamara, 'Irish Gospel Books and Related Texts', *Proceedings of the Irish Biblical Association* 23 (2000), pp. 60–66.

works of Irish provenance. This latter approach has its limitations, and is to be used with caution, as the citations or allusions may not reflect Irish Gospel tradition.

The Grand Illuminated Codices and Small Irish Pocket Gospels
Among those Irish manuscripts we may distinguish two major groups. On the one hand we have the splendid illuminated codices, the illustrated volumes, such as the Books of Durrow (c. 700 CE), and Kells (c. 800 CE), closely related to the tradition of book illumination also found in the Lindisfarne Gospels (c. 700 CE), the Echternach Gospels (c. 700 CE), the Durham Gospels (c. 700 CE) and the Lichfield Gospel Book of St Chad (eighth century). To these we may also add the Gospel Book Codex 51 of the Stiftsbibliothek, St Gall, written and illuminated in Ireland in the later eighth century. The dimensions of the Book of Kells are 330 × 250 mm (12.9 × 9.9 inches); those of Durrow 245 × 145 mm (9.6 × 5.7 inches). These large, illuminated, works were for liturgical or display purposes.

On the other hand we have a group of some eight Irish Gospels of quite a different kind, for instance the Stowe Saint John of the Royal Irish Academy, the Dimma Gospels, the Mulling Gospels and the Mulling Gospel Fragment (all of Trinity College Dublin), the Cadmug Gospel of Fulda (Germany), and the Mac Durnan Gospels of Lambeth Palace, London. These range in dimension from 125 × 112 mm (4.9 × 4.4 inches) for the Cadmug Gospels to 175 × 142 mm (6.9 × 5.6 inches) for the Dimma Gospels. These manuscripts range in date from the seventh or eighth to the ninth centuries, and are aptly described as 'Irish Pocket Gospels'. Patrick McGurk, who has made a special study of this group, notes that as a whole it is so obviously eccentric and Irish in its connections that Ireland was the home of the particular tradition of book making.[19] Diminutive in format, containing the four Gospels with portraits of the evangelists or their symbols, but with no prefaces of any kind, arranging each Gospel on a separate set of bizarrely sized quires, these Irish books are distinguished by their apparent desire to save space and by the extent of their departure from the scribal tradition of that common classical measure, the uncial or half uncial book of the fourth, fifth and sixth centuries. With regard to the function served by these small Irish pocket Gospels, McGurk thinks that they may have been intended as gifts, for instance from master to pupil, or from pupil to master, as tokens of union, or as relics. The monks may have taken them around with them in their satchels. He gives some illustrative instances from the Lives of Irish saints. The monks of Laisren copied the Gospels for Laisren with miraculous speed. The *Life of Finian* of Clonard says that of the many who went to his school 'none of the 3000 went from him without a bachall or without a gospel or without some well known sign so that round these they built their churches and their cathedrals afterwards'.

The Gospel Texts of Saints Patrick and Columbanus
The Gospels brought by the early fifth-century missionaries probably carried the Old Latin text, although use of the Vulgate cannot be ruled out. The earliest Irish

---

19. P. McGurk, 'The Irish Pocket Gospel Book', *Sacris Erudiri* 8 (1956), pp. 249–70, at 149–25.

Gospel manuscript we have is the Ussher Gospels (Codex Usserianus Primus, TCD MS 55; A.IV.15), probably from c. 600 CE. Any evidence for the Gospel text used in the period earlier to this will have to be drawn from the two writers Patrick (c. 432–63 CE) and Columbanus (died 615 CE). Patrick's biblical text has been studied by Ludwig Bieler in 1947.[20] The number of Gospel texts used by Patrick whether as citations or allusions, he notes, is relatively small – about 20 of 22 in all. From his study Bieler concludes that Patrick has no special agreement with the African text; he has none of the special readings of *d* (the Latin text of the Codex Bezae); he shows no special relationship with the later French texts *ff₁*, *g₁₋₂* (Corbeiensis, Sangermanensis); shows no close relationship with the Irish texts of Dimma, Usserianus Primus or Secundus, or Mulling. Patrick very often agrees with those Old Latin or 'mixed' texts, which in the texts he examined have the same reading as the Vulgate, but in some cases Patrick stands clearly *against* the typical Old Latin reading (especially in Mt. 25.40 and Mk 16.15–16). Patrick's relationship to the 'Celtic' group of Vulgate manuscripts is not univocal; he has no notable agreements with D (the Book of Armagh); on the contrary he sometimes agrees with others of the 'Celtic' group against D; he often differs from D and others of the 'Celtic' group. He has a tendency in a series of passages to have readings found in the Vulgate and in Old Latin manuscripts which stand near the Vulgate, but has also some very old variants, some of which agree with d (Codex Bezae), and some with k (Codex Bobiensis) of the African Old Latin text.

The biblical text used by Columbanus has been analysed by G.S.M. Walker (1957).[21] He notes that Columbanus' biblical text has been largely assimilated to the Vulgate, but it preserves a proportion of readings from the Old Latin, and in some places represents a version peculiar to Columbanus himself. Where his biblical text agrees with a known version of the Old Latin, it sometimes bears a resemblance to the 'African' type, but it nowhere agrees with the special variants of the oldest specimen of this type, the Codex Bobiensis believed to have been carried about by Columbanus in his satchel. Columbanus' text, in Walker's view, presents a number of similarities with the Codex Ussserianus and the Book of Armagh, but is not identical with these or any other. Many of his idiosyncrasies may be due to slips of memory. His text, he believes, is in fact a product of a period of transition, in which the native Irish version, already confused by the introduction of variants from other forms of the Old Latin, is gradually being superseded by the Vulgate. In his analysis of Columbanus' text for Matthew, Luke and John (Columbanus never cites Mark), Walker classifies 35 as Vulgate, 14 as Old Latin, 29 as uncertain and 19 as peculiar.

It may be remarked that the biblical text of both Patrick and Columbanus merits re-examination after the critical Stuttgart edition of the Vulgate Gospels (1969) and the fuller collation of B. Fischer (1989–91) where this is relevant.

---

20.   L. Bieler, 'Der Bibeltext des heiligen Patrick', *Bib* 28 (1947), pp. 31–58, 236–63; summary of evidence for the Gospels pp. 259–61.

21.   G.S.M. Walker, *Sancti Columbani Opera* (Scriptores Latini Hiberniae, 2; Dublin Institute for Advanced Studies, 1970).

The Old Latin Text in Ireland

The earliest Gospels introduced into Ireland probably carried the Old Latin text. One can presume that its use was widespread, until transformed or superseded by the Vulgate or a mixed text of Vulgate and Old Latin.

We now posses one Irish text of the Old Latin, namely the Codex Usserianus Primus to which we shall return presently. In the MS St Gall, Stiftsbibliothek in codices 47 and 1395 written in Ireland (eighth century) in fragments of a liturgical text with *Missa pro defunctis* we do, however, have fragments of Jn 11.14–44 with the Old Latin text of the Usserianus kind. In St Gall, Stiftsbibliothek 60, with the text of John of mixed Irish type, there is one section (Jn 1.29–3.26) which has an Old Latin text of the Usserianus and Veronensis type. There are also sections of the Book of Mulling very close to the Old Latin text (of the Usserianus form), although the basic text itself seems to be Vulgate. The Gospel of Matthew in St Gall Stiftsbibliothek Codex 51 has a Vulgate text of the mixed Irish type, but has one section (Mt. 1.20–4.17), which as far as I can see is neither true Vulgate nor mixed text, nor indeed any known Old Latin text. It seems to represent a hitherto unknown Old Latin translation.

The Codex Usserianus Primus.

This MS (TCD 55; A.iv.15), as already noted, has the Irish-Gallic text of the Old Latin. We should note once again that this Irish-Gallic group is not well attested, and for Mark seems to represented only by Usserianus Primus. The attestation for this Irish-Gallic Old Latin text is as follows:

For Matthew: r (Usserianus Primus); g_1 (Codex Sangermanensis; Matthew only; the text of the other Gospels is Vulgate); h (Claromontanus; fifth cent.; from Italy); p (Vienna; fragments from the Passion Narrative according to Matthew; fifth century).

For Mark: The only text extant is Usserianus.

For Luke: Usserianus; β (VL 26; a fragment of Luke in St Paul in Kärnten, Stiftsbibliothek 225.3.19 [XXV a. 1], seventh cent.).

For John: Usserianus; ρ (Fischer Xs; Milan, Amb. M 12 sup.; John 13.3–17; fragment from Gallican Sacramentary; South of France); ρ MS St Gall, Stiftsbibliothek in codices 47 and 1395 written in Ireland (eighth century): fragments of John 11.14–44 in fragments of a liturgical text with *Missa pro defunctis.*

With regard to affiliations of the Irish-Gallic Old Latin text, it has been noted that the text of g_1 (Sangermanensis), and hence of Usserianus Primus believed identical with it, was the text-type used by Hilary of Poitiers (315–367) in the *lemmata* of his commentary on Matthew. We may remark that this, at most, would hold only for the Gospel of Matthew. And even the identity of Hilary's text with g_1 and r (and even the identity of the text of g_1 and r) may merit reconsideration after B. Fischer's complete collation of select passages.

No work, to my knowledge, has been done on the affiliations of the text of Usserianus for Mark.

With regard to the text of Luke in this manuscript (*r*) we may note a peculiar reading at Luke 2.12 (in the nativity scene). Here the Vulgate has: *natus est uobis hodie* **saluator** *qui est Christus Dominus in ciuitate Dauid.* The African and general European texts of the Old Latin do not differ significantly from the Vulgate. The text of *r* has: *quia natus est uobis hodie* **conseruator salutis** *qui est Christus Domini* etc.

The only text of the Irish-Gallic group of Old Latin texts with which to compare the reading of Usserianus is the Kärnten text β. It, too, has the specific r reading *conseruator salutis*, with a few other variants besides. The β text reads: *quia natus est uobis hodie* **conseruator salutis** *qui est Christus Domini in ciuitate Dauid que dicitur Bethe(lem)*.

I can find no evidence of this reading except in texts widely regarded as Hiberno-Latin and connected with Irish tradition on the Continent, for instance a Vienna Commentary on Luke (Vienna Codex. lat. 997), in the commentary on Luke in the Irish *Reference Bible* and in catechetical and homiletic material on the Nativity Gospel in the Catechesis Celtica (MS Vatican Reg. lat. 49) and in a Verona Homiliary.

With regard to *John*, in his introduction to his edition of Usserianus Primus (1884),[22] T.K. Abbott said that *r*'s text of the Woman taken in adultery (Jn 8.11) is not Old Latin, but drawn from the Vulgate, an indication for him that the original being copied by the scribe of *r* lacked this passage. This would be evidence that the scribe of Ussher knew a Vulgate text. On this we may observe, that while *r*'s text in question is very close to the Vulgate, it is not quite identical, and further examination is needed before one can say it was burrowed from the Vulgate.

This leads to the question of the date, the place of origin and the ultimate background of the Ussher codex. There seems to be general agreement among paleographers and textual critics that Usserianus Primus was written in Ireland about the year 600 CE. It is less certain from what part of Europe its original (which belongs to the Irish-Gallic group of Old Latin texts) was brought to Ireland. It may be from Southern France (the Milan palimpsest text has a close relationship to the text of Hilary). However, since one manuscript of the group to which it belongs (Claromontanus) was written in Italy, it might have come from Italy. In more recent times the possibility of an earlier (fifth-century) date and a Continental original for this TCD MS 55 has been advanced.[23]

Whatever of its date and place of origin, the Usserianus Old Latin text seems to have been widely used in Ireland. It is found for the text of Jn 11.14–44 preserved from an office for the dead, or a missal (not a lectionary) in the fragment, St Gall, Stiftsbibliothek Collectanea 1395, pp. 430–33, given the siglum p in Old Latin texts. Usserianus (r) has also heavily influenced most Irish mixed texts of the Vulgate. We may also note that the text of the Usserianus has a number of dry point glosses dating from the seventh century. One of those is an Old Irish gloss, others seem to

22.   T.K. Abbott, *Euangeliorum uersio antehieronymiana ex codice Usseriano* (2 vols.; Dublin: 1884), p. vii.

23.   Thus D.N. Dumville, *A Palaeographer's Review: The Insular System of Scripts in the Early Middle Ages* (Kansai University Institute of Oriental and Occidental Studies; Sources and Materials Series 20–1; Suita, Osaka: Kansai University Press, 1999, I, pp. 35–40, at 39.

indicate commentaries on the text, or an alternative biblical reading, presumably the Vulgate.

In the present state of research what seems indicated with regard to the Ussher Codex is an intense analysis of the biblical text and affiliations of all four Gospels. This would seem to be a necessary complement to any paleographical and art historical study of the manuscript.

The Vulgate Text in Ireland

Of the 27 or so Latin Gospels known to us only one, the Book of Durrow, can be said to have a true Vulgate text. It is generally agreed that its text is of a good Vulgate kind, but apparently without close parallel, although attempts have been made to link it with the Northumbrian texts of the Amiatinus or Lindisfarne Gospels. In his grouping of Latin Gospel manuscripts Bonifatius Fischer places Durrow third (after Durham A.II.10 and A.II.17) in his list of 'English' texts (outside of the group 'Northumbria' which he regards as descending from a sixth-century Gospel Book from Naples). He regards Durrow as the work of an English scribe, written in Northumbria (Lindisfarne?), about 675 CE. The more probable place of origin would seem to be the monastery whose name it bears, Durrow in Co. Offaly, Ireland.

While Durrow is the sole true Vulgate text among Irish Gospel books, its text seems to have been without influence in Ireland. It does not appear that any later copies of Durrow or of its original were made in Ireland. It remains for future research to see if any of its readings can be found in biblical writings of Irish origin or with Irish affiliations.

The question as to where the Book of Durrow was written (whether Ireland, Lindisfarne or Iona) need not detain us here, as our chief interest in the biblical text.

It is not clear when Jerome's revision, whether in its pure or developed (mixed text) form, first reached Ireland. It may have been in the sixth century. The *Life of Colum Cille* compiled by Manus O'Donnell (in 1532) contains the well-known story of how the young Colum Cille visited Finnian (*Findéin*) of Druim Finn (= Dromin, Co. Louth) and borrowed a book from him which he copied without Finnian's permission. This led to the famed judgment of Diarmuid Ó Cerbal, King of Tara, on the matter: 'To every cow her young cow (*le gach boin a boinín*), that is her calf, and to every book its transcript' (*le gach lebhur a leabrán*). Although Manus O'Donnell says that the book in question was the Psalter known as the Cathach, it is possible (if the story contains an element of history) that it was a copy of the Four Gospels recently brought from Italy to Ireland. There is a tradition that a Finnian (of Moville?) went to Rome and brought back a copy of the Gospels, presumably Jerome's new Vulgate revision. The identity of the Irish persons by the name Vinnio, Finnio, Finnian, and Findbar is, however, a complicated matter. If the story has any historical substance it would argue to the introduction of a Vulgate form of the Gospels into Ireland in the sixth century.

The Irish Mixed Gospel Text

The vast majority of Irish Latin Gospel texts known to us have neither a true Old Latin nor good Vulgate text, but rather a mixed text of Vulgate and Old Latin, generally with predominance of the Vulgate element.[24] The identification of a Celtic or Irish family of Vulgate texts was in the process of formation from about 1850 onwards on the basis of Irish and other manuscripts then known. The family came to be known as the group DELQR, from the *sigla* for the five texts the Book of Armagh (D), Egerton 609 of the British Library (E), the Lichfield Gospels (L), the Book of Kells (in Latin Cenannensis from the Irish Cenannas; hence Q), and the Rushworth or Mac Regol Gospels R. The possession of certain common variants formed the basis for the identification of this group. The group is not of specifically Irish origin, as the Lichfield Gospels were written in England in a centre near the Welsh border, and the Gospels of Egerton 609 (from a Tours monastery) were apparently written in Brittany.

To this group we must add the marginal glosses to the Gospels of Echternach (to which I give the *siglum* Ep[mg]), which are from a text clearly of the same tradition as DELQR. It is not clear where the Echternach manuscript was written, whether in Echternach, Lindisfarne or even in Ireland (Rathmelsigi).

The Irish mixed text is basically Vulgate. It is evident from the Echternach glosses (written about 700 or 750 CE) that the mixed Irish/Celtic text was circulating in Ireland and elsewhere in the seventh century. We do not know whether this mixed text originated within Ireland, or basically came to Ireland from elsewhere. It might well be that the first Vulgate text(s) which reached Ireland in the sixth or seventh century and later used there from the seventh century onwards had already a mixed form of text, with many influences from the Old Latin.

A number of questions arise with regard to this Irish/Celtic group DELQREp[mg]. Since the variants are not always the same in all or most of the manuscripts, it is clear that it cannot be regarded as a textual family, with all the witnesses descending from a common ancestor. There have been, and still are, a number of views regarding the group, from that of Samuel Roger and others who believed the mixed text of Continental manuscripts derived from Irish originals, to those who practically deny the existence of the Celtic/Irish group as any meaningful entity. Both one and other of these views seem misguided, and not in accord with the evidence. Another view is that the phenomena of the Celtic/Irish group are in keeping with practice in English and Irish scriptoria, and are to be found in Gospel books of both islands. Scribes in the scriptoria of both islands are viewed as indulging to an unusual degree of licence in relatively minor details of the text, frequently, but by no means always, in the interests of elucidation. This licence, together with the frequent Old Latin readings, and the incorporation of readings from other Gospels, both quite marked in some texts, creates a kind of textual overlay which complicates the process of identifying relationships. While granting that some of these laws may have been at work in the origin of the variants in question, I do not believe that the overall phenomenon that is the Celtic/Irish group can be explained in this way, nor can it be explained as a variant of what is common to English and Irish Gospel books. It is possibly too early to put forward any single explanation of the phenomenon.

---

24.   For the Irish mixed text see McNamara, 'The Celtic-Irish Mixed Gospel Text' (as in note 15 above).

When all the Gospel texts have been examined and the evidence they present corre-lated, it may be possible to present a nuanced explanation.

We can now turn to a consideration of some of the Irish Gospel books, paying greater attention to those which thus far have been less studied, bearing in mind that the biblical text of the Irish manuscripts known to us has not yet been fully examined.

We may begin with the biblical text of Book of Kells (Q), studied in detail by Patrick McGurk.[25] McGurk notes that Q has more variants from the Vulgate in later Matthew and in Mark than in early Matthew, in Luke and in John. From evidence that must be regarded as limited, McGurk notes that the best attested Old Latin witness in Q is b (the Veronensis), with nine instances, followed by r^1 (Usserianus Primus) with eight instances and q (Munich, Clm 6224; from Illyria, or Italy s. VI–VII) also with eight. The researches of another scholar (Christopher Verey)[26] has shown that for John Q is of a different tradition from that in DER (there is no L for John), and is very close in John to the text of the Durham Gospels. This indicates that for John Q has either looked to another source or has been revised drastically.

It is clear that in the Gospel text of the Book of Mulling (TCD 60 [A.I.15]; later eighth century) we have the presence of both Vulgate, Irish mixed text and Old Latin. Special studies have been made both of the Gospels of Matthew and Luke. H. J. Lawlor (1897)[27] believed that in both Matthew and Luke he had identified two lengthy Old Latin passages (Mt. 24.12–28.3; Lk. 4.5–9.54). The later scholar Peter Doyle[28] is of the view that the text is basically Vulgate or Irish mixed type, but with very strong Old Latin influences in certain sections. And the Old Latin text type is that of r^1 (Usserianus), together with a text of the Old Latin b (Veronensis) kind

Brief Examination of some Special Texts

Mac Durnan and Armagh Gospel Texts. When examining the marginal glosses of the Echternach Gospels (from 700, or 750 CE) and comparing them with the main text, the present writer noted that in this main text there were a number of readings which agree neither with the Vulgate nor the so-called mixed Irish/Celtic text, but are found in the Mac Durnan Gospels (MS. Lambeth Palace Library 1370). I set forth the evidence and possible conclusions to be drawn from it in an essay 1987–88 and in 1990.[29]

25. P. McGurk, 'The Gospel Text', in P. Cox (ed.), *The Book of Kells. MS 58 Trinity College Library Dublin* (Lucerne: Fine Arts Facsimile Publications of Switzerland, 1990), pp. 37–152.

26. C. Verey, 'Notes on the Gospel Texts', in C.D. Verey, T. Julian Brown and E. Coatsworth (eds.), *The Durham Gospels, together with Fragments of a Gospel in Uncial. Durham, Cathedral Library, MS A. II. 17* (Copenhagen: Rosenkilde & Bagger, 1980), pp. 68–108, at 72.

27. H.J. Lawlor, *Chapters on the Book of Mulling* (Edinburgh: David Douglas, 1897).

28. Peter Doyle, 'A Study of the Text of St, Matthew's Gospel in the Book of Mulling and of the Palaeography of the Whole Manuscript' (PhD Dissertation, National University of Ireland, 1967); P. Doyle, 'The Text of St. Luke's Gospel in the Book of Mulling', *Proceedings of the Royal Irish Academy* 73 C (Dublin: Royal Irish Academy, 1973), pp. 177–200.

29. See McNamara, *Studies on Texts*, pp. 102–11.

The Mac Durnan Gospels were written by Maeilbridus Mac Durnain, *comarb* of Patrick and Columcille who died according to the Annals of Ulster in 926 CE (alias 927). In the essay referred to I listed 103 texts in which hitherto unattested readings of the Gospels of Echternach agree with the Gospels of Mac Durnan, and occasionally with three other Irish texts associated with Armagh, that is BL Harley 1802 (The Gospels of Máel Brigte), BL Harley 1023, and the Book of Armagh.

The essay was merely exploratory, but indicates that the links between these four Gospels connected with Armagh may merit further examination, this time making full use of B. Fischer's full collation of the texts in question.

St Gall, Stiftsbibliothek 60. Codex 60 of the Stiftsbibliothek, St Gall, is an eighth- or ninth-century manuscript with the Gospel of John only. The hand is Irish, which makes an Irish scribe almost certain, even though the miniatures may be continental imitations of insular models. The Gospel begins as basically Vulgate, with Irish readings and with a text somewhat related to that of St Gall 51. Towards the end of chapter 1, it passes from Vulgate to Old Latin, and indeed Old Latin of the type found in Old Latin b and r[1], that is the Veronensis and the Irish Usserianus. It continues principally in Old Latin into chapter 3 (1.29–3.26), where it returns to Vulgate, with many Irish readings. In this text again we may note the influence of the r and b type of Old Latin in Irish text, with regard to John bearing in mind Bonifatius Fischer's observation that in John Usserianus Primus is of the Veronensis (b) type.[30]

St Gall, Stiftsbibliothek 51. Codex 51 of the Stiftsbibliothek of St Gall contains the four gospels. The manuscript was most probably written in Ireland, and in the late eighth century. The text of the Gospel is of the Irish 'mixed type', with non-Vulgate readings throughout in John, which agree with the Book of Armagh and the Rushworth (Mac Regol) Gospels. In Mt. 1.20–2.16 we have non-Vulgate readings otherwise unattested or rarely attested. It would appear that here we are in the presence of an Old Latin text otherwise unknown.[31]

Glossed Gospel Texts
The Bible was not just a series of texts to be recited. It also needed to be understood. In the Christian Church a variety of means emerged in the efforts to explain the texts of Scripture, for instance exposition, commentary, and the gloss. The

---

30. See M. McNamara, *Studies on Texts of Early Irish Latin Gospels (A.D. 600–1200)* (Instrumenta Patristica, 20; Steenbrugge & Dordrecht: Kluwer, 1990), pp. 102–11; a slightly earlier and different form of the study appeared in 'The Echternach and Mac Durnan Gospels: Some Common Readings and their Significance', Peritia 6–7 (1987–88), pp. 217–22.

See M. McNamara, *Studies on Texts*, pp. 161–78; J. Mizzi, 'The Old-Latin Element in Jn. I,29-III,26 of Cod. Sangallensis 60', *Sacris Eruditi* 28 (1978–79), pp. 33–62.

31. See McNamara, *Studies on Texts*, pp. 112–26. For a more detailed introduction to St Gall Codex 51 see M. McNamara, 'Bible Text and Illumination in St Gall Stiftsbibliothek Codex 51, with Special reference to Longinus in the Crucifixion Scene', in M. Redknap, N. Edwards *et al.* (eds.), *Pattern and Purpose in Insular Art* (Proceedings of the Fourth International Conference on Insular Art held at the National Museum & Gallery Cardiff 3–6 September 1998; Oxford: Oxbow Books, 2001), pp. 191–202.

explanation of biblical texts through glosses, both in Latin and in Irish, was early established in Ireland. We have the text of the Pauline Epistles heavily glossed in both Irish and Latin from c. 800 CE in the well-known Würzburg manuscript (M.p.th.f. 12). From about the same time we have the Irish glosses on the Psalter in the Milan Codex Amb C 301 inf. We have a glossed text of Matthew in the Würzburg MS M.p.th.f.61. The glosses to Matthew in the manuscript are very close to those in the as yet unpublished (Hiberno-Latin) commentary on Matthew in the Vienna Nationalbibliothek 940.

We have one glossed Gospel Book: the Gospels in MS BL Harley 1802, written in Armagh in 1138 by the scribe Máel-Brigte húa Máel-Úanaigh. It is glossed heavily, especially in the Gospel of Matthew. In his work *History of the Vulgate in England from Alcuin to Roger Bacon* (1933) H. H. Glunz expressed the view that the glosses represented the new learning, of the *Glossa Ordinaria* type, introduced into Ireland through Armagh.[32] However, Jean Rittmueller has shown that the glosses in Matthew are derived from Hiberno-Latin commentaries, such the *Liber questionum in euangeliis,* which appear to have been used, if not composed, in Ireland in the eight and ninth centuries.[33] The gloss on Mt. 2.11 cites a text from the apocryphal *Gospel according to the Hebrews* (by which *The Gospel of the Nazarenes* may be intended). The glosses also include a number of items in Irish on material related to Matthew's text.

Bilingual Greek and Latin Gospels
In the ninth century some Irish scholars on the Continent showed a special interest in the Greek texts of the Psalter, the Gospels and the Pauline Epistles. We have bilingual copies of all three texts from an Irish hand. The bilingual Gospel text is in Codex 48 of the Stiftsbibliothek of St Gall.

Interpolated texts in Irish Gospels
A feature of Irish Gospel texts is the presence of certain interpolated passages, or when the interpolated passage is found also in other manuscripts (as for Jn 5.4) specific variant readings in the passage. Here I wish to draw attention to two particular interpolated passages, at Mt. 27.49 and Jn 19.34, both with regard to Jesus' death. At Mt. 27.49, after the words *ceteri uero dicebant sine uideamus an ueniat Elias liberans eum* (there are some minor variant readings to the text), 'Others however said: "Let us see whether Elias will come to save him" ', Irish textual tradition inserts a text dependent on Jn 19.34, as follows: *Alius autem accepta lancea pupungit latus eius et exi(i)t aqua et sanguis,* 'Another person, however, having taken a lance, pricked [or: stabbed] his side and water and blood came out'. This interpolation is found in almost all the Irish texts, with the exception of the Old

---

32. H. Glunz, 'The Gospel Glosses in the Harleian MS 1802 (about 1140), from Armagh', in *idem* (ed.), *History of the Vulgate in England from Alcuin to Roger Bacon* (Cambridge: Cambridge University Press, 1933), pp. 328–41.

33. See J. Rittmueller, 'The Gospel Commentary of Máel Brigte ua Máeluanaig and its Hiberno-Latin Background', *Peritia* 2 (1983), pp. 185–214; also *eadem*, 'Afterword: The Gospel of Máel Brigte', *Peritia* 3 (1984), pp. 215–18.

Latin Usserianus Primus. It occurs in DELQREp^{mg}, Usserianus Secundus, Dimma, Mulling, BL Harley 1023, BL Harley 1802 (Máel Brigte Gospels), Oxford CCC 122, and in the (probably Irish-related) Gospels of St Gatien. Furthermore, the only non-Irish text to carry it is the Anglo-Saxon Gospel Book in BL Royal 1 E VI + Canterbury, Cathedral Library additional 16 (from Kent; end of eighth century). The corresponding Greek text *allos de labôn lonchên enuxen autou tên pleuran kai exêlthen hydôr kai haima* is found in the fourth-century codices Sinaiticus and Vaticanus, and some other texts, but not in the earlier Greek papyri. The Latin interpolated text must be a translation of the Greek as given above, not taken from an Old Latin or Vulgate text, from both of which it differs.[34]

While transmitted principally, in fact almost solely, in Irish tradition, the interpolation did not originate in Ireland. The ancient interpolation, mentioning together at the Calvary death scene both the sponge bearer and the lance bearer, may have been preserved in Ireland for devotional if not liturgical reasons. In the crucifixion scene in Irish art, whether in manuscripts or in metal work, the sponge bearer (named Stephaton) and the lance bearer (named Longinus) are almost invariably present. It is possible that the presence of the interpolation in Greek tradition may have a similar origin. Both the lance bearer (named Longinus) and the sponge bearer are present already at the crucifixion scene in the Rabbula Gospels (Mesopotamia, 586 CE).

The other interpolated text occurs at Jn 19.30. This interpolation is found in Latin only in Irish Gospel texts: in Usserianus Primus of the Old Latin and in the other Irish texts (DREp^{mg}, BL Harley 1023; BL Harley 1802; Fulda Cadmug Gospels; St Gall Codex 51; St Gall Codex 60). After the words *tradidit spiritum* ('he handed over the spirit') of Jn 19.30 the Irish texts add from Mt. 27.51 or Mk 15.38: *Cum ergo expirasset uelum templi scis(s)um est a summo usque deorsum*, 'Now, after he had expired the veil of the temple was rent from the top down to the bottom'. This interpolation is found in no early Greek text, but occurs in later (12th–14th century) Greek minuscule manuscripts. It is found, however, in earlier Syriac and Syro-Palestinian translations.

Arguments for the Study of Irish Latin Gospel Texts

Textual criticism is neither the most attractive nor most rewarding of callings. Yet there are strong reasons, which argue towards the desirability of an intense and sustained study of the text of the Latin Bible in Ireland.

For one thing this Gospel text forms part of the Irish inheritance. It is in the interests of all involved in the study of Irish civilization to be in a position to have access to the Gospel texts used by Irish monks and Irish scholars at home and on the Continent.

Knowledge of the Latin Gospel texts available and used in Ireland can be informative for the study of Hiberno-Latin and vernacular Irish literature, and both these forms of Irish literature in their turn can throw light on the 'Irish' nature of a particular Gospel reading. Take for instance the oft-cited text of Mt. 25.34 where

---

34. On this interpolated text, especially as found in St Gall, Codex 51, see M. McNamara, 'Bible Text and Illumination' (n. 31 above).

the blessed are called by Christ to come, possess the kingdom prepared for them from the foundation of the world. The Vulgate here reads: *possidete paratum uobis regnum* **a constitutione** *mundi,* 'take possession of the kingdom prepared for you from the *foundation* of the world'. Thus also the Old Latin, apart from the texts c d ff₁. The Irish textual tradition reads *possidete quod uobis paratum est regnum* (DR; variant: *regnum paratum uobis,* L*Q) *ab* **origine** *mundi,* 'from the *beginning* of the world'. In the use of *ab origine* the Irish textual tradition is fairly constant here (for instance DER, *Usserianus Secundus,* St Gall 51). Similarly in the inversion at the beginning of the text. What is significant is that this reading (both with the inversion and presence of *ab origine*) is found in Latin citations in vernacular Irish texts, and sometimes in Irish translation, and also in Hiberno-Latin ones, right down from the early Old-Irish Homily (c. 800 CE) to eleventh-century homilies and even later. This is an indication that there is more than a grain of substance to the designation 'mixed Irish' biblical text.

These ancient Latin biblical texts can be significant for Irish literature in other ways also, for instance in *e* peculiar orthography of some biblical names. Thus, for instance, the place where Jesus changed water into wine in the Irish Gospel texts almost invariably ends in the letter n: *Canan (Cannan, Caanan...) Galilaeae.* Thus also in the description of the miracle in the Poem of Blathmac (i Canan na Galile), even though the critical edition sees fit to correct to the normal *Cana.*[35]

Conclusion

Over the last 150 years intense research has gone into the study of the text of the Latin Gospels, and the work still continues. While no little attention has been devoted to the Irish Latin Gospel tradition, the full collation of a number of the Irish texts still remains a *desideratum.* Much more remains to be done in the entire field.

From the examination already carried out we see that from this ancient Irish tradition there remains one full Old Latin text (Usserianus Primus), which seems to have heavily influenced the later Irish mixed text tradition. We also have a section of true Old Latin, of the Usserianus Primus and Veronensis kind, in St Gall Codex 60. Given the evidence it is possible that an Old Latin of the Veronensis kind circulated in early Ireland. There also seems to be, embedded in St Gall Codex 51, a section with a hitherto unknown Old Latin rendering.

We have one good Vulgate text in the Book of Durrow. We cannot say whether this was copied from an earlier Irish original. There is no evidence that either Durrow or its Vulgate original was later copied or used in Ireland.

The so-called mixed 'Celtic/Irish' Gospel text has been the subject of much discussion over recent decades. While this debate is ongoing, and while attention is paid to the caution required by reason of the complexity of the evidence, it still

---

35. See J. Carney (ed.), *The Poems of Blathmac Son of Cú Brettan together with the Irish Gospel of Thomas and a Poem on the Virgin Mary* (Irish Texts Society, 47; Dublin: Educational Company of Ireland, 1964), pp. 12–13 (§ 35).

appears that the designation 'mixed Irish/Celtic Text' is meaningful, both in the field of textual criticism and in the examination of Gospel texts used in Irish vernacular and in Hiberno-Latin literature.

If a *desideratum* were to be added at the end of this essay it would be for a plan and project to fully collate the hitherto unexamined Irish Latin Gospel texts and to publish the more significant of them.

Part II

THE CHESTER BEATTY GOSPEL CODEX (P[45])

THE SIGNIFICANCE OF THE CHESTER BEATTY PAPYRI IN EARLY CHURCH HISTORY[*]

Barbara Aland

The significance of the Chester Beatty New Testament papyri (P^{45-47}) can hardly be overestimated.[1] They support the reconstructed text of our editions of the New Testament in a way that earlier generations could not have imagined. With a bit of exaggeration one can state that the papyri give us essentially the same textual form that we find in Westcott and Hort. Where changes have been made in recent years in the established text, these are frequently supported by the papyri. And yet, the papyri contain mistakes of every variety. And that is what concerns us here. We would like to look at the papyri from a different angle than the usual one, asking whether or how the scribes' view of their profession affected their products, and whether or to what extent the codices they produced met the expectations of the communities that commissioned them. Thus we may hope for insight into the writing practices and literacy of Christian communities in third-century Egypt. The familiar themes of paleography, scribal exemplars (the *Vorlage*), text types and individual scribal habits will play a role in our inquiry, but they will be interrelated and will be considered at the same time in the light of contemporary quotation practice and also of certain statements by contemporary writers, in order to draw some overall conclusions about the significance of the papyri in the communities they served.

1. *The Writing Style of the Biblical Papyri*

It cannot be determined with any confidence whether the Chester Beatty papyri survived the perils of the Diocletian persecution by being in a library in the Fayum.[2] Certainly the papyri were not written originally for a library. The lack of any adequate control of the manuscripts by correctors (*diorthotes*) argues against it.

The writing style of these as well as of other New Testament papyri exhibits certain distinctive characteristics despite the range of scribal skills represented.

[*]   My sincere gratitude is due to Erroll F. Rhodes, New York, for his careful translation, and also to Stephen Emmel, Münster, who reviewed it for last-minute changes.
1.   Chester Beatty Library Biblical Papyri I, II and III.
2.   G. Kilpatrick, 'The Bodmer and Mississippi Collection of Biblical and Christian Texts', *Greek, Roman and Byzantine Studies*, 4 (1963), pp. 33–47 (38).

Colin H. Roberts, in his fundamental study of early Christian papyri, describes this style as follows: 'To judge from their hands, the earliest Christian books were essentially books for use, not, as Jewish Rolls of the Law sometimes were, almost cult objects'.[3] The scribes are experienced writers of documents. They aim for and achieve a high degree of 'regularity and clarity', a style of writing which Roberts calls 'reformed documentary'.[4] They are well aware that they are copying books, and they make use of certain 'literary devices such as spacing, iota adscript, and paragraph marks', but they do it so irregularly that it is obvious they have not been trained to copy literary texts.[5] 'In all of them there is a family resemblance; in none can be traced the work of the professional calligrapher or the rapid, informal hand of the private scholar. Works of secular literature are also written in such hands, but there is not the same preponderance of them.'[6]

Roberts describes the group behind these papyri as tradesmen, peasants and minor government officials, for whom a knowledge of Greek was necessary but who had no literary interests.[7] The copyists served them as writers of documents as well as – if they were Christians – transcribers of their sacred books. In the earliest Christian papyri there are frequently reading aids such as 'accents, breathings, punctuation, marks to indicate foreign words'.[8] These are not characteristic of the documentary style, but reflect the function of the papyri in the community. They were designed for reading in worship services, and possibly also for private devotions.

Should such an appreciation of the scribal function and such a concern for regularity and clarity not affect in some way the quality of copies produced and the special nature of variants that occur?

In answering this question we should begin by assuming that the copyists of the early papyri were both willing and able to make accurate copies, as much as is generally expected of anyone transcribing documents. Just as scribes do not make changes in documents arbitrarily, the same principle applies to their copying of books, and especially sacred books. And further, they might even be expected to be even more painstaking because of the special honour of their task. And yet errors creep in, errors completely consonant with their scribal function. From these very errors we can tell what kind of exemplars the copyists used, and also how they understood their responsibility.

3.   C.H. Roberts, *Manuscript, Society and Belief in Early Christian Egypt* (Schweich Lectures, 1977; London: British Academy [Oxford University Press], 1979), p. 15.
4.   Roberts, *Manuscript, Society and Belief*, p. 14.
5.   Roberts, *Manuscript, Society and Belief*, p. 14.
6.   Roberts, *Manuscript, Society and Belief*, p. 15.
7.   Roberts, *Manuscript, Society and Belief*, p. 21.
8.   Roberts, *Manuscript, Society and Belief*, p. 21.

2. *The Chester Beatty New Testament Papyri as Examples of the Scribal Reformed Documentary Style*

In the following consideration of the papyri we will focus on P[45], the great codex of the Gospels and Acts,[9] and then see whether the results gained there can also be verified in P[46], the earliest Pauline codex,[10] and P[47], the Apocalypse.[11]

A first impression of the quality of a manuscript can be gained from its singular readings, as Colwell and after him Royse and others have shown.[12] P[45] has a great number of them. They almost always make sense, leading Colwell to say that 'P[45] must be given credit for a much greater density of intentional changes than the other two [i.e. P[66] and P[75]]'.[13] But is this conclusion really justified? Are 'intentional changes' a peculiarity of scribes of the documentary style as this suggests? Quite obviously not, because document transcribers are not entitled to make changes in their exemplars. Only two reasons for making changes are at all probable. The *Vorlage* may be ambiguous or lacking in clarity so that its meaning is doubtful to the reader. But that cannot be the case here, because the exemplar of the papyrus is generally of good quality, as a glance at the critical apparatus of any edition of the New Testament will demonstrate. It will show that P[45] frequently reads with the good, authoritative majuscules. Or again, in rapidly copying a text the scribe may be unaware of making any changes. He perceives the sense of the text as a whole and

---

9. Kenyon II, *Text* and *Plates*. Cf. T.C. Skeat and Brian C. McGing, 'Notes on Chester Beatty Biblical Papyrus I (Gospels and Acts)', *Hermathena (A Trinity College Dublin Review),* 150 (1991), pp. 21–25; G. Zuntz, 'Reconstruction of One Leaf of the Chester Beatty Papyrus of the Gospels and Acts (P45)', *Chronique d'Égypte* 51 (1951), pp. 191–211; J. Hering, 'Observations critiques sur le texte des Évangiles et des Actes de P45', *Revue d'Histoire et de Philosophie religieuses,* 14 (1934), pp. 145–54; A. Merk, 'Codex evangeliorum et actuum ex collectione papyrorum Chester Beatty', *Miscellanea Biblica* II (1934), pp. 375–406. Cf. now also the new treatment of the Vienna fragments of P[45] by Thomas J. Kraus, '*Ad fontes*: Gewinn durch die Konsultation von Original-handschriften am Beispiel von *P. Vindob. G* 31974', *Bib* 82 (2001), pp. 1–16.

10. Kenyon III, *Text*; III, *Stext*; III, *SPlates*. H.A. Sanders (ed.), *A Third-Century Papyrus Codex of the Epistles of Paul* (University of Michigan Studies; Humanistic Series, 38; Ann Arbor: University of Michigan, 1935); cf. the review on Sanders' edition by F.G. Kenyon, *American Journal of Philology* 57 (1936), pp. 91–95; K. Junack *et al.* (eds.), *Das Neue Testament auf Papyrus.* II. *Die paulinischen Briefe* (Teil 1; ANTF, 12; Berlin: de Gruyter, 1989); K. Wachtel and K. Witte (eds.), *Das Neue Testament auf Papyrus.* II. *Die paulinischen Briefe* (Teil 2; ANTF, 22; Berlin: de Gruyter, 1994); cf. P. Collomp, 'Notes et étude critique. Les Papyri Chester Beatty. Observations bibliologiques', *Revue d'Histoire et de Philosophie religieuses* 14 (1934), pp. 130–43.

11. Kenyon III, *Text* and *Plates*.

12. E.C. Colwell, 'Method in Evaluating Scribal Habits, A Study of P45, P66, P75', in *Studies in Methodology in Textual Criticism of the New Testament* (NTTS, 9; Leiden: Brill, 1969), pp. 106–24; J.R. Royse, 'Scribal Habits in Early Greek New Testament Papyri' (ThD thesis, Graduate Theological Union, Berkeley, CA, 1981). The method is still useful, although it should be underscored that there are no singular readings in the strictest sense. There is no way of knowing that what we regard as singular readings were not also to be found in the great mass of manuscripts that have been lost.

13. Colwell, 'Method', p. 112.

reproduces it clearly, whereby small changes creep in which do not affect the sense as a whole.[14] This explains why the scribe produces very few nonsense readings.

In order to recognize the nature of the copyist's work it is especially helpful to consider his frequent transpositions and omissions. I take my examples from the singular readings, thus demonstrating as clearly as possible the particular nature of our copyist's scribal habits.

Mt. 26.1 και εγενετο οτε ετελεσεν ο Ιησους παντας τους λογους τουτους, ειπεν τοις μαθηταις αυτου] (And it happened when Jesus had finished all these sayings, he said to his disciples)] και εγενετο [οτε ετελεσεν το]υς λογους τουτους ο ι[ησους παντας ειπεν τ]οις μαθητα[ις αυτου] P[45] (And it happened when he had finished these sayings, Jesus, all of them, he said to his disciples).[15]

This variant does not suggest that the scribe intended to change the text, but rather that with the whole context in mind he followed the verb (ετελεσεν) immediately with its direct object (τους λογους τουτους), then he noted that in his Vorlage the subject (ο Ιησους) is explicit and proceeded to add it, and finally he noticed the qualification of the direct object (παντας) and added it to complete the clause. The reader loses none of the information.[16] It can be assumed with confidence that the scribe's *Vorlage* was the normal text.

The next example of transposition is more difficult, but it is still in accordance with the meaning of the text: Mt. 26.12 βαλουσα γαρ αυτη το μυρον τουτο επι του σωματος μου προς το ενταφιασαι με εποιησεν ('In pouring this ointment on my body she has done it to prepare me for burial'). P[45] transposes τουτο following μυρον to the end of the sentence, possibly because the demonstrative pronoun was at first overlooked and then restored as soon as possible at a suitable place.[17] And by using the same words the whole sentence is even stylistically improved.

The text in Jn 10.34–36 is abridged and altered rather problematically, yet obviously without any conscious attempt to improve the style:

απεκριθη αυτοις [ο] Ιησους· ουκ εστιν γεγραμμενον εν τω νομω υμων οτι
εγω ειπα · θεοι εστε; ει εκεινους ειπεν θεους προς ους ο λογος του θεου
εγενετο, και ου δυναται
λυθηναι η γραφη, ον ο πατηρ ηγιασεν και απεστειλεν εις τον κοσμον υμεις
λεγετε οτι βλασφημεις, [...]

(Jesus answered them: 'Is it not written in your law,
"I said you are gods"? If he called them gods to whom the word of God came (and scripture cannot be broken), do you say of him whom the Father consecrated and sent into the world, "you are blaspheming" [...]').

14.   Colwell, 'Method', p. 117: 'This scribe does not actually copy words. He sees through the language to its idea-content, and copies that – often in words of his own choosing, or in words rearranged as to order'. Considering the text of P[45] on the whole Colwell may go too far but one has to agree with his basic judgement.

15.   According to the reconstruction of the Vienna fragments of P[45] by G. Zuntz, 'Reconstruction', pp. 208–209; cf. Royse, 'Scribal Habits', p. 91.

16.   Cf. the good analysis of all the transpositions by Royse, 'Scribal Habits', pp. 131–137.

17.   See Zuntz, 'Reconstruction', pp. 208–209; cf. Royse, 'Scribal Habits', p. 91. P[45]: βαλουσα γαρ αυτη το μυρος επι του σωματος μου προς το ενταφιασαι εποιησεν τουτο.

P⁴⁵ gets confused in this difficult sentence structure. After γεγραμμενον it adds the obviously suggested εν τη γραφη, omits προς ους ο λογος του θεου εγενετο (producing an error thereby), and at the end of v. 35 it drops η γραφη which had been used earlier. The total thrust of the difficult sentence becomes even clearer: 'Is it not written in Scripture, in your law, "I said, you are gods"? If he called them gods (and that cannot be broken), do you say of him whom the Father consecrated and sent into the world, "You are blaspheming" [...]'[18] This may not be accurate copying, but it does keep the essential meaning. We agree with Royse when he writes, 'Whatever the cause of the transpositions and however long the text involved, the scribe ends up with understandable Greek'.[19]

The nature and method of copying in P⁴⁵ is both intelligent and liberal: intelligent, because the sense of the exemplar is quickly grasped and in essence precisely reproduced; and liberal, because involved expressions and repetitious words are simplified or dropped. The text of its exemplar, and we can assume that this was the normal text without any substantive variants, provided causes sufficient to invite some immediate improvement in all the examples given.[20]

We may conclude that P⁴⁵ represents the kind of manuscript one might expect from an experienced transcriber of documents.[21] On the whole a reliable copy has been produced. The conspicuous omissions[22] and transpositions are not the work of a scholar carefully comparing exemplars, nor are they the result of intervention by a stylistic editor polishing the text.[23] They are due rather to the standards of regularity and clarity imposed on scribes by their profession. Especially in P⁴⁵ there

18. ουκ εστιν γεγραμμενον/ [εν τη] γραφη εν τω νομω οτι εγω ειπα θεοι εστε· εκεινους ε[ι/πεν θ]εους και ου δυναται λυθηναι ον ο πατηρ ηγιασεν και απεστει/[λεν ει]ς τον κοσμον· υμεις λεγετε οτι βλασφημεις [...]

19. Royse, 'Scribal Habits', p. 133; Colwell's overall assessment of the scribal habits of P⁴⁵ (Colwell. 'Method', pp. 118–19) is far too influenced by the view that the scribe clarified the text intentionally.

20. This is likely in general because P⁴⁵ frequently reads with the text of the *Novum Testamentum Graece* and a majority of good witnesses. There are also some (but not many) variants where P⁴⁵ reads with a few other witnesses; these may be derived from an exemplar that can no longer be reconstructed, as for example in Jn 10:

Jn 10.8   ηλθον προ εμου] om. προ εμου P⁴⁵vid P⁷⁵ℵ* Γ Δ 892ˢ.1424 pm lat syˢ·ᵖ sa
          ac² pbo; Aug
Jn 10.11 τιθησιν] διδωσιν P⁴⁵ ℵ* D lat syˢ pbo bo
Jn 10.12 τα προβατα ιδια] ιδια τα προβατα P⁴⁵ Θ it
Jn 10.15 τιθημι] διδωμι P⁴⁵ P⁶⁶ℵ* D W pbo
Jn 10.39 om παλιν P⁴⁵vid ℵ* D 579.1241 al lat ac²
Jn 10.42 om εκει P⁴⁵vid 1241 lat sy s·p ac² boᵐˢˢ

21. I doubt that the slave (copyist) was properly speaking an educated person, as Kraus now believes (see p. 14 n. 49). Surely what we have here is a 'Beauftragter, ein professioneller Schreiber' (Kraus, 'Ad fontes', p. 18).

22. See especially Royse, 'Scribal Habits', pp. 126–31.

23. Cf. Colwell, 'Method', pp. 118–19: 'The most striking aspect of his style is its conciseness'.

is a broad correlation between the professional standards and skill of the scribe and the product of his work. The scribe spares the reader obviously superfluous elements. If the scribe is a Christian he may draw upon the other gospels for harmonizations in parallel passages. And while this does not happen too often (Royse notes 11 instances), it would be inconceivable for a non-Christian scribe.

This assessment of the papyrus is now also clearly corroborated in Mark (I omit Acts). The textual character here is admittedly different. Since we cannot assume that the scribe has changed his writing style, he must have had a different *Vorlage*. This is quite conceivable, because there were not many manuscripts of the Gospel of Mark, and the community would have to use what was available. The text of Mark in P[45] is marked by far fewer agreements with the early text than in the other gospels. It reads more often with the Majority Text, proving that here it must have used an exemplar influenced by an early tributary to the later Byzantine tradition.

Significantly the same kind of singular readings are found in Mark as are met in the other gospels based on other exemplars. Superfluous elements and repetitious words are dropped, parallels are restored, conjunctions are inserted and intended meanings are clarified. But it must be stated clearly that here again there is no question of scholarly or stylistic revision, but only of such half-conscious changes as transcribers of documents make in seeing that exemplars are reproduced accurately, but also clearly and intelligibly. I offer just a few examples from the Gospel of Mark.[24]

Mk 6.41   om πεντε P[45]
Mk 6.41   om δυο P[45]
Mk 6.49   om επι της θαλασσης P[45vid].[25]

In each of these instances the omitted words have just occurred in the context. It was just said that they had only five loaves and two fish (v. 38) and similarly it was already said that he came to them 'walking on the water'. The omission makes for more rapid reading.[26] This may also be true of the following addition and the small omisson and stylistic change:

Mk 12.14 δωμεν η μη δωμεν] δωμεν ουν η μη δωμεν P[45] ('should we pay them – the taxes – or should we not?' P[45] adds: 'should we pay – 'then' – or not?')

Mk 9.28 και εισελθοντος αυτου εις οικον οι μαθηται αυτου κατ ιδιαν επηρωτων αυτον] εισελθοντι αυτω προσηλθον οι μ[αθηται αυτου κατ ιδιαν αυτ]ω και ηρωτησαν αυτον λεγοντες P[45vid].[27]

24. These are taken from the impressive collection of all the singular readings in P[45] compiled by Royse (see note 15).

25. The omission is inferred as it occurs in a lacuna; cf. also Royse, 'Scribal Habits', p. 93.

26. It would be interesting to investigate the extent to which the variants in New Testament manuscripts may be related to these half-conscious attempts to make the text more readable. This might well lead to a study of literacy in the third century. And remember, being able to read need not mean being able to read fluently.

27. Cf. possibly also Mk 7.8 παραδοσιν] εντολην P[45].

It is difficult but perhaps not impossible to judge whether the problem of the Caesarean text in Mark may be related to the skills of professional scribes. It has often been said that P^{45} and W represent a textual form established by scholars in Caesarea. Actually there are agreements between P^{45} and W which cannot be coincidental and must point to a common ancestry.[28] But they do not give the impression of intentional changes based on philological principles, nor are they distributed over the text in a manner or frequency that lead one to suspect any consistent purpose. I would accordingly have doubts about the Caesarean text as a redacted text.

Rather we should assume with Metzger 'that the Caesarean text is really a textual process'.[29] This process was not initiated by P^{45}, but it could have been prompted and further developed by a series of scribes similar to the scribe of P^{45} in their professional attitude and approach – quickly grasping the sense of their exemplar's text, and copying it 'accurately' but in a 'readable' form.

How did the community that commissioned the manuscripts respond to them? It could have been dissatisfied for many reasons with the codex they received: The number of singular readings was large and all the more dangerous because they made good sense. The scribe had made very few corrections (Royse counts nine), and only two were from a second hand. Thus no official corrector had been appointed. Even the difference of the textual character of Mark (and Acts) could have been embarrassing. Could it be that this was not all that noticeable, because the community agreed that Mark was in any case still Mark? Or was it noticed, but no one took the trouble to obtain a codex with a trustworthy text from a neighbouring community?

In any event the codex represented a sizable investment. On the basis of scribal fees and the cost of materials, Theodore Skeat has estimated the total expenditure

---

28. The following are some of the significant examples:

Mk 6.45   om εις το περαν P^{45} W f¹ q sy^s (but note the lack of agreement in the same context at 6.47: add. παλαι P^{45} D f¹ 28.2542; 6.48 om της νυκτος P^{45vid} sing.; 6.48 om προς αυτους only D W Θ 565 it)

Mk 6.48   add. σφοδρα και p. αυτοι $P^{45\ vid}$ W Θ f¹³ 28. (565.700)

Mk 8.38   om λογους $P^{45\ vid}$ W k sa

Mk 8.38   om ταυτη $P^{45\ vid}$ W a i k n

Mk 9.2   Add (p) εν τω προσευχεσθαι αυτους (αυτον Θ 28) P^{45} W Θ f¹³ (565); cf. Lk 9.29.

Mk 9.2   p. μετεμορφωθη add ο ιησους P^{45} W f¹³

Mk 9.25   om τω ακαθαρτω P^{45} W f¹ sy^s

Mk 9.27   om και ανεστη $P^{45\ vid}$ W k l sy$^{s.p}$

But then there are some characteristic readings where P^{45} does not read with W:

Mk 7.4   om και κλινων $P^{45\ vid}$ ℵ B L Δ 28* (sy^s) sa^{ms} bo (without W)

Mk 7.5   κοιναις χερσιν και ανιπτοις P^{45}sing. (f¹³: κοιναις χερσιν ανιπτοις), that means P^{45} presents a mixed reading from the established text (κοιναις χερσιν) and the Byzantine reading (ανιπτοις χερσιν). W reads κοιναις ταις χερσιν.

29. Bruce M. Metzger, 'The Caesarean Text of the Gospels', in *idem* (ed.), *Chapters in the History of New Testament Textual Criticism* (NTTS, 4; Leiden: Brill, 1963), pp. 42–72 (67). A fresh study would be welcome.

at 43 to 44 drachmas.[30] Although the real value of this sum is difficult to gauge because of the inflation in the third century,[31] for the Fayum in the first half of the third century this amount would not have been cheap although it would not have been prohibitively expensive.[32] What this meant for the commissioning community depends upon its size.

We will look further at the community's expectations after glancing at the two other papyri, P[46] and P[47]. This can be brief. Both these papyri differ from P[45] with regard to the quality of both their text and its copying. But when we come to how satisfied the church was with the finished product, we have the same problem as with P[45]. P[46] and P[47] also had good exemplars on the whole, but the quality of their copying was (each in various respects) not unobjectionable.

As for P[46], the hand is graceful and flowing, almost calligraphic 'with some pretensions to style and elegance'.[33] The quality of the copy is not comparable with the beautiful hand. The picture is marred by numerous errors – errors not only of orthography and badly written nomina sacra, but also numerous omissions due to a wandering eye (parablepsis) if not to pure carelessness. At times the writer did not understand the exemplar, and he produced a great number of nonsense readings. Particularly striking among them is 1 Cor. 15.51 παντε ου κοιμηθησομεθα ου παντες δε αλλαγησομεθα P[46]A[c]. ('We shall not all die, but we shall not all be changed'). A later reader placed a dot in the margin at this point, apparently questioning its meaning.[34] Harmonizations with the immediate context are frequent, indicating also a degree of carelessness on the part of the writer.[35] Omissions of one or

30.　Cf. T.C. Skeat, 'A Codicological Analysis of the Chester Beatty Papyrus Codex of Gospels and Acts (P45)', *Hermathena (A Trinity College Dublin Review)*, 155 (1993), pp. 27–43 (pp. 41–42).

31.　Prices increased more slowly in Fayum/Arsinoë than in other regions of Egypt. Cf. H.-J. Drexhage, *Preise, Mieten, Pachten, Kosten und Löhne im römischen Ägypten bis zum Regierungsantritt Diokleians* (St. Katharinen: Scripta Mercaturae, 1991), 407.

32.　For comparison: in 215 CE one temple guard earned 28 drachmas, another earned 19 drachmas, a head librarian 30 drachmas, a scribe 40 drachmas, a supervisor of the monthly procession 12 drachmas. In the years 248/258 CE a cattleman received 64 drachmas, an ox driver 52 drachmas, a scribe or bookkeeper 40 drachmas, and beginning in 255 the rates exploded, with a scribe (in Memphis) charging 120 drachmas, or three times the going rate in 215. See for all of these examples Drexhage, o.c. (see note 31), 428–34. Yet comparing the amount for P[45] with the rates for entertainment artists and performers (mimes, flautists, dancers, etc.), the latter are much higher. Cf. Drexhage, o.c. (see note 31), 434–39. Since P[45] comes from the first half of the third century we are on fairly firm ground: the community paid for their codex a little more than a scribe's monthly income, but a little less than a cattleman would have earned.

33.　Kenyon III, *Text*, xiii.

34.　Cf. 1 Cor. 15.2, where the writer calls attention to a difficulty in the text (or the *Vorlage?*) which he is unable to cope with. On this passage cf. G. Zuntz, *The Text of the Epistles: A Disquisition upon the Corpus Paulinum* (Schweich Lectures of the British Academy, 1946; London: Oxford University Press, 1953), pp. 254–55. Zuntz suspects that the scribe misconstrued the sentence structure, and consequently being puzzled he left a space empty, 'obviously with the idea, "let the corrector settle that"'. That may be true, although I doubt that the corrections in P[46] or even in its presumed predecessors justify the inference that 'philological technique was applied to the text of the Epistles already in the second century' (p. 254).

35.　Royse, 'Scribal Habits', pp. 268–69.

more words occur often, but they seldom lead to nonsense readings.[36] Accordingly P[46] represents a rough and inadequate copy of a good exemplar.[37] What we have here is doubtless a copy, even though an inaccurate one, and not a text intentionally altered by the scribe. The scribe was not capable of it nor was it his task.

We agree with Zuntz: 'The excellent quality of the text represented by our oldest manuscript, P[46], stands out again. As so often before, we must here be careful to distinguish between the very poor work of the scribe who penned it and the basic text, which he so poorly rendered. P[46] abounds with scribal blunders, omissions, and also additions. In some of them the scribe anticipated the errors of later copyists; in some other instances he shares an older error; but the vast majority are his own uncontested property. Once they have been discarded, there remains a text of outstanding (though not absolute) purity.'[38] But there remains the question: to what extent were people really disturbed by such faults?

Finally, P[47] is also written in an experienced hand, but it is unattractive, thicker, and anything but calligraphic. The copyist's orthography is as poor as that of P[46]. He also produces nonsense readings from carelessness. His one peculiarity is a tendency toward certain atticist grammatical and stylistic improvements, such as the

---

36. Royse, 'Scribal Habits', pp. 254–60.

37. The papyrus frequently reads with the great majuscules, especially B, against D F G. Cf. e.g.,

1 Cor. 1.8	ημερα P[46] $\aleph$ B rell] παρουσια D F G
1 Cor. 2.1	μυστηριον P[46 vid] $\aleph$* A C a r sy[p] bo; Hipp BasA Ambst] μαρτυριον $\aleph$[2] B D F G Ψ 33.1739.1881M b vg sy[h] sa
1 Cor. 10.28	ιεροθυτον P[46] $\aleph$ A B H 1175*. 1739* b sa Ambst] ειδωλοθυτον C D F G Ψ 33. 1739[c]. 1881 M lat sy[h] bo Tert
1 Cor. 11.29	om αναξιως P[46] $\aleph$* A B C* 6. 33. 1739 co] αναξιως $\aleph$[2] C[3] D F G Ψ 1881 M latt sy
1 Cor. 13.3	καυχησωμαι P[46] $\aleph$ A B 048. 33. 1739* co Hier[mss]] καυθησομαι C D F G L 6. 81. 104. 630. 945. 1175. 1881 al latt sy[hmg] Tert Ambst Hier[mss]; καυθησωμαι Ψ 1739[c]. 1881[c] M

P[46] frequently follows the reconstructed text against the so-called Western text, which by 200 CE must not already have been current in Egypt. Occasionally the exemplar contained readings attested by D F G. The following readings could hardly be considered independent inventions:

Rom. 8.23	om υιοθεσιαν P[46 vid] D F G 614 t; Ambst against all the rest
Gal. 3.14	ευλογιαν P[46] D[*.c] F G b vg[ms]; Mcion[T] Ambst] επαγγελιαν $\aleph$ A B C D[2] Ψ 0278. 33. 1739. 1881 M lat sy co

Both readings, however, could be explained by an inability to understand the text of the exemplar (Rom. 8.23), or by the influence of the context (Gal. 3.16–17). Other variants which may have been suggested by the context are the following:

1 Cor. 15.47 ο δευτερος ανθρωπος πνευματικος εξ ουρανου P[46] sing., paralleling 15.44–46

It is difficult to assess the reading Heb. 6.2 διδαχην (instead of διδαχης) P[46] B 0150 d. The accusative makes sense in parallel to θεμελιον (6.1). It may have been in the exemplar. But it may also have been chosen because of all the genitives in the context.

38. Zuntz, *Text* (see n.34), pp. 212–13.

use of a neuter plural with a singular verb.[39] Again, his exemplar is good, but he does not always copy it carefully.

We find a similar situation, then, in all three of our papyri. The relatively large number of errors, oversights and imperfections occuring in the sacred text of the New Testament lead us to ask whether the community that commissioned the work could be satisfied with it.

3. *The Commissioning Community and its Reaction to the Completed Manuscript*

The question is whether those who commissioned the work were completely unaware of its errors and oversights, or did they believe that its minor textual differences, which they recognized from other known manuscripts or from worship services of neighbouring churches, were unimportant. The thesis I propose here is that actually for those who commissioned the work these minor differences, including all the differences we have discussed, were inconsequential. And if this can be demonstrated it would be extraordinarily illuminating about attitudes toward the New Testament and its text in the third century.

To find a methodological basis for answering this question let us observe the general usage with regard to quotations of the period. Of course quotations were freer than text manuscripts, but toward the end of the second century the situation underwent a fundamental change. Quotations were no longer pure paraphrases or adaptations of the original text; instead, extensive literal citations from what was recognized as a New Testament became the rule. This 'text consciousness', as I have called it elsewhere, was clearly evolving.[40] It was not yet as fully formed as it became in the fourth century with John Chrysostom, who almost never deviates from the Byzantine text of his period, but still the contrast with the quotations in the first half of the second century is quite striking.

Correspondingly, toward the end of the second century one of the special charges made against heretics was that of making changes in the Scriptures. This charge was unjustified, to the best of our knowledge, and should be understood against the background of a general concern for quotations to be precise and literal.[41] Only when opponents as well as the so-called Orthodox placed such great weight on accuracy in quoting and in copying Scriptural texts does it make sense to accuse the opposition of manipulating the text.

But what constitutes accuracy of quotation in principle, and where do our papyri fit in this context? First with regard to the copyists: are they incapable of complete accuracy, or are they simply not interested in making a slavishly precise reproduction of their exemplar? The answer is probably both, but especially the latter. As yet the scribes are not working within a heritage of transcribing sacred texts as in

39.   Cf. Royse, 'Scribal Habits', p. 360.

40.   Cf. B. Aland, 'Die Rezeption des neutestamentlichen Textes in den ersten Jahrhunderten', in *ETL* 86 (1989), pp. 1–38 (2 et passim).

41.   Cf. Aland, 'Die Rezeption', pp. 13–20.

the Jewish tradition or the period of the Byzantine text, where strict rules are carried out under careful supervision. They are transcribers of documents and writers of literary texts of modest expectations with regard to standards of precision, that is, they are prone to making small changes that at most do not alter the sense. More than this is beyond their capacity, and they do not attempt to do more.

What does this mean for a community's expectations when commissioning a work like our papyri in a period when we may presuppose an emerging text consciousness, even in the Fayum? There are two possibilities. Either they do not notice the manuscript's errors because they have nothing to compare it with, and possibly because the lector in the worship service can quietly smooth over any difficulties; or they do not believe that the errors are very serious, especially when they can be offset by the reader.

As to the first alternative, we cannot assume that communities had an official appointed to supervise the production of texts. Otherwise all the codices would have been proofread better than they actually were. And yet, some corrections were made. We should assume that communities would have had the opportunity to hear the Scriptures read, whether in a neighbouring church or from a guest minister, before getting their own copy. The Fayum was an old Greek settlement, and it was christianized very early. Therefore any errors in a third-century manuscript, and especially nonsense readings, frequent omissions and transpositions, should have been noticed by some members of the church. If they were still not corrected, we are forced to accept the second alternative: the congregation and its minister or its lector did not consider the 'minor' deviations and errors in their manuscript to be important. They tolerated them. Also in evidence is the fact that we must consider the commissioning communities to have been largely illiterate. They were unable to detect the inaccuracies of their codex, and were made even less aware of them by the compensating skill of the lector in the worship services. The text was heard more than it was read, even among the educated and the literate.[42]

This is further corroborated by quotations from about the same period. These lack examples of outright errors, but they show numerous examples of transpositions, omissions and changes of verbal forms and vocabulary that nevertheless do not alter the sense of the text. In contexts where the quotation is clearly meant to be accurate, it is obvious that neither the author nor the scribe, nor yet the community commissioning a manuscript is at all concerned with literal or slavish precision. Rather, the concern for an absolute degree of textual precision did not appear before the fourth/fifth century, and then it was chiefly among copyists of the Byzantine text.[43]

42. See the excellent study by Harry Y. Gamble, *Books and Readers in the Early Church: A History of Early Christian Texts* (New Haven and London: Yale University Press, 1995). Gamble made a study of literacy in the early Church as related to the sociocultural studies of William Harris and W. Meeks, and his conclusions on 'the uses of early Christian books', should be noted by every textual critic; cf. pp. 2–11 and 203–41, especially 203–23. See also his contribution in this volume.

43. We should add that insufficient evidence has been preserved of textual witnesses for any

A good example of this kind of text consciousness that did not aim for literal precision is found in Clement's lengthy citation of Mk 10.17–31 in *Quis dives salvetur* 4.4–10. The author quite clearly intends to present the readers of his diatribe with the literal text of the parable of the Rich Young Man; otherwise he could have referred to the well known story with a simple allusion. What he actually provides is a closely text-related but very free quotation, which adheres to an exemplar but with frequent changes, which make hardly any difference in meaning and are attested almost exclusively by Clement. Some of these readings are harmonizations with parallel passages of other synoptic gospels, as could be expected from one with Clement's familiarity with the New Testament. We offer some examples only.[44] These include changes in verbs and verbal forms:

10.17	προσδραμων εις] προσελθων τις Cl
	γονυπετησας αυτον επηρωτα αυτον] εγονυπετει λεγων Cl
10.20	εφη] αποκριθεις λεγει Cl
10.21	δος] διαδος Cl

transpositions:

10.18	λεγεις αγαθον] 2 1 Cl
10.20	ταυτα παντα] 2 1 Cl
10.21	οσα εχεις πωλησον] 3 1 2 Cl
10.23	εις την βασιλειαν του θεου εισελευσονται] 6 1–5 Cl
10.24	ο δε Ιησους παλιν] 4 2 1 3 Cl
10.29	λεγω υμιν] 2 1 Cl

choice of synonyms:

10.22	κτηματα] χρηματα Cl (cf. 10.23)
10.25	ευκοπωτερον] ευκολως Cl
10.29	ος αφηκεν οικιαν ...] ος αν αφη τα ιδια ... Cl
10.29	η μητερα η πατερα] και γονεις Cl

omissions:

10.21	εμβλεψας αυτω ηγαπησεν αυτον] 1 3 4 Cl
10.21	om υπαγε Cl
10.29/30	om ουδεις εστιν Cl (et εαν μη λαβη] αποληψεται Cl)
10.29	om η τεκνα η αγρους Cl
10.29	om η αδελφας Cl

additions:

10.22	add και αγρους post πολλα Cl
10.29	add και χρηματα post αδελφους Cl
10.30	add εχειν ante μετα διωγμων et add εις που (or εις τι) post διωγμων Cl

harmonization to the synoptic context :

10.21	add ει θελεις τελειος ειναι Cl (cf. Mt. 19.21)

other so-called text types. It can be assumed that even here in the fourth/fifth century there was a higher degree of precision in copying than was characteristic of earlier periods.

44.   Major variants which are also supported by other witnesses are ignored here. The numerous minor variants are sufficient to demonstrate just how freely Clement could treat his exemplar.

This list of minor variants found in the text of Clement's lengthy citation and not attested in any other Greek manuscripts clearly shows the quality of these 'minor' differences. Clement neither adjusts his citation syntactically to the context of his immediate text, as would have agreed with ancient citation practice, nor does he alter the text of Mark to make stylistic improvements. His readings, then, cannot be explained by any literary ambitions. The divergences from his exemplar have to do with banalities (with the exception of 10.30, where Clement improves the clarity of the difficult sentence).[45] They go back to the rapid dictation of the author to his stenographer and were not regarded as worth correcting.

But this is important: if Clement could expect his Alexandrian church to accept the text he gave them as the text of the New Testament, then we can infer that for him and for his readers these 'minor' matters did not matter. The variations Clement allowed himself define precisely the range of what was considered insignificant. If such variations were possible for the sophisticated Clement in Alexandria, in a passage so lengthy that it was midway between a citation and a text manuscript, they are also conceivable and even probable in manuscripts produced in the Fayum. We may also draw the inference that the readers of the manuscripts we have presented here were well aware of the divergences, omissions and transpositions, but regarded them as trivial because they did not yet have a highly developed tradition of holy Scripture with corresponding procedures of controlling its transmission. Only when the sense of the text was considered to be distinctly disturbed (cf. 1 Cor. 15.51 παντες ου κοιμηθησομεθα ου παντες δε αλλογησου εθα in P[46]) would a reader – cautiously – place a mark in the margin by the passage. Banalities did not call for intervention or correction.

In conclusion it may be said that the Chester Beatty papyri reflect the situation of the New Testament in a particular region of Egypt in the third century, both precisely and revealingly. They attest the significance of the New Testament as a most influential constant in the self-consciousness of the communities. They are witnesses to the awareness of a distinctive canon of Scripture. They show that alternative sequences of the New Testament writings were possible (P[45]: Matthew, John, Luke, Mark, Acts,[46] and P[46]: Romans, Hebrews, 1 and 2 Corinthians, Ephesians, Galatians, Philippians, Colossians, 1 Thessalonians), but that the collection of these writings was essentially closed. The Chester Beatty papyri are far from including any apocryphal writings, as is true also of the other early New Testament papyri (with the exception of P[72]). Finally, the papyri are a witness to the beginnings of a text consciousness in the community in the sense of the New Testament text to be cited and subject to exegesis. The text critical work of Origen had obviously not yet reached the Fayum. But even Origen is willing to examine the possible meaning of every variant at one passage carefully than to reject them – possibly – too hastily.[47]

---

45. It probably contained elements of D and W.
46. Cf. Skeat, 'A Codicological Analysis', pp. 31–42.
47. Cf. Aland, 'Die Rezeption', pp. 22–23.

This kind of circumspection is an appropriate attitude to take toward manuscripts such as the Chester Beatty papyri, which are accurate in principle, but full of distinctive variants that do no violence to the meaning of the text. These papyri are an extremely informative and eloquent witness for the history of the church in the third century.

SINGULAR READINGS IN THE GOSPEL TEXT OF P[45]

J. Keith Elliott

As a hand-written copy P[45] is by definition unique. Unlike multiple copies of a modern book reproduced by printing, manuscripts are distinctive. No two manuscript copies of the Greek New Testament agree in all particulars – idiosyncratic errors and peculiar orthography as well as more significant textual variation separate one manuscript from another.

Although we know that scholars such as Origen[1] and Jerome[2] were occasionally alert to textual differences in the manuscripts they had access to, few ordinary readers and users of the books that came to be known as the Christian scriptures would in antiquity have been in a position to compare their church's or monastery's copy of the Bible with another manuscript. Such scholarly exercises would pre-sumably have been possible in an academic centre such as Caesarea or Alexandria. But, in general, multiple versions of the same text would not have been readily accessible. In any case the average Christian was not concerned with the niceties of textual variation – for him it was sufficient to be told that book 'a' was approved reading, whereas document 'x' was apocryphal.[3] To read Matthew, Mark, Luke or John was all that was important. Those defining the extent of the canon as such did not specify that the copy of, say, Mark had to be the one that contained (or did not contain) the last 12 verses of Chapter 16, for example.

Readers and users of the Gospels in a particular ancient Christian community accepted the version of those books, which happened to be in their personal or local copy. We may compare this to a modern situation where Christians hear and accept as canonical the distinctive text of a particular translation of the New Testa-ment being read, be it the Authorised Version, Revised Version, or a more recent version. For instance, worshippers at a modern wedding service are likely to hear without questioning in 1 Cor. 13.3 the words '[…] I give (up) my body to be burnt' or '[…] I hand over my body so that I may boast' which depend on the translation

---

1.   See B.M. Metzger, 'Explicit References in the Works of Origen to Variant Readings in New Testament Manuscripts', in J.N. Birdsall and R.W. Thomson (eds.), *Biblical and Patristic Studies in Memory of Robert Pierce Casey* (Freiburg: Herder, 1963), pp. 78–95.

2.   See B.M. Metzger, 'St. Jerome's Explicit References to Variant Readings in Manuscripts of the New Testament', in E. Best and R. McL. Wilson (eds.), *Text and Interpretation: Studies in the New Testament Presented to Matthew Black* (Cambridge: Cambridge University Press, 1979), pp. 179–90.

3.   As in lists such as those found in the Gelasian Decree, the List of the Sixty Books or the Stichometry of Nicephorus.

being read (cf. Good News Bible and Revised English Bible or New Revised Standard Version).

Similarly, the users of the Gospel text of P^{45} are unlikely to have indulged themselves with a comparison of their manuscript with any differing wording remembered from another manuscript. The copyist of that manuscript (or a predecessor) may of course have consciously altered the wording of the exemplar he was copying from when transcribing this text. Much deliberate alteration took place in effect to assimilate parallel texts, the commonly recognized harmonizing of Gospel parallels especially to conform Mark and Luke to the wording in Matthew being the most frequent. (Examples of this cause for textual variation may be seen throughout.)

We now turn to P^{45}. As we read through the remaining pages of its Gospel text[4] we are first struck by the fact that this is a perfectly acceptable copy of these books. It reads well and logically, there being only a couple of places where the sense is obscured by an unusual wording. Readers familiar with the Gospels will identify some places where P^{45} supports a reading differing from another text; at other times the alert reader may see a form of words hitherto unknown from other Gospel manuscripts. It is those unique readings that form the basis of the current investigation. I shall concentrate on the distinctive readings of P^{45}.

Text-critics dub such distinctive readings 'singular'. I shall also refer to some so-called 'sub-singular' readings too, where the distinctive text of P^{45} is shared by one or two other manuscripts. 'Sub-singular' seems a strange and self-contradicting term but by its use text-critics are pointing to a distinctive text that, probably coincidentally, is shared by another manuscript, usually without their having any recent common close ancestry or their ever having been influenced by the other. 'Singular' (or even 'sub-singular') are dangerous words. What we mean by these terms is that these are readings not found in the bulk of other manuscripts, but we must remember that the vast majority of other manuscripts, especially minuscules, have not been read in their entirety. So, it may be argued, today's singular reading could tomorrow turn into a reading shared by other recently read manuscripts. That may indeed be a working possibility, but for most practicable purposes we may accept that, as the singular readings of an early manuscript like our P^{45} are not shared with other early manuscripts (and most of the manuscripts written up to the ninth century have been read in detail by modern scholars), they are for the most part unique to that manuscript. The other thing that must be said at the outset is that even if the currently extant fund of manuscripts reveals that a reading in one manuscript is unique, singular and distinctive, that does not of course mean that it was ever thus. The sheer chance of survival may deny our ever knowing if that distinctive reading was once shared (commonly) in its own day. All we may do is to say that of the manuscripts that happen to be extant today we have at this or that verse a text otherwise unattested elsewhere.

Obviously when trying to fit P^{45} into the overall picture of the history of New Testament manuscripts, the distinctive readings are only one part of the evidence. One needs of course to see how its text compares with representatives of the gen-

---

4.   I leave aside the pages of this manuscript containing Acts in a collection of articles examining the fourfold Gospels.

erally agreed text-types into which the New Testament text has been divided, although Epp's warning that it is somewhat anachronistic to make the text-type of a third century manuscript fit categories of text derived from manuscripts of later centuries is fair.[5] One may, however, see which readings it shares with say D or with ℵ or with W or the Majority text. Kenyon made a preliminary investigation in his introduction.[6] Others have refined this work.[7] It may be that the conclusion is that P[45] is a 'free' text, to use the Alands' term.[8] But whether it is concluded that the manuscript cannot be classified or could perhaps be an early representative of a particular text-type is not our concern now.

Those who aspire to a so-called thoroughgoing solution to text-critical problems would put into the melting pot the readings of all manuscripts before deciding where the original reading of the original author lies.[9] Those who convince themselves that they know which manuscripts are more reliable than others are obviously prejudiced in favour of readings found in their favourite manuscripts. As far as P[45] and other early papyri are concerned there has been a certain prejudice in favour of their readings especially if B (Codex Vaticanus) also supports them.[10] We see in our most frequently consulted Greek New Testament (Nestle-Aland[27]) that occasionally P[45] and a few others have influenced the text printed especially if those few others are favoured manuscripts. The papyri have not influenced textual decisions as much as one could have imagined given the early date of many of them but there are places where P[45] and a few allies (notably B) have influenced the 'original' text in the modern printed editions, as may be seen in the apparatus of Nestle-Aland e.g. Lk. 9.62 [προς αυτου] where the words are omitted by P[75], B and our manuscript.[11] See also Lk. 6.34 [εστιν]: the verb is also absent from P[75], B; Lk. 10.35 word order with P[75], B; Lk. 10.38 αυτον *sine add.;* Lk. 11.11 shorter text after υιος with P[75], B. At Lk. 11.22 our text with P[75] and D (against B) omits αυτου; that reading is not accepted by Nestle-Aland. In general though our manuscript and other early papyri have not influenced modern editors of the Greek New Testament as much as some would have expected.

5.   Eldon J. Epp in, among other places, 'The Significance of the Papyri for Determining the Nature of the New Testament Text in the Second Century: A Dynamic View of Textual Transmission', in W.L. Petersen (ed.), *Gospel Traditions in the Second Century* (Indiana and London: Notre Dame University Press, 1989), pp. 71–103.

6.   Kenyon II, *Text*, pp. xi–xx.

7.   For instance see Larry Hurtado's contribution to this volume with reference to parallels with manuscript W in Mark.

8.   Kurt Aland and Barbara Aland, *The Text of the New Testament: An Introduction to the Critical Editions and to the Theory and Practice of Modern Textual Criticism* (trans. Erroll F. Rhodes; Grand Rapids: Eerdmans; Leiden: Brill, 2nd edn, 1989), esp. pp. 56–64.

9.   See J.K. Elliott, 'Thoroughgoing Eclecticism in New Testament Textual Criticism', in B.D. Ehrman and M.W. Holmes (eds.), *The Text of the New Testament in Contemporary Research: Essays on the* Status Quaestionis (SD, 46; Grand Rapids: Eerdmans, 1995), pp. 321–35.

10.   Martini's work on P[75] and B comes to mind: C.M. Martini, *Il Problema della recensionalità del codice B alla luce del papiro Bodmer XIV* (Rome: Pontifical Biblical Institute, 1966).

11.   E.J. Epp, 'The New Testament Papyri in Historical Perspective' in M.P. Horgan and P.J. Kabelski (ed.), *To Touch the Text: Biblical and Related Studies in Honor of Joseph A. Fitzmyer SJ* (New York: Crossroad, 1989), pp. 261–88 esp. 56–64.

I am interested here in trying to appreciate what the original users of P^{45} would have read. To identify the singular and sub-singular readings I have access of course to modern tools such as printed *apparatus* and collations which readily enable me to see where the readings of P^{45} have not been repeated in any other manuscript (or which are different from over 99 percent of all other known manuscripts).[12] Do those readings make a substantial difference to the type of Gospel text they read, heard and lived their Christian lives by?

The first thing that must be concluded is that the text of this early manuscript, 'free' though it may be dubbed, is no aberrant text like Codex Bezae is often said to be. There are no real surprises, no startling deviations or unusual glosses.

There are however a few places where P^{45} gives us a shorter text than that found elsewhere. Sometimes the shortening of the text is probably due to the accidental omitting of the words due to an optical reason such as hom. and our scribe like many another is prone to parablepsis.

Occasionally our manuscript has a longer text than any others. We shall look at some of the most significant of these, but, before we do so, I should say something about nomenclature. Words like 'add' or 'omit' are loaded in favour of the view that we know precisely what the original text contained. That is not certain. All we can note is by comparing one manuscript with another is that one has a longer or a shorter text. Nevertheless I do draw attention to the Synoptic parallels because those readings need to be taken into account when assessing the reasons for all types of change within manuscripts of the Synoptic Gospels. (We should of course bear in mind that because of its fragmentary nature it is not usually possible to compare many Synoptic parallels within the manuscript itself.)

Among shorter readings P^{45} has the following absences:

Mark
6.40 κατα^1[...] πεντηκοντα (absent from the Synoptic parallels)
6.41 πεντε (in the Matthaean and Lukan parallels)
6.41 δυο (in the Matthaean and Lukan parallels)
6.48 της νυκτος (in the Matthaean parallel)
8.11 ζητουντες παρ' αυτου (an omission through hom. seems likely here: αυτω ... αυτου) but this makes nonsense of the verse
9.25 τω ακαθαρτω with W (cf. Lukan parallel)
9.25 αυτω with Θ Fam1

Two other shorter readings in Mark are at 8.38 (where the lacunae in the manuscript make it unlikely that the words λογους and ταυτη could have been there. These variants happen – coincidentally – to agree with the readings in W).[13] The apparatus in Kenyon II, *Text* does not note these variants.

---

12.   P^{45} like most other papyri is regularly cited in the apparatus of modern critical editions, such as Nestle-Aland^{27} but not consistently (e.g. Mk 6.37 (word order); 6.39 (omit definite article); 8.11 (omit ζητουντες παρ' αυτου); 8.19 (om. τους) are absent from Nestle-Aland^{27}).
13.   P^{45} agrees with W elsewhere in this verse in the sub-singular reading και for μετα. Cf also at Mk 9.2 + ο Ιησους with W.

Luke

In Lk. 6 it seems from the space available in v. 48 that our manuscript has a shorter text than in other manuscripts, all of which have either (a) τεθεμελιωτο γαρ επι την πετραν or (b) δια το καλως οικοδομησθαι αυτην after σαλευσαι αυτην. There is a good and clear example of hom. if the exemplar had (b). The readers of this parable in P[45] lack an apparently otiose explanation why the flood failed to shake this house. Thus its readers may gain a rather different impression of the storyteller's skill than readers of other accounts.

12.2 P[45] lacks και κρυπτον ο ου γνωσθησεται (also probably an omission due to hom –θησεται […] -θησεται) without any significant loss of meaning or sense. (The words occur in the Matthaean parallel.)

12.9 P[45] lacks the verse.

John

Folios 16–17 contain a good portion of Jn 10–11. Reading through the remains of these chapters in P[45] an observant reader, familiar with a printed Greek New Testament text, would note the absence of και η ζωη at 11.25. Knowledge of this unique reading has had a great impact. Among modern English versions, the New Revised Standard Version has this shorter reading in its margin. Barrett's commentary refers to this variant and he is prepared to argue for the originality of the shorter text.[14]

11.7 There is no reference to the disciples after λεγει.

As far as *longer* readings are concerned, we note the following:

Mark

6.47 + παλαι with D Fam1, a reading found in the WH margin (cf. Mk 15.44).

7.5 + κοιναις χερσιν και ανιπτοις, which looks like a conflation of the readings κοιναις χερσιν and ανιπτος χερσιν. Fam13 has a similar longer text. κοινοις χερσιν ανιπτοις.

9.19 + και διεστραμμενη (in the Matthaean and Lukan parallels)

Luke

11.15 P[45] reads ελαλησαν οχυροι λεγοντς instead of ειπον *cett*.

A reading in P[45] which modern critics would dub a conflate reading is the longer reading at Lk. 12.24: before τους κορακας the manuscript has τα πετεινα του ουρανου which agrees with the Matthaean parallel.

John

10.34 + εν τη γραφει

11.43 + ελθε (apparently) after δευρο.

We may conclude this survey by stating that by comparison with other manuscripts, singular readings in P[45] that offer a shorter text do not generally remove the

14. C.K. Barrett, *The Gospel according to St. John* (London: SPCK, 2nd edn, 1978).

sense from the passage. We could deduce either that the scribe was responsible for pruning what may have been seen as redundant expressions or that later scribes of other manuscripts added to the short original text (unnecessary) detail.

***

Let us now read through more consistently the remains of the Gospel text of P⁴⁵ and see what its readers would have encountered that would make their reading and understanding of the text differ from the text encountered by readers of other manuscripts.

Matthew

Very little remains, but we have parts of chs. 20–21 and (together with the Vienna fragments of folio 2 *recto* in the Austrian National Library Pap. G 31974) parts of 25–26.

In the story of the two blind men in Jericho, P⁴⁵ has ηκολουθησαν οχλοι πολ-λοι and no αυτω at 20.29. That makes this reading differ from that in D (and a few others), which also have the plural but with αυτω. The rest of the manuscript tradition has the singular. Commentators may wish to explain the significance of these differences and text-critics may wish to discuss which reading gave rise to the other(s), but all that we wish to do now is to point out that the reading of our manuscript gives a picture (uniquely so it seems) of various groups of people with Jesus. Also in this story at 20.31, P⁴⁵ has the aorist εκραυγασαν against the more common εκραζον, εκραξαν (cf. v. 30) or εκραυγαζον. A change of verb could suggest a more sensitive literary style or that a stronger verb was needed to express a louder, more dramatic cry (as μειζον implies). We do however note that the Lukan and Markan parallels to this verse have forms of κραζω. It is not our intention here to pronounce on the originality or secondariness of the different readings but merely to note the distinctiveness of P⁴⁵.

In the verses extant from Mt. 25 in the manuscript in folio 2 *recto* (not folio 2 *verso* as shown in the Text volume)[15] there is a higher incidence of the particle και than in other manuscripts (see vv. 42–44). Readers of P⁴⁵ here would thus gain a different impression of the author's style than readers of other manuscripts of Matthew.

In the Vienna fragments of this section at Mt. 26.7 the rare word order αλαβασ-τρον εχουσα μυρου may, as in many a differing sequence of words, merely be the result of a scribe's having memorized a run of words which he then transcribes in a slightly different order that does not alter the overall meaning of the passage. [We note many such changes of sequence when comparing singular readings in P⁴⁵ with other manuscripts: e.g. Mk 6.37; 9.1 (where ωδε now has a less prominent position); 9.3; Lk. 10.35, 38, 41 (to emphasise κυριος perhaps); 11.19, 44; 12.7, 11, 28, 36, 52–53 (where there are many variations in sequence throughout the manuscript tradition); 13.10, 15, 24, 31; 14.5; Jn 10.18 *bis*, 41; 11.9, 33.]

---

15.   Correction noted in Kenyon II, *Plates*, p. v.

Mark

The extant fragments of Mark are more extensive than those containing Matthew They contain parts of Mk 6–8 including the stories of John the Baptist's death, the Feeding of the Five Thousand and its aftermath, the Qorban question, the Healing of the Deaf-mute, the Transfiguration and the Healing of the Epileptic Boy.

There are some oddities in the story of the Baptist's death. The reading αυτου γυν[αικα at 6.17 is puzzling. So too is η]ρωδιας δε at v. 19 which suggests that this proper name is anarthrous. A minor difference at 6.21 is the addition of the preposition εν but whether such redundancy implies an original or a secondary reading is an open question. A fuller investigation into the use of prepositions in the manuscript is needed – cf. in this context Lk. 14.1 (+εν). At 6.22 is a rare instance when our scribe has provided a correction or maybe an addition above the line of the text. Ειπεν ο Ηρωδης (a singular reading) stands in the text with βασιλεως added above the proper name; that longer text—if that is what is intended—is also a singular reading. Another unique longer reading adds αιτησαι at 6.24, presumably to the mother's otherwise verbless reply.

The observant reader of 7.8 will miss the familiar την παραδοσιν των ανθρωπων (which balances την παραδωσιν των πρεσβυτερων in v. 5). Readers of P⁴⁵ have εντολην instead of παραδοσιν which repeats this noun in v. 8a.

In the Healing of the Deaf-mute, P⁴⁵ has the compound ενεβαλεν at 7.33 instead of the usual simple verb (but cf. επεβαλεν in Fam13).

At 8.12 the generation asks for (αιτει) a sign in P⁴⁵. Other manuscripts read επιζητει or ζητει. The former parallels Matthew *bis*. ζητει v. l. επιζητει is in the Lukan parallel.

At Mk 9.6 P⁴⁵ (with W) reads λαλει. This tense seems odd. The imperfect ελαλει in Θ, λαλησει in A D fam13, and λαληση in Byz. make better sense. This verb is preferable to forms of αποκρινομαι (ℵ reads απεκριθη *pace* Kenyon's apparatus); B reads αποκριθη (printed as the current Nestle text). Its very difficulty may make the P⁴⁵ text original.

9.19 ο ΙΗ ειπεν: the addition of the subject—a singular reading—may be contrasted to Lk. 13.12 where P⁴⁵ lacks the name 'Jesus', thus showing that we cannot argue that our scribe consistently adds or omits proper names, or that these changes are inspired in one particular direction from the liturgy.

9.19 προς εμε cf. the same stylistic feature at Lk. 14.26.

9.23 has given rise to a variety of text forms but our manuscript with ει δονη is the most compact and is to be understood as a simple quoted repetition of the words preceding. It gives his rendering of the verse a dramatic impact.

Luke

Of all the Gospels Luke's has survived best in P⁴⁵. Seven folios contain extensive portions of Lk. 6–7 and 9–14. We can therefore gain a good impression of the text its original readers accepted as one of their Christian writings.

9.29 προσ]ευξασθαι (with ℵ*) as in v. 28; προσευχεσθαι *cett*.

9.31 εμελλον – this creates a difficult reading but could it be that it was one that perplexed the original readers? Certainly all other manuscripts have a 3rd person singular (μελλει, ημελλε, εμελλεν).[16]

An interesting sub-singular reading in P⁴⁵ (shared with X) is at Lk. 9.33, which has Peter address Jesus as διδασκαλε. Other manuscripts read επιστατε here. The parallels are κυριε (Matthew) and ραββι (Mark).

9.36 + εγενετο after και¹. That verse also lacks ουδεν and the emphatic αυτοι after και² in our manuscript.

9.37 της ημερας in P⁴⁵ gives a different meaning from 'on the next day' (in various forms of wording) in other manuscripts, but note δια της ημερας in D.

9.40 αυτον (for αυτο) suggests it is not the spirit but the man (!) who is cast out (cf. D: απαλλαξωσιν αυτον).

9.48 By placing an article before μεγας our manuscript balances better ο μεικροτε[ρος earlier.

9.50 A difficult reading – ου γαρ εστιν καθ' υμων ουδε υπερ υμων. The following verse also reads awkwardly and are also likely to have confused the readers of this manuscript: 9.52 προσωπου (*sine add.*); 9.53 προσωπον ην αυτου πορευομενου!

9.62 The sequence of words following ουδεις differs in various manuscripts. The sequence in P⁴⁵ is shared with only D.

11.13 π̅ν̅α αγαθον (with L) against πνευμα αγιον *cett.*; other readings are αγαθον δομα D; δοματα αγαθα Θ. (cf. 10.21 πνευματι without qualification.) Also at

11.13 note that P⁴⁵ has Jesus address God as ο π̅ρ̅ υμων ο ουρανιος (against ο πατηρ [ο] εξ ουρανου); ουρανιος is a hapax in Luke.

11.19 The absence of τα δαιμονια is characteristic of our scribe's having avoided words clearly understood from the context.

11.42 has ανηθον which parallels Matthew. Other manuscripts in Luke have πηγανον, but note Fam13 has *both* nouns.

12.4 When analysing questions of Lukan style it is to be noted that Luke according to P⁴⁵ has πτοηθητε, possibly to avoid an excess number of examples of φοβεισθαι in this context.

13.32 Ποιουμαι, a singular reading: the alternatives are επιτελω/αποτελω/αποτελουμαι.

John

As far as word-order is concerned, our manuscript's reading ο καλος ποιμην *bis* at 10.11 instead of the more Semitic order ο ποιμην ο καλος may be significant when one assesses the style used either by the original author or by copyists. Similarly on stylistic grounds we see that P⁴⁵ follows the neuter plural τα προβατα with ηκουσεν at 10.8 – all other witnesses read a plural form. Our manuscript uniquely has και before καθως at 10.15 thereby reading και seven times in vv. 14–16 (or

---

16. On the related issue of the orthography see J.K. Elliott, 'Textual Variation Involving the Augment in the Greek New Testament', *ZNW* 69 (1978), pp. 247–52 esp. 249ff.

eight times if we include κακεινα). Note also the use of the relatively uncommon απερ for α at 10.16.

Although not qualifying as a singular or sub-singular reading we note also in the Good Shepherd passage that the shepherd *gives* (διδωσι) his life at 10.11 (with ℵ* D) and at 10.15 (διδωμι with P⁶⁶, ℵ* D W). Most other manuscripts read τιθησι or τιθημι in these verses.

10.39 δε is read instead of και/ουν/anacolouthon (cf. also + δε at Jn 10.22; γαρ at Lk. 11.11). Particles are an obvious area for scribal preferences in a 'free' text.

11.4 ο υιος αυτου (against the 'normal' reading ο υιος του θεου), possibly to avoid a repetition of του θεου earlier in the verse.

11.45 We merely speculate on the significance of the *v.l.* εωρακοτες in P⁴⁵ with D; και θεασαμενοι *cett.*

11.52: εσκορπισμενα. All other manuscripts have the form compounded with διε-. The simple verb is found elsewhere in John at 10.45 (a reading extant in P⁴⁵)

11.57 P⁴⁵ refers to πρεσ[βυτεροι. No other manuscript refers to 'elders' in this context. The standard reading is 'Pharisees' and our manuscript recognises this group at 11.47. Nowhere else in John (outside the disputed Pericope Adulterae) are 'elders' mentioned.

Conclusion

All manuscripts have their share of singular readings (often nonsense readings) but the meaningful singular and sub-singular readings of this early papyrus manuscript deserve our attention. These distinctive readings—readily culled from a good *apparatus criticus* or from the edition by Kenyon (even though neither source gives every example, as we observed above)—ought not to be dismissed as aberrant. All the readings deserve our attention if we are to understand what the readers of as important an early witness as P⁴⁵ were confronted with as they heard and studied their Gospels.

Excursus

One place in Luke where it would have been of interest to see what a third century reader would have found in P⁴⁵ is the Paternoster. Unfortunately our manuscript is deficient here. At the bottom of folio 11r the words visible come from Lk. 11, then Kenyon estimates that seven lines are missing from the manuscript: folio 12r begins with isolated words from vv. 6, 7. That is a disappointment because the text of the Lord's Prayer in Luke in some manuscripts has the longer readings paralleling the Matthaean form of the Paternoster (notably in Lk. 11.2 +ημων ο εν τοις ουρανοις, + γενηθητω το θελημα σου ως εν ουρανω και επι της γης and 11.4: αλλα ρυσαι ημας απο του πονηρου). These longer readings are found in manuscripts from the fourth century onwards. P⁷⁵ of the third century supports the shorter form of the Paternoster in Luke. A rough calculation of the amount of text contained originally in the lacunae in fol. 11r. suggests (on the basis of the average number of letters per line and the average number of lines per page) that there was space in P^{45} for some but not all three of these longer readings (which total about 86 letters in all). But I doubt if we can go further along this line of enquiry with any confidence to reconstruct the missing text here or to pronounce on which form of the Paternoster was known to this third century witness other than to conclude that its text is unlikely to have been the same as that found in P^{75}.

P[45] AND THE TEXTUAL HISTORY OF THE GOSPEL OF MARK

Larry W. Hurtado

The Chester Beatty Codex of the Gospels and Acts (P[45]) was a find of sensational importance for the textual history of the New Testament. Like a flare bursting over a night time battlefield, it cast light upon the previously darkened pre-Constantinian centuries of the textual history of the New Testament, forcing revisions of scholarly views on several major matters. In one giant step, P[45] brought scholarship on the text of the Gospels from the mid-fourth century practically to the doorstep of the second century. First made available to the scholarly world in the 1933 edition by Frederic G. Kenyon, for New Testament scholars P[45] is the jewel in the crown of the 12 Greek biblical manuscripts acquired by Alfred Chester Beatty about 1930.[1] My purpose here is to focus specifically on the relevance of P[45] for the textual history of the Gospel of Mark. Before I take up this matter, however, some basic information is required to set the scene and by way of explanation of why the textual history of the Gospel of Mark should be such an important topic.

Introductory Matters

First, though some offer other views, most New Testament scholars are persuaded that the Gospel of Mark is the earliest of the four canonical gospels, and probably the earliest extant narrative book about Jesus, assigning its composition to about 70 CE. Most further agree that Mark was quickly very widely circulated and influential, becoming the pattern and major source for the authors of the Gospels of Matthew and Luke (which are commonly thought to have been composed within a decade or two after Mark appeared). This makes the Gospel of Mark particularly important as a source for the study of early Christianity, the history of early Christian literature, and, of course, for Jesus of Nazareth.

Second, through the dedicated efforts of various scholars in the nineteenth century, the textual history of the New Testament writings became an important subject of investigation and debate. The highwater mark of the nineteenth-century work was the 1881 critical edition of the Greek New Testament by B.F. Westcott and F.J.A. Hort, and the accompanying introductory volume published in 1882, which provided a still very valuable discussion of the text-critical principles by which they worked and their views on the textual history of the New Testament.[2]

---

1.   For Kenyon's publications of the Beatty papyri, see Charles Horton's article in this volume.
2.   Brooke Foss Westcott and Fenton John Anthony Hort, *The New Testament in the Original*

The broad effect of their work was to consolidate the view that the New Testament writings had undergone a history of transmission characterized both by the accidental variations that happen to any text copied by many hands, and also deliberate changes arising from various concerns of those who copied these writings.

Westcott and Hort showed that the task of restoring the likely 'original' text of New Testament writings involves reconstructing the history of their textual transmission. This means that it is important to study the earliest copies of such writings that we can obtain. It also means that we should inquire about the historical relationships of manuscripts to one another, and about the scribal characteristics of each manuscript before making final judgements about which are likely to be the original readings in the many cases where there are variants.[3]

Prior to the acquisition of P^{45}, the earliest Greek manuscripts of the New Testament Gospels were three codices dated to the mid-to-late fourth or early fifth century: the famous Codex Sinaiticus (fourth century, now kept in the British Museum), Codex Vaticanus (fourth century, kept in the Vatican Library), and the subsequently-acquired Codex Washingtonianus (also known as the Freer Gospels Codex late fourth or early fifth century, purchased by Charles Freer in 1906 and now kept in the Freer Gallery of the Smithsonian Institution in Washington DC). It is easy to appreciate, therefore, the excitement generated immediately when news of P^{45} broke upon the scholarly world in the early 1930s.

Dated sometime in the third century (usually 200–250 CE), P^{45} was at least one hundred years earlier than any other then previously known Greek manuscript of the Gospels.[4] Although only a portion of the original codex survives (30 leaves of an original 112), and none of the five New Testament writings in it is completely preserved, P^{45} provided scholars with a sufficient amount of the text of the four Gospels and Acts to make it enormously important for the textual history of these writings as well as for other matters.[5] For example, along with evidence then

---

Greek (Cambridge and London: Macmillan, 1881); *idem*, *The New Testament in the Original Greek: Introduction and Appendix* (Cambridge and London: Macmillan, 1882).

3.   'Knowledge of documents should precede final judgement upon readings' (Westcott and Hort, *The New Testament*, p. 31). In supporting this principle, I dissent from the approach called 'thoroughgoing eclecticism'. Cf., e.g., J.K. Elliott, 'Thoroughgoing Eclecticism in New Testament Textual Criticism', in Bart D. Ehrman and Michael W. Holmes (eds.), *The Text of the New Testament in Contemporary Research: Essays on the* Status Quaestionis (SD, 46; Grand Rapids: Eerdmans, 1995), pp. 321–35; Gordon D. Fee, 'Rigorous or Reasoned Eclecticism – Which?' in Eldon J. Epp and Gordon D. Fee (eds.), *Studies in the Theory and Method of New Testament Textual Criticism* (SD, 45; Grand Rapids: Eerdmans, 1993), pp. 124–40.

4.   Kenyon II, *Text*, x; Kurt Aland, *Repertorium der griechischen christlichen Papyri.* I. *Biblische Papyri* (Patristische Texte und Studien, 18; Berlin and New York: de Gruyter, 1976), p. 269; Joseph van Haelst, *Catalogue des papyrus littéraires Juifs et Chrétiens* (Paris: Publications de la Sorbonne, 1976), p. 136 (MS no. 371).

5.   Shortly after the acquisition of P^{45} by Chester Beatty, additional fragments of the same manuscript (several fragments of Luke and one small scrap each of Mark and John) were discovered as having been acquired by the University of Michigan and were transferred to Mr. Beatty. For further details of Beatty's acquisition see Horton's contribution to this volume. Further portions of the same manuscript were also found in Vienna (Österreichische Nationalbibliothek, Pap.

emerging from the Oxyrhynchus papyri, P^{45} demanded radical revision of earlier views about when early Christians had adopted the codex as their preferred form of book production. It is now clear that the codex was already being programmatically used by Christians in the mid-second century (and probably much earlier).[6]

Until the identification of the small Rylands fragment of John (in 1935) and the publication of the Bodmer Gospels Papyri (P^{66} in 1959 and P^{75} in 1961), P^{45} was by far the earliest Greek witness to the text of the Gospels.[7] It remains one of our most important witnesses to the text of the New Testament generally, and in at least two specific matters it still holds an unrivalled importance. First, although T.C. Skeat recently proposed that three fragments of Matthew and Luke (P^{64}, P^{67}, and P^{4}) belong to the same manuscript which he dated to the late second century CE, and, further that this manuscript originally contained the four canonical Gospels, P^{45} is still the earliest undeniable example of a four-gospel codex.[8] Secondly, in any case P^{45} remains the earliest witness to the text of the Gospel of Mark.[9]

It is also worthwhile to note some general features of the manuscript. I depend here almost entirely on the analysis of physical features of the codex given by Kenyon in his 1933 edition, and the more recent codicological study by T.C.

Vindob. Graec. 31974) by Hans Gerstinger ('Ein Fragment des Chester Beatty-Evangelienkodex in der Papyrussammlung der Nationalbibliothek in Wien', *Aegyptus* 13 [1933], pp. 67–72).

6.   On the Christian preference for the codex, see, e.g., C.H. Roberts and T.C. Skeat, *The Birth of the Codex* (London: Oxford University Press, 1987); Harry Y. Gamble, *Books and Readers in the Early Church* (New Haven and London: Yale University Press, 1995); L.W. Hurtado, 'The Earliest Evidence of an Emerging Christian Material and Visual Culture: The Codex, the *Nomina Sacra* and the Staurogram', in Stephen G. Wilson and Michel Desjardins (eds.), *Text and Artifact in the Religions of Mediterranean Antiquity: Essays in Honour of Peter Richardson* (ESCJ, 9; Waterloo: Wilfrid Laurier University Press, 2000), pp. 271–88.

7.   P^{52}, a fragment of one codex leaf with a few lines of the Gospel of John, is usually dated c. 130–50 CE (C.H. Roberts, *An Unpublished Fragment of the Fourth Gospel in the John Rylands Library* [Manchester: Manchester University Press, 1935]). P^{66}, a Greek codex of John, is dated c. 200 CE (Victor Martin, *Papyrus Bodmer II: Évangile de Jean Chap. 1-14* [Cologny-Geneve: Bibliotheca Bodmeriana, 1956]; *idem*, *Papyrus Bodmer II, Évangile de Jean, Supplément, Chaps. 14-21* [Cologny-Geneva: Bibliotheca Bodmeriana, 1958]; Victor Martin and J.W.B. Barns [eds.], *Papyrus Bodmer II, Supplement, Nouvelle édition augmentée et corrigée* [Cologny-Geneva: Bibliotheca Bodmeriana, 1962]). P^{75} (containing portions of Luke and John) is dated c. 175–225 CE (Victor Martin and Rodolf Kasser, *Papyrus Bodmer XIV* [Cologny-Geneva: Bibliotheca Bodmeriana, 1961]).

8.   T.C. Skeat, 'The Oldest Manuscript of the Four Gospels?', *NTS* 43 (1997), pp. 1–34. Skeat had also suggested that P^{75} may have been a four-gospel codex in 'The Origin of the Christian Codex', *ZPE* 102 (1994), pp. 263–68. See also Skeat, 'Irenaeus and the Four-Gospel Canon', *NovT* 34 (1992), pp. 194–99; G.N. Stanton, 'The Fourfold Gospel', *NTS* 43 (1997), pp. 317–46.

9.   Recent volumes of Oxyrhynchus papyri have reported a number of fragments from very early codex manuscripts of Matthew (P.Oxy. 4401 [P^{101}], 4402 [P^{102}], 4403 [P^{103}], 4404 [P^{104}], 4405 [a new page P.Oxy. 2683; P^{77}], 4406 [P^{105}]; *The Oxyrhynchus Papyri, Volume LXIV*, ed. by E. W. Handley, U. Wartenberg, R. A. Coles and others [London: Egypt Exploration Society, 1997]) and John (P. Oxy. 4445 [P^{106}], 4446 [P^{107}], 4447 [P^{108}], 4448 [P^{109}]; M.W. Haslam, A. Jones, F. Mattomini, M.L. West *et al.* (eds.), *The Oxyrhynchus Papyri Volume LXV* [London; Egypt Exploration Society, 1998]).

Skeat.[10] Although the damage that the codex suffered before being acquired by Chester Beatty is extensive (as Kenyon noted, '[…] nearly every line is more or less mutilated […]'), significant portions of all four of the Gospels and Acts survive.[11] In Skeat's words, 'When complete the codex would have formed a substantial volume, about 25 cm [about 10 inches] in height and 20 cm [about 8 inches] in width, and a thickness of perhaps 5–6 cm [about 2–2.5 inches] apart from any binding'.[12] P⁴⁵ was composed of 56 four-page quires, each quire made up by a single sheet of papyrus folded once to make two leaves, these 56 quires sewn together to make a single codex of 112 leaves or 224 pages.[13] Papyrus sheets are made up of strips of the papyrus plant, and on any sheet of the material one side has the papyrus fibres running horizontally (the *recto* side) and the other side has them running vertically (the *verso* side). In P⁴⁵ the quires were arranged so that wherever one would open the codex the facing pages would match, either *recto* to *recto* or *verso* to *verso*. On each page there is a single column of writing in 'a small and very clear hand' about 19 cm (7.5 inches) in height and 16 cm (6.25 inches) in width, estimated to have averaged 39 lines of text per page. The upper margin was at least 3 cm (about 1.25 inches) and the bottom margin probably as much or a bit more (no part of the lower margin of any page survives). The inner margin (between the column of text and the fold of the sheet) is about 2 cm (about .75 inch), and the outer margin was probably about 2.5 cm (about an inch).[14]

It is very interesting to note that the likely order of the four Gospels in P⁴⁵ was not what became the more familiar one but rather the so-called 'Western' sequence—Matthew, John, Luke, Mark—the Gospels attributed to apostles coming first (in order of decreasing length), followed by those attributed to figures connected with apostles (likewise in order of decreasing length).[15] This order is also found in several manuscripts of the Old Latin version, the Greek-Latin bi-lingual Codex Bezae (late fourth century CE), and the Freer Gospels codex (late fourth/early fifth century CE).[16] As I shall note later in this discussion, there are further reasons for

10.   Kenyon II, *Text*, esp. v–xi; T.C. Skeat, 'A Codicological Analysis of the Chester Beatty Papyrus Codex of the Gospels and Acts (P45)', *Hermathena* 155 (1993), pp. 27–43.

11.   The table of contents given by Kenyon is as follows: Mt. 20.24–32; 21.13–19; 25.41–26.3, 6–10, 19–33; Jn 10.7–25, 31–11.10, 18–36, 43–57; Lk. 6.31–41, 45–7.17; 9.26–41, 45–10.1, 6–22, 26–11.1, 6–25, 28–46, 50–12.12, 18–37, 42–13.1, 6–24, 29–14.10, 17–33; Mk 4.36–40; 5.15–26, 38–6.3, 16–25, 36–50; 7.3–15, 25–8.1, 10–26, 34–9.8, 18–31; 11.27–33; 12.1, 5–8, 13–19, 24–28; Acts 4.27–36; 5.10–20, 30–39; 6.7–7.2, 10–21, 32–41, 52–8.1, 14–25, 34–9.6, 16–27, 35–10.2, 10–23, 31–41; 11.2–14, 24–12.5, 13–22; 13.6–16, 25–36, 46–14.3, 15–23; 15.2–7, 19–26, 38–16.4, 15–21, 32–40; 17.9–17.

12.   Skeat, 'A Codicological Analysis', p. 41.

13.   Skeat's calculations ('A Codicological Analysis', p. 41), correcting Kenyon's estimate of '55 sheets, forming 110 leaves or 220 pages' (Kenyon II, *Text*, viii). Kenyon's reference on p. vi to '220 leaves' is an obvious error in wording.

14.   Kenyon II, *Text*, pp. vi, viii.

15.   See now Skeat, 'A Codicological Analysis', pp. 31–32, confirming Kenyon's suggestion that the Gospels were in the 'Western' order in P⁴⁵ (Kenyon II, *Text*, p. viii).

16.   The more familiar order (Matthew, Mark, Luke, John) reflects the order of mention of the Gospels in Irenaeus, *Adv. Haer.* 3.1.1. See the recent discussion of these matters by Hengel, *The Four Gospels*, pp. 34–47.

associating P[45] with the Freer Gospels codex. But let us turn now to the importance of P[45] for the textual history of the Gospel of Mark.

The Initial Impact

In his fascicle on *General Introduction* and the fascicle on the text of *The Gospels and Acts*, Kenyon drew attention to the great importance of the Chester Beatty manuscripts for the textual history of the biblical writings, both Old Testament and New Testament writings.[17] Collectively, the 12 Chester Beatty Biblical Papyri attested in general the text of the biblical writings as conveyed in the Greek manuscripts of the fourth century. In Kenyon's words, 'The first and most important conclusion derived from the examination of [the Chester Beatty Biblical Papyri] is the satisfactory one that they confirm the essential soundness of the existing texts', with 'no striking or fundamental variation', and 'no important omissions or additions of passages, and no variations which affect vital facts or doctrines'. The many variations in readings have to do with 'minor matters, such as the order of words or the precise words used', on which questions the Chester Beatty manuscripts give 'evidence of great value to Biblical critics'. But Kenyon emphasized that the 'essential importance' of the Chester Beatty Papyri was 'their confirmation, by evidence of an earlier date than was hitherto available, of the integrity of our existing texts', and he urged, 'In this respect they are an acquisition of epoch-making value'.[18]

With specific reference to the Gospels and Acts, he judged that P[45] provided evidence 'of the first importance for its bearing on the early history of the text of these books'.[19] At the time when the Chester Beatty Papyri were published, there was a continuing difference of scholarly opinion for and against the view of Westcott and Hort that the fourth-century Codex Vaticanus and its close allies (especially Codex Sinaiticus) represented what they called a 'Neutral Text' that preserved the original readings of the New Testament writings better than either the great mass of medieval-period manuscripts (the 'Received Text' represented in the Authorised [King James] Version) or the other early witnesses that were thought to reflect the so-called 'Western Text' (such as Codex Bezae and Old Latin manuscripts). The damage that P[45] had suffered did not prevent scholars from seeking to determine what kind of text it reflected, and what it contributed to this debate.

It was certainly not an early witness to the Byzantine text, but P[45] was also not 'an out-and-out supporter' of either the 'Neutral' or the 'Western' type of text. The manuscript differed at numerous small points from the readings that characterize the 'Neutral' text; but at the same time P[45] did not have the more notable variants that distinguish the 'Western' text. That is, P[45] did not easily fit into either of the two early text-types identified by scholars, and was not easily enlisted to serve by either side in the scholarly disputation of the day over the priority of the 'Neutral' or the 'Western' text-type. Instead, in general P[45] justified a re-examination of the

17.   Kenyon I, *General Introduction*, pp. 14–18; *idem* II, *Text*, pp. xi–xx.
18.   Kenyon I, p. 15
19.   Kenyon I, p. 15

terms of the debate, and should have provoked an inductive approach to the question of the early textual history of the Gospels.

Unfortunately, though very understandably, what quickly happened instead was that P[45] was enlisted in support of a fourth textual grouping that had then only recently been posited, the so-called 'Caesarean' text-type. As we shall see, however, P[45] was a poor conscript for that particular cause; for it actually provoked doubts about the validity of the 'Caesarean' text-type as then defined.

P⁴⁵ and the Caesarean Text-Type

There is not the space here to give more than a brief explanation of what the 'Caesarean' text-type was thought to be and how it came to be such an important category of text-critical thought in twentieth-century New Testament scholarship.[20] Building on observations by W.H. Ferrar (published 1877) that four medieval Greek Gospel manuscripts seemed to be related textually, and on further work by several other scholars, Kirsopp Lake and close colleagues produced several important studies that added to this 'Ferrar Group' a number of other manuscripts, and they initially designated this expanded collection as 'Family θ'.[21]

It was, however, B.H. Streeter who gave the name 'Caesarean' to this grouping in his widely-successful book, *The Four Gospels*, first published in 1924.[22] Agreeing with the work of Lake and Blake, his own main contributions consisted of adding several more manuscripts to the group and connecting the type of text of Mark, witnessed in the putative grouping, to the Gospel quotations in the writings of the important third-century figure Origen, produced during his residence in Caesarea. From this last observation Streeter proposed the term 'Caesarean text' for what Lake and Blake had referred to as 'Family θ', and thereby the 'Caesarean' group/ text quickly became a well-established item in text-critical discussion of the following decades.[23] Writing in 1933, Kenyon referred to Streeter's conclusions as a 'turning point' and claimed 'the assured place in textual criticism' thereafter of the Caesarean text.[24]

We also should note that it was Streeter who in 1926 added Codex W (the Freer Gospels codex) to the growing list of putative witnesses to the 'Caesarean' text in

---

20.   For a more detailed review of scholarship, see esp. Bruce M. Metzger, 'The Caesarean Text of the Gospels', in *idem* (ed.), *Chapters in the History of New Testament Textual Criticism* (NTTS, 4; Leiden: Brill, 1963), pp. 42–72; L.W. Hurtado, 'Codex Washingtonianus in the Gospel of Mark: Its Textual Relationships and Scribal Characteristics' (PhD thesis, Case Western Reserve University, 1973; Ann Arbor, MI: University Microfilms), pp. 13–46.

21.   See esp. Kirsopp Lake and R.P. Blake, 'The Text of the Gospels and the Koridethi Codex', *HTR* 16 (1923), pp. 267–86.

22.   B.H. Streeter, *The Four Gospels: A Study of Origins* (London: Macmillan, 1924, reprinted 1926, 1927). In this essay I cite the second impression of 1926. See esp. pp. 79–107.

23.   Streeter is most remembered in New Testament textual criticism for his theory of 'local texts', each text-type associated with a major centre of Christianity in the early centuries. See *The Four Gospels*, pp. 26–76.

24.   Frederic G. Kenyon, *Recent Developments in the Textual Criticism of the Greek Bible* (London: Oxford University Press, 1933), p. 47.

the Gospel of Mark.[25] As we shall see shortly, Codex W remains particularly important for characterizing properly the text of P[45] in Mark, even though Streeter's view
of the matter has been shown to be incorrect. Streeter claimed that in the Gospel of
Mark Codex W 'represents the Caesarean text in a very pure form', and that it furnished 'conclusive evidence' of a 'single type of early text' behind the Caesarean
grouping.[26] Indeed, Streeter wrote that in the Gospel of Mark Codex W 'is far the
oldest, and much the purest, authority for this ancient and interesting type of
Eastern text [...]'[27]

Two years after Streeter published his views, Lake, Blake, and Silva New (later
Silva Lake) published an extensive study that dealt with all information on the
Caesarean text-type available at that point; and they attempted a reconstruction of
the supposedly archetypal text in three sample chapters of Mark.[28] This scholarly
troika proposed still further additions to the witnesses for the Caesarean text, but
also differed with Streeter on a couple of matters. For our purposes, the important
disagreement was over the value of Codex W in Mark for reconstructing the Caesarean text. Lake and his colleagues concluded that in Mk 6–16 Codex W was
'clearly Caesarean, though not one of the best witnesses'.[29]

The reason for all the energetic efforts of scholars in this debate was that Streeter
and his followers believed that they had found in the Caesarean text-type a textual
tradition at least equal in age and importance to the other two early textual groups,
the 'Neutral' and the 'Western' texts. Lake was more hesitant about the date and
origin of the Caesarean text; but the view that became dominant was that the Caesarean text was another early and very important text-type.[30]

Nevertheless, there were critics of the theory of the 'Caesarean text' from the
start; but we do not have the space here to rehearse the debate in any detail. It is
interesting, however, that they included such giants as F.C. Burkitt, who to his death
remained unconvinced that supporters of the Caesarean text had actually demonstrated an identifiable group sufficiently distinct from other 'Eastern' witnesses,
and M.J. Lagrange, who doubted the *close unity* of the putative Caesarean witnesses

---

25.   Streeter put this claim into an appendix to the second impression of *The Four Gospels*
(London: Macmillan, 1926), pp. 598–600, which I cite in this essay, and expanded his case in two
articles: 'The Washington MS of the Gospels', *HTR* 19 (1926), pp. 165–72, and 'The Washington
MS and the Caesarean Text of the Gospels', *JTS* 27 (1926), pp. 144–47.

26.   Streeter, 'The Washington MS of the Gospels', pp. 168–69.

27.   Streeter, *The Four Gospels*, p. 599.

28.   Kirsopp Lake, Robert Blake, Silva New, 'The Caesarean Text of the Gospel of Mark', *HTR*
21 (1928), pp. 207–404.

29.   Lake, Blake and New, 'The Caesarean Text', p. 212. Lake also believed that he saw
evidence that Origen had used a 'Caesarean' manuscript of Mark in his Alexandrian period ('The
Caesaean Text', p. 263).

30.   In the large 1928 study, Lake gave three options as to the origins of the Caesarean text, and
did not see any clear basis for choosing among them ('The Caesarean Text of the Gospel of Mark',
p. 333). Shortly afterward, however, he seems to have settled for the view that the Caesarean text
had resulted from the revision of a 'Western' text by a 'Neutral' textual standard; see Kirsopp
Lake, *The Text of the New Testament* (London, rev. 6th edn, 1928; reprinted London: Rivington's,
1959), p. 84.

and also proposed that the *kind* of Markan text represented by the Caesarean witnesses reflected scribal efforts to meet perceived popular needs of the church for copies of the Gospels that were pleasing and inoffensive in style and contents.[31]

But Streeter's view prevailed, and Kenyon's identification of P⁴⁵ as a witness to the Caesarean text in Mark initially meant that Egypt, not Caesarea, might have been the place of origin of the 'Caesarean' text, and, more importantly, that the Caesarean text was attested in the earliest manuscript of Mark.[32] The latter claim obviously enhanced considerably the perceived importance of the Caesarean text-type, as it had support from among the oldest manuscripts of the Gospels then available (particularly Codex W and P⁴⁵), and was thus a competitor in Egypt with the 'Neutral/Alexandrian' text in the earliest period of extant evidence.

Kenyon also proposed that P⁴⁵ had another major impact, contributing substantially towards the 'disintegration' of the so-called 'Western' text considered as a single family'. Although P⁴⁵ shared many readings with the principal witnesses of the 'Western' text (e.g. Codex Bezae), it had none of their 'more striking variations'. So, P⁴⁵ showed that the notion of a cohesive 'Western text' had to be given up, and that 'throughout the second and third centuries there was in existence a considerable variety of readings which had not yet crystallised into families', the text-types identified by scholars in later witnesses.[33]

But in light of further studies, it was not even clear that P⁴⁵ really supported the Caesarean text any better than it did the Western text. A year after Kenyon's 1933 publication of P⁴⁵, P.L. Hedley showed that in the Gospel of Mark P⁴⁵ was not in fact a frequent supporter of the principal Greek witness of the Caesarean text, Codex θ, or of the putative 'archetype' text reconstructed by Lake, Blake and New. Hedley did see a close relationship between P⁴⁵ and Codex W (the Freer Gospels codex) in Mark; but he viewed the low levels of agreement of both P⁴⁵ and W with the Codex θ and other Caesarean witnesses as indicating that the 'Caesarean text' was not really a cohesive and distinct text-type. He accused Streeter and others of lumping into their 'Caesarean' text-type a diversity of witnesses that did not easily fit into either the 'Neutral' or 'Western' text-types, thereby creating a text-type out of a miscellany of manuscripts.[34]

In a 1934 article devoted to the then newly available P⁴⁵, Lagrange, too, criticized the theory of a cohesive Caesarean text-type, noting that 'the agreement of P [P⁴⁵] with the Caesarean text is especially the agreement of P [P⁴⁵] with [Codex] W'.[35] He suggested that P⁴⁵ and Codex W might represent an early stage of a

31. F.C. Burkitt, 'Review of *The Four Gospels: a Study of Origins* by B.H. Streeter', *JTS* 26 (1925), pp. 278–94; *idem*, 'Review of "The Caesarean Text of the Gospel of Mark" by K. Lake, R.P. Blake, S. New', *JTS* 30 (1929), pp. 347–56; M.J. Lagrange, 'Le group dit césaréen des manuscrits des Évangiles', *RB* 38 (1929), pp. 481–512.

32. Kenyon, I, *Text*, p. 17; *idem, I Text*, p. 16.

33. Kenyon, I, *Text*, pp. 16–17.

34. P.L. Hedley, 'The Egyptian Texts of the Gospels and Acts', *CQR* 118 (1934), pp. 23–39, 188–230. See esp. pp. 32–35.

35. M.J. Lagrange, 'Le papyrus Chester Beatty pour les Évangiles', *RB* 43 (1934), pp. 5–41. I have translated a statement from p. 17.

textual tradition that led to the kind of text found in the later Caesarean witnesses; but he noted that P[45] and Codex W form a distinctive group and cannot simply be called 'Caesarean' in the same sense of the word as manuscripts such as Codex θ.[36]

In other studies of the period as well, P[45] was recognized as a crucial witness for the early textual history of Mark. But it was clear that P[45] and Codex W were placing great strains upon the credibility of the Caesarean text-type theory. The Spanish scholar Teofilio Ayuso published an extensive study in 1935 in which he proposed that P[45] and Codex W were the principal members of an early sub-group of the Caesarean witnesses, and that the Egyptian provenance of both of these manuscripts suggested Egypt as the place of origin of the Caesarean text-type. Contrary to Lagrange's view that all the Caesarean manuscripts reflected a Markan text that was recessional in nature, Ayuso contended that this recessional quality was restricted to the later Caesarean manuscripts (e.g. θ, 565, 700), and that P[45] and W actually represented a *primitive* kind of text of Mark. Ayuso called this the 'pre-Caesarean' text (meaning the early stage of the Caesarean text), and claimed that it had good claims as representing the original readings of New Testament writings.[37] In a later study, he argued that this 'pre-Caesarean' text and the 'Western' text were the only two 'pre-recessional' kinds of text and, thus, were the two *most valuable* bodies of evidence for reconstructing the original text of the New Testament writings.[38]

In 1937, Silva Lake wrote of the diversity apparent among the putative Caesarean manuscripts and mentioned two sub-groups similar to those proposed by Ayuso, P[45] and W forming the key members of the early sub-group.[39] In their 1939 tribute to Lagrange, Kirsopp and Silva Lake noted that the discovery of P[45] and its accord with Codex W (and to a lesser extent Family 13) had tended at first to promote the identification of these two manuscripts as good Caesarean witnesses, but that later study led them to view P[45] and W as the two 'poorest' representatives of the Caesarean text. P[45] and W, they suggested, reflect the kind of text of Mark *on which* the later Caesarean text proper was established.[40]

For the next several decades the dominant view enshrined in handbooks on New Testament textual criticism and echoed in scholarly studies was that the P[45] and W formed an early stage of the Caesarean text, and were in some way specially

---

36. Lagrange, 'Le papyrus Chester Beatty', pp. 40–41.

37. Teofilio Ayuso, '¿Texto cesariense o precesariense?', *Bib* 16 (1935), pp. 369–415, esp. 379–84. Cf. Lagrange, 'Le papyrus Chester Beatty pour les Évangiles'.

38. Teofilio Ayuso, '¿Texto arrecensional, recensional o prerecensional?', *Estudios Biblicos* epoca segundo 6 (1947), pp. 35–90, esp. 79–89.

39. Silva Lake, *Family Pi and the Codex Alexandrinus* (SD, 5; London: Christophers, 1937), p. 4 (n. 5), pp. 62–64.

40. Kirsopp and Silva Lake, 'De Westcott et Hort au Père Lagrange et au-dela', *RB* 48 (1939), pp. 497–505, esp. p. 503. In a study released two years later, they revised their reference to P[45] and W as 'poor' Caesareans, preferring then to regard them simply as 'early' Caesarean witnesses of a 'pre-Origenien' text that was 'revised into the true "Caesarean"' *Family 13 (The Ferrar Group): The Text according to Mark with a Collation of Codex 28 of the Gospels* (SD, 11; London: Christophers, 1941), pp. 7–8.

related to the later Caesarean witnesses such as Codex θ.[41] At the same time, there was vigorous dissent from scholars such as Hollis Huston, whose study of P^{45} confirmed its special relationship to Codex W, but led him to conclude that neither of these manuscripts supported the Caesarean witnesses well enough to be connected with them at all.[42] In several published articles on P^{45}, C.C. Tarelli reached similar conclusions.[43] This unsettled state of opinion was to continue until the underlying problems in method were adequately addressed.

The Methodological Problem

In his 1963 analysis of research, Bruce Metzger referred to Kenyon's publication of P^{45} as having an effect like an acid upon the supposed unity of 'the elaborately constructed Caesarean text'.[44] Study of P^{45} exposed with particular force the specific erroneous assumptions in Streeter's theory of the 'Caesarean text', and also revealed the broader problems in practically all efforts to determine textual relationships of manuscripts.

Those who accepted the claims of Streeter and Kenyon that P^{45}, a third-century manuscript written in Egypt, agreed with the 'Caesarean text' began to realize that it was scarcely correct to refer to that text as 'Caesarean'; and Streeter's theory of localized texts was rather decisively shown to be wrong. On the other hand, those who denied any special relationship of P^{45} with 'Caesarean' manuscripts such as Codex θ contended that P^{45} could not be invoked to provide the origins of the Caesarean text and to give it high value as a primitive textual tradition. Metzger summarized matters by saying, 'it must be acknowledged that at present the Caesarean text is disintegrating'.[45]

A large part of the reason was P^{45}. Behind the difficulties in dealing with P^{45} was a larger problem. As I wrote in 1981 in a study concerned with the question of whether in fact P^{45} and W were really related to the later 'Caesarean' manuscripts,

> The major problem in the discussion of whether the Caesarean witnesses formed a sufficiently homogeneous group to be regarded as a text-type was that no one had formulated an adequate definition of a text-type relationship, nor had anyone determined an adequate method for discovering such a relationship between two or more witnesses.[46]

41. For example, J. Harold Greenlee, *The Gospel Text of Cyril of Jerusalem* (SD, 17; Copenhagen: Munksgaard, 1955), p. 32.

42. Hollis W. Huston, 'Mark 6 and 11 in P^{45} and in the Caesarean Text', *JBL* 74 (1955), pp. 262–71, esp. 270.

43. See esp. C.C. Tarelli, 'The Chester Beatty Papyrus and the Caesarean Text', *JTS* 40 (1939), pp. 46–55; also 'Some Linguistic Aspects of the Chester Beatty Papyrus of the Gospels', *JTS* 39 (1938), pp. 254–59; 'The Chester Beatty Papyrus and the Western and Byzantine Texts', *JTS* 41 (1940), pp. 253–60; 'Some Further Linguistic Aspects of the Chester Beatty Papyrus of the Gospels', *JTS* 43 (1942), pp. 19–25.

44. Metzger, 'The Caesarean Text of the Gospels', p. 62.

45. Metzger, 'The Caesarean Text of the Gospels', p. 67.

46. L.W. Hurtado, *Text-Critical Methodology and the Pre-Caesarean Text: Codex W in the*

This will perhaps seem astonishing to those not well acquainted with New Testament text-critical scholarship. Since at least the early nineteenth century scholars had been attempting to identify manuscript groups, that is, to identify manuscripts that had some sort of special textual relationship to one another, as a necessary condition for reconstructing the textual history of the New Testament. From the beginning of this effort, it mainly consisted in comparing readings of manuscripts and trying to measure the frequency of agreement in readings. However, until the last few decades of the twentieth century this remained a highly unreliable effort. There were really two problems: one with what scholars chose to count and the other with how they counted. Once again, P^{45} contributed toward making these problems very apparent.

Here is the basic problem in what they counted. After the historic work of nineteenth-century scholars such as Westcott and Hort, most scholars were persuaded that the text-type that lay behind the 'Received Text' (the text-form translated in the Authorised/King James Version), variously referred to as the 'Antiochian', 'Ecclesiastical', or 'Byzantine' text-type, was a recensional text-type produced in the fifth or sixth century. The 'Western' and 'Neutral/Alexandrian' text-types, by contrast, were regarded as much older, both probably going back to the second century or earlier. On this basis scholars tended to assume that the readings characteristic of the Byzantine text-type were likewise all comparatively late. So any Byzantine readings in manuscripts of the fifth century and later simply reflected the influence of the Byzantine text-type, which became the standard text-type to which readings of manuscripts were thought to have been revised. 'Non-Byzantine' readings were taken as remnants of early text-types that pre-dated the rise of the Byzantine text-type. So, the procedure followed by scholars was usually to tabulate agreements of two manuscripts in these non-Byzantine readings (that is, in readings that differed from the Textus Receptus), ignoring what they regarded as Byzantine readings in manuscripts. It was believed that agreements between two manuscripts in the 'non-Byzantine' readings indicated that the manuscripts were related and belonged to a common textual group.[47]

The publication of Codex W (the Freer Gospels) in 1912 should have alerted scholars to the error, for this manuscript has numerous readings that were regarded as Byzantine. But perhaps the dating of Codex W to the late fourth or early fifth century allowed scholars to assume that these readings simply showed that the Byzantine recension was a bit earlier than they had thought. When, however, P^{45}

Gospel of Mark (SD, 43; Grand Rapids: Eerdmans, 1981), p. 5. This book is a revised form of my 1973 PhD thesis (see n. 20 above).

47.   Perhaps the most outspoken proponent of this method of reconstructing early texts was Streeter, *The Four Gospels*, pp. 81–82; *idem*, 'Origen, Aleph and the Caesarean Text', *JTS* 36 (1935), pp. 178–80; 'Codices 157, 1071 and the Caesarean Text', in R.P. Casey, S. Lake and A.K. Lake (eds.), *Quantulacumque: Studies Presented to Kirsopp Lake* (London: Christophers, 1937), pp. 149–50. The approach was also used, however, by Kirsopp Lake, for example, in his reconstruction of the supposed archetype of Family 1 (*Codex 1 of the Gospels and its Allies* [TS, 7.3; Cambridge: Cambridge University Press, 1902], pp. xxiii–iv); and by Lake and his colleagues in their putative reconstruction of the Caesarean text of selected chapter of Mark, 'The Caesarean Text of the Gospel of Mark'.

appeared on the scholarly scene, to those with eyes to see it quickly became apparent that the commonly used procedure for determining manuscript relationships, counting only 'non-Byzantine' readings, was based on a serious fallacy. For even this third-century manuscript had numerous readings that had been thought to be 'Byzantine'; and it was impossible (at least for most scholars) to imagine that the supposed Byzantine recension could be dated early enough to account for this. That is, the 'Byzantine' readings in P^{45} could not have been 'revised' into the text from some manuscript of the Byzantine text-type. Clearly, restricting the counting of agreements to supposedly 'non-Byzantine' readings was fallacious and totally unjustifiable.

It was partly these 'Byzantine' readings in P^{45} that accounted for its poor agreement with the reconstructed Caesarean text of chapters of Mark published in 1928 by Lake, Blake and New. In 1939, under the impact of P^{45} particularly, they lamented that the principle upon which this reconstruction had been based was 'clearly false'.[48]

There was also a problem in the way scholars counted agreements. There was no agreed standard as to what constituted *sufficient* agreement to demonstrate group relationships among manuscripts. Scholars regularly cited numbers of agreements of this or that pair of manuscripts and this use of numbers gave a misleading air of science to their work. But in the absence of some agreed standard of reference numbers are virtually meaningless, and in such a circumstance scholarship that uses numbers is pseudo-scientific.[49] Furthermore, scholars usually paid little attention to the amount of *disagreement* between two manuscripts. Let us suppose, for example, that two manuscripts agree 50 times in variants from the Textus Receptus, and that one of the manuscripts has another 60 variants from the Textus Receptus not shared by the other manuscript. How significant in this case is the amount of agreement of these two manuscripts in their variations from the Textus Receptus?

---

48.   K. Lake and S. Lake, 'De Westcott et Hort au Père Lagrange et au-delà', *RB* 48 (1939), pp. 497–505 (503). The 1928 proposed 'reconstruction' of the Caesarean text of Mk 1, 6 and 11 was originally intended as a preliminary publication, with a full reconstruction of the whole of Mark to follow. As late as 1941 the Lakes still wrote of the future publication of this work, but they also referred to the need for a 'complete rewriting' of it in view of newer evidence, in particular P^{45}: K. Lake and S. Lake, *Family 13 (The Ferrar Group)*, p. 8. See also S. Lake, *Family Pi and the Codex Alexandrinus*, p. 60 (n. 12), where she says that a full reconstruction was prepared and 'will, *hoffentlich* be published in 1937'. The publication never appeared, and the likely reason is that the Lakes lost confidence that the Caesarean manuscripts constituted a real group. Note the reference to the delay by A.H. White, 'The Problem of the Caesarean Text', *Journal of the Manchester University Egypt and Oriental Society* 24 (1942–45; published 1947), pp. 39–59, esp. 41. J. Harold Greenlee mentioned a letter from Silva Lake to H.J. Cadbury dated 18 October 1946 in which she wrote that by then she thought that the two supposed Caesarean sub-groups 'are so distinct that they represent two distinct textual types' (*The Gospel Text of Cyril of Jerusalem*, p. 13).

49.   I mean no implication of dishonesty on the part of any of the scholars mentioned. They were sincerely operating on the basis of fallacious assumptions and insufficiently thought-out procedures. But their counting of manuscript agreements was to scientific analysis of manuscript agreements comparable to what leeching was to modern medical treatment.

Moreover, scholars rarely gave serious attention to the *nature* of the agreements of manuscripts, whether, for example, some agreements in readings might be pure coincidence or were more unusual and significant.[50] Along with the need for a more objective standard and procedure for counting agreements of manuscripts, there was a need for some more systematic way of characterizing the *kind* of text represented in a manuscript.

The Methodological Breakthrough and the Results for P[45]

It was Ernest C. Colwell who provided the methodological breakthrough upon which virtually all subsequent study of New Testament manuscript relationships has built. Colwell was especially concerned with the need for soundly based methods in New Testament textual criticism, and in a number of essays that were then re-published as a collection in 1969 he provided the key insights that pointed the way forward.[51] Perhaps the most influential of these essays (written in collaboration with E.W. Tune) proposed a method for establishing quantitative relationships of manuscripts that clearly sought to address the major fallacies and problems in previous scholarship.[52] The essential features of the method were these: (1) a broad selection of manuscripts must be used that will include representatives of all putative text-types; (2) the amount of text studied should be large enough to give several hundred places of variations in readings; (3) at any given place of variation in reading among the manuscripts, all the variant readings must be noted and the reading of each manuscript must be recorded at each place of variation; (4) the agreements of every possible pair of manuscripts of those studied must be tabulated over all places of variation, and the number of times that any manuscript agrees with any one of the others can be converted into percentages of the total number of places of variation in the portion of text studied. This all allows for a fully *comparative* picture of the levels of agreement of any one manuscript with any other, which is perhaps the essential contribution that gives numbers of agreements any meaning. Finally, (5) noting that Vaticanus and Sinaiticus are commonly accepted as primary witnesses to the same type of text, Colwell proposed that their levels of agreement in such a study should be taken as a rough quantitative criterion of text-type relationship.[53]

---

50.   To his credit, Hedley drew attention to these problems in his 1934 study, 'The Egyptian Texts of the Gospels and Acts', esp. pp. 33–34.

51.   Ernest C. Colwell, *Studies in Methodology in Textual Criticism of the New Testament* (NTTS, 9; Grand Rapids: Eerdmans, 1969). On the development of better quantitative methods of assessing manuscript relationships see also Bart D. Ehrman, 'Methodological Developments in the Analysis and Classification of New Testament Documentary Evidence', *NovT* 29 (1987), pp. 22–45; Thomas C. Geer, Jr, 'Analyzing and Categorizing New Testament Greek Manuscripts: Colwell Revisited', in Bart D. Ehrman and Michael W. Holmes (eds.), *The Text of the New Testament in Contemporary Research: Essays on the* Status Quaestionis (SD, 46; Grand Rapids: Eerdmans, 1995), pp. 253–67.

52.   Colwell, *Studies*, pp. 56–62.

53.   I have summarized and attempted to express more simply in my own words the itemized procedures and principles listed by Colwell, *Studies in Methodology*, pp. 57–59.

Colwell gave only a small illustration of his proposed procedure in an analysis of Jn 11. It was Gordon Fee who first applied a slightly improved form of Colwell's method in two important publications on the textual relationships of Codex Sinaiticus and P^{66} in the Gospel of John.[54] Encouraged by Fee's study, and appropriating his modifications of Colwell's method, in my 1973 PhD thesis I applied the basic approach in a study focused on Codex W and the 'pre-Caesarean' text in Mark.[55] A revised form of this study was published in 1981, and the results appear to have been accepted in the scholarly guild.[56] These and subsequent studies have shown that Colwell's proposals were basically sound and produce reliable indications of manuscript relationships.

On the basis of my application of Colwell's method to the question of the textual relationships of P^{45} in the Gospel of Mark, the following results seem assured. In Mark, the closest ally to P^{45} is Codex W, and these two apparently Egyptian manuscripts, though separated chronologically by perhaps as much as two hundred years, show a level of agreement that approaches that which signifies primary witnesses of a text-type. Colwell's proposal, which has been generally validated in several studies, is this: 'the quantitative definition of a text-type [relationship] is a group of manuscripts that agree more than 70% of the time and is separated by a gap of about 10% from its neighbours'.[57]

At 103 places of textual variation in Mark where P^{45} is extant and clearly readable, it agrees 69 percent with Codex W, and all of its quantitative relationships with the other witnesses used in the study (the 1873 Textus Receptus, Alexandrinus, Sinaiticus, Vaticanus, Bezae, Koridethi, and 565) range from 37 to 55 percent.[58] That is, the quantitative relationship of P^{45} and W is both strong and separated by nearly 15 percentage points from the next closest relationship of P^{45}, a very significant gap in terms of the Colwell quantitative method. After Codex W, the next closest relationship of P^{45} is with Family 13 (55 percent). The relationships of P^{45} with the putative Caesarean witnesses used in my study are completely unremarkable: P^{45}-θ = 37 percent; P^{45}-565 = 44 percent. There is no way that P^{45} can be regarded as having any special connection with the 'Caesarean' text of Mark.

But there are two interesting things about the textual relationships of P^{45} in Mark: (1) It is clearly related to Codex W, and (2) it is not particularly related to any of the other witnesses of any known text-type. It appears that P^{45} and Codex W form a small group of their own and attest a particular kind of text of Mark that

54.   Gordon D. Fee, 'Codex Sinaiticus in the Gospel of John: A Contribution to Methodology in Establishing Textual Relationships', *NTS* 15 (1969), pp. 23–44, reprinted in Epp and Fee, *Studies in the Theory and Method of New Testament Textual Criticism*, pp. 221–44. See also Gordon D. Fee, *Papyrus Bodmer II (P^{66}): Its Textual Relationships and Scribal Characteristics* (SD, 34; Salt Lake City: University of Utah, 1968).

55.   Hurtado, 'Codex Washingtonianus in the Gospel of Mark', see n. 20 above.

56.   Hurtado, *Text-Critical Methodology and the Pre-Caesarean Text*.

57.   Colwell, *Studies in Methodology*, p. 59.

58.   I cite percentages of agreement from my published study, *Text-Critical Methodology and the Pre-Caesarean Text*, p. 94. I have rounded off the percentage figures given there to the nearest full percent.

circulated in Egypt (and perhaps elsewhere). This suggestion is confirmed by a look at the textual relationships of Codex W. Like P^{45}, its next closest relationship is with Family 13 (59 percent), which is still ten percentage points less than the W-P^{45} agreement. W's other relationships range from 34 percent (Sinaiticus) through 40 percent agreement with the Textus Receptus and Bezae, to 42 percent agreement with the Caesarean witness, manuscript 565. None of these levels of agreement signifies any special relationship with Codex W. For Codex W, as for P^{45}, each is the other's closest ally by far.

In another important essay, Colwell also proposed that it was important to characterize the scribal habits and preferences evidenced in key manuscripts; and he demonstrated the value of this data in a path-finding study of P^{45}, P^{66}, and P^{75}.[59] In an insufficiently noted ThD thesis that was directly inspired by Colwell's essay, James Royse conducted a more thorough study of the scribal habits of the six earliest extensively-preserved New Testament papyri (P^{45}, P^{46}, P^{47}, P^{66}, P^{72}, and P^{75}).[60] Regarding P^{45}, Royse essentially confirmed and elaborated Colwell's judgments. I cite from Royse's summary: (1) 'The scribe is concerned to produce a readable text and is successful', with few nonsense readings or other errors and few corrections; (2) there is 'a marked tendency to omit portions of the text, often (as it seems) accidentally but perhaps also by deliberate pruning'; (3) there is frequent harmonization, particularly harmonization of readings to the immediate context, but also cases where readings in Mark are harmonized to the readings of other canonical gospels, especially Matthew; (4) stylistic and grammatical improvements are often attempted, with some of them perhaps showing Attic or Classical Greek standards; (5) the scribe of P^{45} is 'rather rarely' subject to accidental copying errors of sight, and seems on the whole to have been a careful and rather competent worker, who copied by sense units and not (as in the case of some scribes) mechanically letter by letter or word by word.[61]

In my 1981 book, I offered a somewhat similar characterization of the scribe of Codex W, particularly with reference to the scribal preference for a clear, readable and inoffensive text of Mark.[62] That is, P^{45} and Codex W reflect a kind of Markan text that was likely intended for edification of an ecclesiastical readership. These manuscripts show the efforts of scribes whose high regard for the biblical text was

59.   Colwell, 'Method in Evaluating Scribal Habits: A Study of P^{45}, P^{66}, P^{75}', in *Studies in Methodology*, pp. 106–24.

60.   James R. Royse, 'Scribal Habits in Early Greek New Testament Papyri', (ThD thesis, Graduate Theological Union; Berkeley, CA, 1981). A revised version of Royse's thesis is forthcoming as a volume in the series 'Studies and Documents', published by Eerdmans. See also *idem*, 'Scribal Tendencies in the Transmission of the Text of the New Testament', in Ehrman and Holmes (eds.), *The Text of the New Testament in Contemporary Research*, pp. 239–52; and Peter M. Head, 'Observations on Early Papyri of the Synoptic Gospels, Especially on the "Scribal Habits"', *Bib* 71 (1990), pp. 240–47. Skeat, 'A Codicological Analysis', p. 42 (n. 1), referred to Günter Zuntz, 'Reconstruction of One leaf of the Chester Beatty Papyrus of the Gospels and Acts (P^{45})', *Chronique d'Egypte* 51 (1951), pp. 191–211, as 'containing the only detailed description of the script and the scribal habits of the writer' [of P^{45}].

61.   Royse, 'Scribal Habits', pp. 156–57.

62.   Hurtado, *Text-Critical Methodology and the Pre-Caesarean Text*, pp. 67–84.

thoroughly compatible with a freedom to amend it in the interests of readability and religious edification. In this, they reflect scribal concerns different from those that appear to have been more characteristic in those manuscripts that are usually referred to as witnesses of the 'Neutral', or today more commonly the 'Alexandrian' text-type. The Neutral/Alexandrian manuscripts seem to represent a scribal practice that results in comparatively fewer deliberate changes and (probably) more faithful copying of the exemplar. P[75], for example, the earliest primary witness to the Alexandrian/Neutral text and likely a few decades earlier than P[45], shows a scribe who was often less careful than the scribe of P[45], that is more given to accidental errors but also far less given to intentional changes.[63] When studied alongside the other very early extant papyri of the New Testament writings, P[45] demonstrates that in the very first centuries of textual transmission we have to reckon with varying scribal tendencies and approaches, some concerned with simple copying and others ready to exercise some freedom to amend in the interests of the text serving perceived religious needs.

Conclusion

The Chester Beatty Gospels codex certainly remains one of the most important witnesses to the history of the Gospels and Acts, and is particularly important for the textual history of the Gospel of Mark. P[45] has also had profound effects upon scholarly opinion. Initially greeted as support for the theory of an early 'Caesarean text', P[45] ultimately helped to bring about the demise of the theory. Together with the Freer Gospels codex (Codex W), its closest known ally, P[45] forms an apparently distinct group that, though small in number, is an important witness to the variety of scribal purposes and historical forces that affected the transmission of the Gospels in the earliest centuries.

Its many lacunae are frustrating for some matters. For example, we cannot be sure what the ending of Mark was in P[45] (and, as is well known, there were several Markan endings from which scribes could choose!).[64] But in spite of its fragmentary condition, P[45] is a priceless piece of evidence of the state of the text of the Gospels and Acts in the early third century.

Though P[45] received considerable scholarly attention in the first few decades after it was made available, with many other important New Testament manuscripts it has largely lain fallow in more recent years. Unfortunately, because of changing

---

63. Royse, 'Scribal Habits', p. 538; Colwell, 'Method in Evaluating Scribal Habits', p. 121: 'In P[75] the scribe's impulse to improve style is for the most part defeated by the obligation to make an exact copy'. On P[75], see also Gordon D. Fee, ' P[75], P[66], and Origen: The Myth of Early Textual Recension in Alexandria', in Eldon J. Epp and Gordon D. Fee (eds.), *Studies in the Theory and Method of New Testament Textual Criticism* (SD, 45; Grand Rapids: Eerdmans, 1993), pp. 247–73.

64. Skeat concluded that 'the codex cannot […] be claimed to support either the inclusion or the exclusion of the controversial verses', Mk 16.9–20, the so-called 'long ending' of Mark ('A Codicological Analysis', p. 39). On the long ending of Mark, see now James A. Kelhoffer, *Miracle and Mission: The Authentication of Missionaries and their Message in the Longer Ending of Mark* (WUNT, 2/112; Tübingen: Mohr–Siebeck, 2000).

fashions in New Testament scholarship, for several decades now young scholars have not been encouraged to work closely with biblical manuscripts. So it is likely that we have not yet received the full benefits that P^{45} can provide toward a fuller understanding of the textual history of the Gospels and Acts. I hope, however, that future scholars will not neglect this and other important manuscripts, our earliest Christian artefacts, and that P^{45} will be able to provide its full measure of testimony about how Christians in the second and third centuries regarded, read, copied, and circulated the New Testament.

THE CHESTER BEATTY BIBLICAL PAPYRI:
A FIND OF THE GREATEST IMPORTANCE

Charles Horton

1. *Introduction*

For textual historians, the re-discovery of works that have lain forgotten in collections or which have otherwise been 'lost' to scholarship is normally a once-in-a-lifetime experience. For the generation of biblical scholars active in the early- to mid- twentieth century, the discoveries of lost texts happened much more frequently. For the general public, each new discovery eclipsed the previous one in the headlines of the day, as attention was drawn to the latest sensation. In many respects this was the fate that befell the biblical texts acquired by Alfred Chester Beatty in the 1930s; from the syndicated headlines in the world's newspapers, the papyri became the 'preserve' of academic journals as public attention was drawn to the discoveries of the Dead Sea Scrolls, the Nag Hammadi codices and other finds now shared by the Bodmer Library, the Chester Beatty Library and the University of Michigan. As a group the Chester Beatty Biblical Papyri remain the single most important find of early Christian manuscripts so far discovered and individually they have provided scholarship, and by extension the laity, with direct contact with the formative years of Christianity.

This paper explores the background to their discovery, their acquisition by a private collector and the eventual publication of the *editio princeps* by Frederic Kenyon.

2. *The Papyrus Collector*

Although various aspects of the life of Alfred Chester Beatty (1875–1968), American mining engineer, industrialist and book collector have been published, the history of Beatty as a book collector has yet to be written.[1] Beatty assembled a small

---

1.   For a summary account of the biblical collection see Kevin Cathcart, 'The Biblical and Other Early Christian Manuscripts of the Chester Beatty Library' in Kevin Cathcart and J.F. Healy (eds.), *Back to the Sources: Biblical and Near Eastern Studies in honour of Dermot Ryan* (Dublin: Glendale, 1989), pp.129–63 and Albert Pietersma, 'Chester Beatty Papyri', in *ABD* (New York: Doubleday, 1992) [on CD-Rom]. For Beatty's business career see: A.J. Wilson, *The Life and Times of Alfred Chester Beatty* (London: Cadogan, 1985). For Beatty's decision to move his collection to Ireland, see Brian P. Kennedy, *Alfred Chester Beatty and Ireland 1950–1968: A Study in Cultural Politics* (Dun Laoghaire: Glendale Press, 1988). For an introduction to his book collecting, see

but choice collection of manuscripts, printed books and prints, ancient, medieval and modern, as well as the rare, unusual and even the bizarre from both the occidental and oriental worlds. Collected over 60 years, Beatty's library was regarded in the 1950s as one of the finest private collections in England and possibly, the last great collection of manuscripts to be assembled by one individual.

Beatty's collecting had started as a schoolboy habit but this trait developed into a serious occupation in his 30s, by which time he had made his first millions in the gold and silver mines of North America. Having shaken off the dust of the mining towns, Beatty began to assemble the vestiges of a self-made millionaire. In 1907, he acquired a new home on 5th Avenue, New York and maintained a large household staff. He lavished diamonds and a Studabecker on his wife and he travelled to Europe to buy art and antiques. And as he said himself, 'I still have beer tastes but I hope to get to champagne someday'. After the death of his first wife in 1911, Beatty decided to leave New York and move to London. He married again and on 31 January 1914 embarked for Egypt on his honeymoon.

Cairo was then a popular winter resort for international travellers, some of whom were great collectors. Two fellow American collectors, J. Pierpont Morgan and Charles Freer paid frequent visits and Freer's correspondence with his friend Frank Heckler, gives a vivid impression of an American's view of life in the Middle East in the years immediately prior to Beatty's visit. Freer wrote:

> Business practices here are shocking, I have bought a few things and have struck some pretty tough men. Honor in business affairs is unknown and many other of the traits in mankind which we in America are taught to admire, here are entirely unseen.[2]

The business practices Freer found so disturbing did not prevent him from acquiring an early Greek biblical manuscript from a Cairo dealer for £1600 (Freer Gospels or *Codex Washingtonianus*).[3] Increasingly, European and American newspapers carried reports of new finds of early manuscripts in Egypt. These reports and notices of the academic discoveries excited public interest, as Pentland Mahaffy, Provost of Trinity College, Dublin recalled:

> The days passed quickly in which, we lived over again the days of the Renaissance. Now, as then, lost fragments of classical literature were constantly coming to light along with copies of existing works centuries older than any manuscripts of them previously known. Day after day we pored over the precious texts in my College rooms until the dinner hour arrived, when we discussed our discoveries and hopes with other scholars over the dessert and wine of the Common Room. It was an ideal time.[4]

Charles Horton, 'It was all a great adventure': Alfred Chester Beatty and the formation of his library', *History Ireland* 8.2 (2000), pp. 37–42 and *ibid.*, *Alfred Chester Beatty: From Miner to Bibliophile* (Dublin: Townhouse, 2003).

2.   Freer to Heckler, 20 January 1907 in Thomas Lawton and Linda Merrill, *Freer: A Legacy of Art* (Washington, DC: The Freer Gallery of Art, 1993), p. 68.

3.   Washington DC, Freer Gallery of Art, MS 032. Lawton and Merrill, p. 66.

4.   A.H. Sayce. *Reminiscences* (London: Macmillan, 1923), p. 297.

The publication of the first catalogue to Beatty's library - the descriptive catalogue to the Western illuminated manuscripts (1927), established Beatty's fame as a book collector.[5] It contained lavish illustrations and descriptions to over 150 examples of medieval illumination and established Beatty as the most important book collector in England at the time but surprisingly, he sold the best of this collection in 1932. Why did he do it? The answer lies, I believe, in the *modus operandi* of Beatty the collector; whereby one part of the collection was sold in order to acquire another.[6]

At the time of Sotheby's announcement of the sale of Western manuscripts in March 1932, Beatty was in the process of acquiring manuscripts that would make his collection even more famous. These manuscripts were ancient Egyptian papyrus rolls and early Christian papyrus codices. Beatty was to make substantial purchases and unlike his other collections, the papyri demanded extensive conservation, editing and publication expeniture in addition to the purchase price.

It is worth noting that in 1912, (the year that Beatty moved from New York to London), Sir Edward Thompson wrote in his *Introduction to Greek and Latin Palaeography,* that in the early nineteenth-century, the existence of Greek papyri 'was scarcely suspected'[7] and the known papyri texts amounted to approximately 200 items.[8] The publication between 1897 and 1907 of the excavations of B.P. Grenville and A.S. Hunt would change that perception but generally, interest in papyri had largely been the preserve of archaeologists and academics and being for the most part undecorated, few private collectors had ventured into this area except to purchase individual pieces as examples of ancient writing.[9]

Beatty's interest in papyri had grown throughout the 1920s, whether this was a result of *Egyptomania,* after Howard Carter's discoveries, or the persuasive attempts of the British Museum's curators to imbue him with a sense of re-discovery of lost texts, we will probably never know. But by now Beatty had build a villa beside the Pyramids at Giza and he returned to Egypt every winter until 1938.

5.   Eric Millar, *The Library of A. Chester Beatty: A Descriptive Catalogue of the Western Manuscripts* (Oxford University Press, 1927). Between 1911–28, Beatty collected over 250 Western manuscripts, only the best were kept for the catalogue, the remainder were generally sold or exchanged for better quality works.

6.   Previous commentators have cited financial reasons for the sales but archival evidence does not support this argument. The proceeds of the sales (£16,968 in 1932 and £17,750 in 1933) would have made little difference to the overall wealth of Beatty at this time.

7.   Edward Thompson, *Introduction to Greek and Latin Palaeography* (Oxford: Clarendon Press, 1912), p. 93

8.   Eric Turner cites the work of Ulrich Wilcken, *Urkunden der Ptolemäerzeit* (1891), which lists 200 Greek and Latin manuscripts. Eric G. Turner, *Greek Papyri. An Introduction* (Oxford: Clarendon Press, 2nd edn, 1980), pp. 17–24. In 1958 this figure had risen to an approximate 30,000 Greek and 400 Latin papyri. Colin Roberts and T.C. Skeat, *Birth of the Codex* (Oxford: Oxford University Press), p. 28 n. 4.

9.   Some nineteenth-century collectors such as the Irish peer Lord Valentia, or Lord Amherst had assembled collections of ancient Egyptian papyri, mostly funerary texts, see James Baikie, *Egyptian Papyri and Papyrus-Hunting* (London: Religious Tract Society, 1925). Some Christian papyri entered private collections in the 1890s, most notably that formed by Mrs John Rylands in memory of her husband. See Christopher de Hamel, *The Book: A History of the Bible* (London: Phaidon, 2001), pp. 310–22.

Very early on in his collecting career, Beatty had learnt that if he wanted to secure the best pieces he needed the best advice. This had proved very successful when he was assembling his collection of European, Persian and Turkish illuminated manuscripts and these advisors were now about to produce spectacular results for Beatty. Throughout the twenties and early thirties, the single most important group of advisors composed almost all of the senior curators in the British Museum's Department of Egyptian Antiquities and Department of Manuscripts as well as allied Oxford and Cambridge academics. Harold Idris Bell, Frederic Kenyon, Alan Gardiner, and Edward Edwards, as well as Herbert Thompson, Charles Alberry and W.E. Crum, were on retainers to Beatty as advisors, exclusively for his extensive papyrus collection.[10] The chief papyri were purchased through dealers, but Beatty's correspondence with Harold Bell shows that Beatty also acquired papyri through a museum syndicate whereby several sponsors of excavations distributed the finds among themselves. By 1925 Beatty's interest in papyri was well established, but as Bell reported, there was not enough good papyri to warrant a catalogue, to which Beatty replied:

> There is no hurry about the question of my issuing a catalogue, as I intend to pick up during the next two or three years fine examples of papyri, and eventually when I have a more or less comprehensive lot, to throw out the poorer ones, and then bring out a catalogue.[11]

Less than a year later in May 1926, Bell had completed the preliminary copying of the Greek documentary papyri, having chosen them 'mainly as specimens of hand-writing, but nearly every one contains something of interest quite apart from the palaeographical aspect'.[12] These acquisitions had been made in a fairly *ad hoc* way, and were generally the rewards for sponsoring British archaeological work in Egypt. A few months later, however, another of Beatty's advisors would chance on a find that would eclipse all of Bell's work for Beatty.

Alan Gardiner, an assistant keeper in the Department of Egyptian Antiquities, had discovered that several Cairo dealers were about to disperse a collection of ancient Egyptian papyrus rolls, which had survived what he termed, the 'destructive hands of the feelaheen' but which would now in all likelihood, be scattered to various institutions and collectors. Gardiner informed Beatty that one papyrus in particular, which tells the story of Horus and Seth, had on the verso, a new literary text of 'almost alarming importance'. He suggested to Beatty that he should purchase the entire find as 'I just hate the idea of the rest of this find passing into other hands, and [the dealer] is quite ruthless and cares not one jot for scientific interests [he is] a shark and too well off to reduce his prices'.[13]

---

10. For brief biographies of the aforementioned academics as well as Chester Beatty, see Warren Royal Dawson and Eric P. Uphill, *Who Was Who in Egyptology: A Biographical Index of Egyptologists, of Travellers, Explorers...from the year 1500 to the present day, but excluding persons now living* (London: Egypt Exploration Society, 1972).

11. Chester Beatty Papers (CBP) Beatty to Bell, 6 July 1925.

12. CBP. Beatty to Bell, 17 May 1926.

13. CBP. Gardiner to Beatty, 8 April 1928.

Beatty had authorized Gardiner to acquire items up to a limit of £400 and this proposal now required a far greater investment. Gardiner encouraged Beatty further by suggesting to him that he would acquire a papyrus which was unrivalled in interest in any collection - excepting perhaps for one, the story of Sinute in the Berlin collection. Gardiner said at the time that he never dreamed that such interesting papyri would pass through his hands.[14]

Beatty was won over and he gave authority to Gardiner to acquire as much of the find as possible. Gardiner, to disguise his interest, discreetly sent agents to all the dealers and gradually he acquired most of the find. This acquisition began to turn the emphasis of Beatty's collection away from illuminated manuscripts towards rare texts and in several newspapers he was referred to as 'a British Egyptologist'. Indeed, Beatty's papyrus collection developed into one of the most important private collections in the world, which no other private collector, and only the largest public institutions, could match. He was now in active competition with some of the great imperial museums of Europe and in some cases his acquisitions were made against the background of rivalry between British and German national collections.

It was in this context that the greatest of all of Beatty's acquisitions was made.

3. *The Chester Beatty Biblical Papyri*

Even during the financial crisis of late 1929, Beatty, as usual, prepared to spend the winter in Cairo. He and his family were now regular visitors, staying at their large villa at Giza. Shortly after their arrival in late December 1929, Beatty toured the usual dealers who had previously supplied him with manuscripts. Beatty had become such a regular customer of the Cairo dealers that they very often gave him first option on their new stock. One dealer in particular had acquired a cache of papyrus codices that he now offered for sale.[15] From later accounts it would appear that this cache had been seen by German and American academics. Professor Carl Schmidt of the University of Berlin was one of the first people to respond to the stories that the Cairo dealers were about to disperse a group of *Hebrew manuscripts written in Greek*. He immediately attempted to secure it, but as G.S. Wegener later stated in *6000 Years of the Bible*, (1958) 'the dealers, scenting a killing, put up their prices

14. CBP. Gardiner to Beatty, 8 April 1928. The papyrus in question is now Papyrus Chester Beatty I, a unique literary roll dating from 1160 BCE; the other 20 scrolls collected at the same time were primarily surgical and magical texts. See Alan Gardiner, *The Library of A. Chester Beatty. Description of a Hieratic Papyrus with a Mythological Story, Love-Songs and other miscellaneous texts* (London: privately printed, 1931) and *idem, Hieratic Papyri in the British Museum. Third Series: Chester Beatty Gift* (London: British Museum, 1935). Papyrus Chester Beatty II–XX were donated by Beatty to the British Museum. For more details of the discovery see P.W. Pestman, 'Who were the owners, in the "Community of Workmen", of the Chester Beatty Papyri' in R.J. Demaree and Jac. J. Janssen (eds.), *Gleanings from Deir El-Medina* (Leiden: Nederlands Instituut voor het Nabije Oosten, 1982).

15. Maurice Nahman, an antiquities dealer, was originally a banker but he found it more profitable to supply collectors with books and objects. He features not only in the Chester Beatty Papers but also in the Pierpont Morgan and Charles Freer's archives.

beyond the reach of any but a millionaire'. [16] That millionaire was Beatty, but the dealers had already divided the manuscripts, mostly quire by quire, but in some instances, page by page or individual pages torn in two, selling the sections to each other and other collectors before Beatty made his purchases. Beatty knew that the dealers 'tested the market' before revealing how much of a find they possessed and bearing in mind his experience with Gardiner and the acquisition of the ancient Egyptian rolls, he suspected that he had been shown only a fraction of what was available. Beatty was also very cautious; he would never buy anything unseen and he always sought approval regarding authenticity from his advisors. To disguise his interest in this purchase, Beatty sent a coded telegram (and presumably photographs) in January 1930 to Eric Millar of the Manuscripts Department of the British Museum for his opinion. [17] In reply, and in keeping with Beatty's code, Millar responded on 3rd February 1930:

> SILVER MINE VERY RICH HAS 3 SHAFTS (STOP)
> GOLD MINE RICH HAS FOUR SHAFTS (STOP)
> SHOULD BUY BOTH WITHOUT FAIL ESPECIALLY SILVER MINE

In short, Beatty's telegram caused a sensation in the British Museum as Millar had sought the advice of Kenyon, Bell and Edwards, all of whom replied in various excited if perhaps reserved tones, stating the importance of the find. Millar also copied the telegram to Beatty's secretary with a key to the code which explained that 'mines' represented the manuscripts, 'rich' meant old and the number of 'shafts' gave the date. Millar's note provides some added details, which allows us to identify these manuscripts. The silver mine, a third century manuscript consisted of 13 leaves, in single columns, (corresponds to the Book of Daniel, now CBL Biblical Papyrus X) while the gold mine manuscript had 21 leaves, in double columns, which equates to the fourth century Book of Genesis (CBL Biblical Papyrus VI). [18] Within a month, the papyri were in the British Museum awaiting examination. Harold Bell, as Beatty's advisor on Greek papyri, undertook the first appraisal and his cursory report is dated 11 April 1930. He wrote to Beatty:

> [...] You have made a very valuable purchase. The literary papyri are all biblical
> or religious, which personally I regret, as I should have liked texts of Greek
> literature, but their early date gives them a quite special interest and value. They
> go back as far as the second century and do not come lower than the fourth; the
> find must certainly rank with the most important ever made.

Intriguingly, Bell then goes on to state that the find consisted of codices *and rolls*, a fact that nobody else mentions and oddly a reference, which does not appear in the printed literature. [19] He went on to report:

---

16.   G.S. Wegener, *6000 Years of the Bible* (trans. Margaret Shenfield; London: Hodder & Stoughton, 1963), p. 90.

17.   No photographs of the biblical papyri in their original state have been traced.

18.   In a later report by Kenyon's the number of leaves of the Genesis codex had increased to 45.

19.   Kenyon does not mention this in his newspaper articles or in his *General Introduction*, Kenyon I.

As regards the non-literary documents, they are so brittle that I have not ventured to handle them much before they are dampened out, but they too are good papyri. One roll contains copies of two first century documents (from the period of Titus and Vespasian). If these should prove to be part of the same find as the Christian texts it might be very interesting.[20]

It is a great pity that Bell's description is so vague and unfortunately there is no mention of the content of the rolls. The first written appraisal by Frederic Kenyon is a quick scribbled note to Beatty, dated several months later (3 September 1930). Kenyon listed the books in canonical order, noting the number of leaves and assigning a rough date. He reassuringly tells Beatty that, 'there is no doubt that this is by very much the most important Biblical discovery that has been made for very many years'. Kenyon's list provides evidence of Beatty's first purchases from the dealers but as the months progressed other acquisitions added more leaves. Kenyon listed the folios as follows:

I	Genesis IX.1–XLII.2, 45 leaves. All somewhat mutilated, but text of G[enesis] for the greater part recoverable. Two columns to a page, large rather heavy hand. ? 4th cent. Partly transcribed.
II	Genesis. 12 leaves in non-literary hand, 3rd cent. Not examined
III	Numbers and Deuteronomy. 16 leaves, containing Num. VI.4–VIII.19, Deut I.20–VII.3. Two columns to a page, well written, 2nd cent. Transcribed.
IV	Isaiah, fragments, 2nd cent. Not examined.
V	Jeremiah, a few small fragments, in rather heavy hand, 2nd–3rd cent. Not examined.
VI	Daniel, Septuagint version, 13 leaves containing Dan. III.72–VI.18, Imperfect, one tall column to a page, of which nearly half is lost. Upright square hand, 2nd cent. Transcribed.
VII	Ecclesiasticus, 1 leaf, 3rd cent. Not examined.
VIII	Luke, considerable fragments of 7 leaves with two fragments of John in same hand, 2nd–3rd cent. Only slightly examined.
IX	Acts, small portion of one quire, much frayed at edges, 2nd–3rd cent. Not examined.
X	Romans, 1 leaf, ? 3rd cent. Not examined.
XI	Revelations, 9 leaves containing X.2–XVII.2, a few lines lost at the top of each leaf. Rough hand, ? 4th cent. Transcribed.
XII	Homily, unidentified, 1 leaf, ? 3rd cent. Not examined.[21]

A few days later, Kenyon sailed to America to investigate the papyri from the same find, purchased by the University of Michigan. Kenyon entered into negotiations with the University of Michigan concerning reuniting different portions of the find. Several proposals were made, including one which would have required Beatty to surrender his portion of the Pauline Letters (P^{46}) in exchange for Michigan's leaves of the Gospel-book (P^{45}), Book of Numbers (Rahlfs 963) and Book of Isaiah (Rahlfs 965)[22]. This proposal did not suit Beatty and negotiations continued

---

20. CBP. Bell to Beatty, 11 April 1930.
21. CBP. Kenyon to Beatty, 3 September 1930.
22. At this stage of the negotiations, Beatty only had nine leaves of P^{46} while Michigan

until Michigan agreed to sell all its leaves (with the exception of the Pauline Letters) at the price that they had paid. At this stage Beatty the businessman started to quibble, as he was now being asked to pay, £100 per leaf, more than double what he had paid the Cairo dealer for his leaves. Kenyon became concerned as he was particularly anxious to re-unite those leaves of P^{45} which had been torn apart by the dealers and the negotiations were beginning to delay his publication. He worked on persuading Beatty to agree to Michigan's terms and eventually Beatty bought a sizable section of the Michigan leaves but the codex of the Pauline Letters (P^{46}) and the Book of Enoch was to remain split between the two collections. The negotiations over the Michigan leaves and the pressure from academics, who now knew about the papyri, meant that Beatty could not keep his purchases secret for very much longer. He authorized Kenyon to prepare an announcement, which duly appeared in *The Times* on 19 November 1931, which began: 'I have now [...] the privilege of making known a discovery of Biblical manuscripts which rivals any of the [recent discoveries] in interest and surpasses all of them in antiquity'.[23] The announcement caused a flurry of letters of congratulations from fellow collectors, academics, curators and expectant publishers all of whom were eager to see the texts in print. It also meant that Beatty's fame as a book collector was assured. He was now known internationally as a collector of rare texts and not just illuminated manuscripts and letters flooded into his London home offering him rare books and manuscripts, including one supposedly written 'by Jesus'. Many of these letters bear Beatty's customary response to books he did not like: 'No good. Fetched away.'

Both Kenyon and Beatty knew that the dealers still retained other leaves and perhaps complete books from the find and as time went by they were afraid that other parties would try and buy what was left. Kenyon, however, was under pressure to publish and within a year of *The Times* announcement, he had completed his transcription of P^{45}, re-united the fragments acquired by Michigan and personally saw the text through to publication.[24] The publication of the Chester Beatty Biblical Papyri was an enormous undertaking, particularly at a time when the economy was in crisis and the demand on Beatty's personal finances extraordinary.[25] As Beatty and Kenyon had been heavily involved in securing the biblical papyri, other advisors working on different parts of the Library, had sought his attention but had found it

---

possessed 30. Beatty was in favour of selling his portion until he made his second acquisition of 46 Pauline leaves, thus altering the balance in his favour.

23.   *The Times* announcement was syndicated to other newspapers all over the world, resulting in hundreds of clippings, which were kept in a special scrapbook for Beatty.

24.   Kenyon sent the completed text and plates for the *General Introduction* to Emery Walker 26 December 1932 and the first volume appeared by July 1933.

25.   Beatty weathered the financial storm but to give an example of his financial commitments, the household staff at his London residence, country estate and Cairo villa numbered nearly 40. He also maintained several relatives (a brother and his parents) and paid the school or university fees of the children of some of his advisors. He also managed substantial donations to help the British Museum purchase the Luttrell Psalter, Bedford Hours and Codex Sinaiticus. He also produced at his own expense, the sumptuous catalogues to his Western manuscripts and Egyptian papyri - all between 1928–33.

increasingly difficult to make contact with Beatty. In one reply to an exasperated scholar, Beatty tried to explain that as

> I am Chairman of a number of companies, and I feel that during these difficult times I must devote all my time to them [...] until we get through this world crisis I feel my first duty is to them and so I cannot devote the time to MSS which I would like and would be able to in normal conditions.[26]

As Kenyon remained in London to oversee the publication and to continue the editing of the various texts, Beatty continued his search for any remaining leaves. In 1934 Beatty brought back photographs of further leaves of the Book of Daniel but he did not buy these and they were eventually bought in the winter of 1935/6 by John H. Scheich, another American collector, who deposited them with Princeton University.[27]

In further correspondence with Kenyon, Beatty also referred to 'other' manuscripts found at the same time and to the background of the find.

> They were found in three jars. In one jar they had nearly all perished and I imagine that was the jar in which Acts were found, because we only had the centre portion of the leaves.[28]

A memorandum in the Chester Beatty archives, 're Discovery of the Chester Beatty Biblical Papyri' and dated 20 April 1934, provides some further detail:

> The Papyri in question were found in 'three earthenware jars about 1928–1930 by some Arabs that were digging near the monastery [here the text is followed by blank spaces]. The jars [...] were found a few feet below the surface in the sand. They were on top of a wooden coffin [...] in approximately the position shown in the sketch below [...]
>
> The jars were about 14 to 15 [inches] high and about 8–10 [inches] wide [...] One of thee jars contained the Papyri in more or less dust. I understand that a few fragments were picked out but broadly speaking this jar yielded practically nothing.
>
> The other two jars contained papyri in fairly good condition. They were placed upright in the jars. They were shoved in rather loosely and there were no bindings. The leaves, however, were held together in some cases by binding cord, the holes of which are shown in the margins of many of the papyri leaves.
>
> There are a series of pages from the New Testament that seem to have had originally about 26 lines and they were in pretty good condition, the bottom margin and a few lines being missing. These apparently were found in one of the jars.
>
> The other jar contained a portion of the Old Testament on very long sheets of papyri. These had been bent double and put in the jar [...]

---

26. CBP. Beatty to Herbert Thompson, 2 May 1932. Beatty was also dealing with the resignation of Eric Millar (advisor on Western Manuscripts) and the appointment of his replacement to oversee the sale of his Western manuscripts at Sotheby's (7 June 1932).

27. Several letters between Kenyon and Beatty in 1935–36 mention leaves of the 'Prophets papyrus', which probably refers to the Book of Daniel, which is split between the Chester Beatty Library (CBBP X, 13 damaged leaves) and Princeton University (26 complete leaves). They were original part of the same codex that included the Books of Ezekiel and Esther (CBBP IX).

28. CBP. Beatty to Kenyon, 30 April 1935

> These were taken out of the jar and placed in moist (Berseem) [Egyptian clover] which made the papyri moist enough to straighten out. This was done. These pages are still in the hands of the Egyptian. A few have been photographed and before photographing they were shown to a bishop of the Greek Church who pronounced them Third Century and stated that they were portions of the Prophets Jeremiah and Isaiah. I have seen fifteen leaves and I understand he has a number more but he will not state how many. They are in fine condition (outside of being slightly damaged in the centre where they were bent.)
>
> The coffin on which the three jars were found was of wood and broken, and close to the coffin a glass lamp was found. Plain glass (not coloured) with date of glass on the outside of the lamp.[29]

This memorandum, with its carefully omitted details regarding the exact location, raises several questions, one of which concerns early Christian burial practices and in particular, the status of the individual who was buried with the equivalent in effect of carefully positioned canopic jars, the contents of which would surely have been as vital for the afterlife as any embalmed organ in ancient Egyptian belief. If this account is correct, it would also appear to dismiss the suggestion that the papyri formed part of an early Christian library, or if they did, then these books were redundant as scribal exemplars at the time of the burial. It would also certainly follow that these books were not casually hidden away during some period of persecution or disturbance with the intention of retrieval but were part of the funerary process.

Kenyon's vague description of the discovery and his inference that they came from the Fayum, must be viewed against Beatty's fear of competition from other private and academic collectors, the desire to obtain the complete find and the shady world of the Egyptian dealers, 'whose statements as to *provenance* are not always reliable'.[30] Amid all the publicity that surrounded the find, only the French language newspaper in Cairo objected to their purchase as it had been made by a wealthy Englishman. Later Professor Carl Schmidt made his own enquires and he concluded that the papyri had in fact came from Aphroditopolis (modern Atfih), situated on the opposite bank of the Nile to the Fayum. His account claimed that they were found in 'clay pots', not in a grave but in a cave.[31]

By 1936, seven years after his first acquisition, Beatty had become resigned to the fact that he had obtained all that he could of the find, even though there were elements still available. He wrote to Kenyon:

29. The memorandum includes several rough sketches, which depict the jars on the coffin, the folded codex and a sample page layout showing dimensions, positioning of binding cord and size of margins. It was compiled by an unknown author 'based on a conference with Shaker Farag, March 17 and 18 1934'. An annotation by Beatty's secretary records that it was sent to Beatty on 20 November 1934.

30. Kenyon, I, p. 5. In a reply to a query where Beatty obtained his books, his Librarian replied: 'Sir Chester buys in many places […] and from many sources, and for various reasons it is not advisable to disclose the position of the pool in which a big fish has been caught. There are too many anglers about!'

31. Wegener, *6000 Years*, p. 306. For references to the provenance of P[45] see Philip W. Comfort and David P. Barrett (eds.), *The Complete Text of the Earliest New Testament Manuscripts* (Grand Rapids, MI: Baker Books, 1999), pp. 145–48.

I got home to England a short time ago and was going to write to you about the position of the leaves of the papyrus of the Old Testament, which were photographed last year. Unfortunately, it is somewhat impossible to deal with the man who owns them. He has an idea that they are worth far more than the whole of the Testament. (I think he is asking £120 a leaf.) However, next year, I may be able to get them at a fair price.

With regard to the leaves of the Epistles [...] there are no more leaves of that portion available or, in fact, any more leaves of the New Testament. [32]

Beatty never acquired these Septuagint leaves and unfortunately there is no other reference to them as his attention was shifting to the acquisition of another major papyrus find: his great collection of Manichaean codices.

4. *Epilogue*

As Beatty acquired more and more biblical texts, he gave away most of his ancient Egyptian papyri to the British Museum, keeping only one major literary piece, the Love Poems and some minor illustrated funerary texts. It is likely that Beatty acquired about 90 percent of this early Christian find but as the dealers had split up the books, some quire by quire, others page by page, it is unlikely that the full extend of the original find will ever be known, or its true archaeological context.

Beatty's collection of biblical papyri was placed in the public domain with the publication of the full colour fasciculus and whereas Kenyon's editing may be wanting in places, he managed, through Beatty's help, to produce the edited text in a very short time. Beatty made sure that no expense was spared in its production. The photography and the production of the colour plates of each page and all the other costs of production were met by Beatty. The publication was not to be a limited edition reserved for the very wealthy but sold at a substantially subsidized price to ensure accessibility by all who needed it.[33] He encouraged and sponsored the best scholars available to work on his collection and he made sure that his manuscripts were expertly conserved. For this and many other acts of generosity in the field of biblical scholarship, Beatty was honoured by the British Academy[34] and later received a special papal blessing[35] and as Kenyon had commented: 'You have certainly written your name large in the history of the biblical text by your acquisition of such a wonderful group of early m[anuscript]s' and later he remarked 'your papyri really mark an epoch in the history of the Bible text'.[36]

---

32. Beatty had acquired P^{45} for £40 ($200) per page.

33. The prospectus issued by Emery Walker for Kenyon's *The Chester Beatty Biblical Papyri* lists the price of each volume, which ranged between 12 shillings and 6d. and £10 (Kenyon III, containing Pauline Epistles with 170 plates). This can be compared to the catalogue of Beatty's Egyptian papyri (1931), which was produced on handmade paper and sold for £185 per copy.

34. British Academy Certificate of Appreciation awarded to Sir Alfred Chester Beatty, 7 February, 1965.

35. CBP. Papal blessing, 26 January 1959.

36. CBP. Kenyon to Beatty, 9 July 1936 and 17 March 1938.

Since then, scholars have pored over every letter, word, and line in order to extract every grain of textual evidence that these books can yield and yet there are still new discoveries to be made. Colin Roberts reported that while examining P^{45} in Dublin in 1950, he 'was astonished to find how many crumbs Kenyon had left for his successors. Not only were there a number of misreadings, some of them [were] of great importance for the text...'[37] It is to be hoped that many of these crumbs will provide excitement for another generation of biblical students.

---

37.   CBP. Roberts to Richard Hayes, Chester Beatty's Librarian, 4 April 1956. Roberts was writing in support of the work of Professor Hollis W. Huston, regarding his revised publication of Kenyon's *Gospels and Acts*. Beatty, although initially reluctant to see Kenyon's work altered, agreed that Huston's revised text should appear as a supplementary volume to the Fascilicus series. Huston's text was submitted and reference made to it in the Preface to Fascilicus V and VI (Plates) but it was never published.

BIBLIOGRAPHY

Abbott, Thomas K., *The Codex Rescriptus Dublinensis of St. Matthew's Gospel (Z); also a new revised and augmented edition; also, fragments of the Book of Isaiah, in the LXX version... Together with a newly discovered fragment of the Codex Palatinus* (Dublin: Hodges, Foster and Figgis; London: Longmans Green, 1880).

—*Euangeliorum uersio antehieronymiana ex codice Usseriano* (2 vols.; Dublin: 1884).

Achtemeier, Paul J., '*Omne verbum sonat*: The New Testament and the Oral Environment of Late Western Antiquity', *JBL* 109 (1990), pp. 3–27.

Aland, Barbara, 'Die Rezeption des neutestamentlichen Textes in denersten Jahrhunderten', *ETL* 86 (1989), pp. 1–38.

—'Marcion/Marcioniten', *TRE* 22 (1992), pp. 89–101.

Aland, Kurt, *Repertorium der griechischen christlichen Papyri*. I. *Biblische Papyri* (Patristische Texte und Studien, 18; Berlin and New York: de Gruyter, 1976).

Aland, Kurt, and Barbara Aland, *Der Text des Neuen Testaments: Einführung in die wissenschaftlichen Ausgaben und in Theorie wie Praxis der modernen Textkritik* (Stuttgart: Deutsche Bibelgesellschaft, 1982).

—*The Text of the New Testament: An Introduction to the Critical Editions and to the Theory and Practice of Modern Textual Criticism* (2nd English edn trans. Erroll F. Rhodes Grand Rapids: Eerdmans; Leiden: Brill, 1989).

Alexander, Loveday C.A., 'Schools, Hellenistic', in *ABD* V, pp. 1005–11.

—*The Preface to Luke's Gospel: Literary Conventions and Social Context in Luke 1.1-4 and Acts 1.1* (SNTSMS, 78; Cambridge: Cambridge University Press, 1993).

—'Ancient Book Production and the Circulation of the Gospels', in Richard Bauckham (ed.), *The Gospels for All Christians: Rethinking the Gospel Audiences* (Edinburgh: T. & T. Clark, 1998).

Allen, W., 'Ovid's *Cantare* and Cicero's *Cantores Euphonionis*', *TAPA* 103 (1972), pp. 1–14.

Attridge, Harold W. (ed.), *Nag Hammadi Codex I (The Jung Codex)*. I. *Introduction, Texts and Translation* (The Coptic Gnostic Library; NHS, 22; Leiden: Brill, 1985).

Aucher, I.B., and G. Moesinger (eds.), *Evangelii concordantis expositio* (Venetiis: Libraria PP. Mechitaristarum, 1876).

Auwers, J.M., 'Le texte latin des Évangiles dans le Codex de Bèze', in P.C. Parker and C.-B. Amphoux (ed.), *Codex Bezae: Studies from the Lunel Colloquium, June 1994* (NTTS, 22; Leiden and New York: Brill, 1966), pp. 183–216.

Ayuso, Teofilio, '¿Texto cesariense o precesariense?', *Bib* 16 (1935), pp. 369–415.

—'¿Texto arrecensional, recensional o prerecensional?', *Estudios Biblicos* epoca segundo 6 (1947), pp. 35–90.

Baarda, Tj., ' "The Flying Jesus", Luke 4.29–30 in the Syriac Diatessaron', *VC* 40 (1986), pp. 313–41.

—'Luke 22.42–27a. The Emperor Julian as a Witness to the Text of Luke', *NovT* 30 (1988), pp. 289–96.

—'A Staff Only, Not a Stick: Disharmony of the Gospels and the Harmony of Tatian (Matthew 10.9f.; Mark 6.8f.; Luke 9.3 & 10.4)', in J.-M. Sevrin (ed.), *The New Testament in Early Christianity* (BETL, 86; Louvain: Peeters, 1989), pp. 311–34.

Baikie, James, *Egyptian Papyri and Papyrus-Hunting* (London: Religious Tract Society, 1925).

Balough, J., 'Voces Paginarum: Beiträge zur Geschichte des lauten Lesens und Schreibens', *Philologus* 82 (1927), pp. 84–109.

Barns, W.B., G.M. Browne, and K.C. Shelton (eds.), *Nag Hammadi Codices: Greek and Coptic Papyri from the Cartonnage of the Covers* (The Coptic Gnostic Library; NHS, 16; Leiden: Brill, 1981).

Barrett, C.K., *The Gospel according to St. John* (London: SPCK, 2nd edn, 1978).

Bauckham, R.J. (ed.), *The Gospels for all Christians: Rethinking the Gospel Audiences* (Grand Rapids: Eerdmans, 1998).

Bauer, Walter, 'Der Wortgottesdienst der altesten Christen', in G. Strecker (ed.), *Aufsätze und kleine Schriften* (Tübingen: Mohr, 1967), pp. 155–209.

Beard, M., 'Writing and Religion: Ancient Literacy and the Function of the Written Word in Roman Religion', in J.H. Humphrey (ed.), *Literacy in the Roman World* (JRASS, 3; Ann Arbor: University of Michigan, 1991), pp. 35–58.

Berger, S., *Histoire de la Vulgate pendant les premiers siècles du Moyen Age*, (Paris, 1893; repr. New York: B. Franklin, 1961).

Bieler, L., 'Der Bibeltext des heiligen Patrick', *Bib* 28 (1947), pp. 31–58.

Böhlig, Alexander, Frederik Wisse and Pahor Labib (eds.), *Nag Hammadi Codices III, 2 and IV, 2: The Gospel of the Egyptians* (*The Holy Book of the Great Invisible Spirit*) (the Coptic Gnostic Series; NHS, 4; Leiden: Brill, 1975).

Boomershine, T.E., 'Peter's Denial as Polemic or Confession: The Implications of Media Criticism for Biblical Hermeneutics', *Semeia* 39 (1987), pp. 47–68.

Bovon, François, and Pierre Geoltrain (eds.), *Écrits apocryphe chrétiens*, I (Bibliothèque de la Pléiade; Paris: Gallimard, 1997).

Bowman, A.K., *Life and Letters on the Roman Frontier: Vindolanda and its People* (London: British Museum, 1994).

Bowman, A.K., and J.D. Thomas, *Vindolanda: The Latin Writing-Tablets*, IV (Britannia Monograph Series, 4; London: Society for the Promotion of Roman Studies, 1983).

—*Vindolanda Writing-Tablets: Tabulae Vindolandensis*, II (London: British Museum, 1994), pp. 40–46.

Bowman, A.K., and G. Wolf (ed.), *Literacy and Power in the Ancient World* (Cambridge: Cambridge University Press, 1994).

Brandt, D., *Literacy as Involvement: The Acts of Writers, Readers and Texts* (Carbondale, IL: Southern Illinois University Press, 1990).

Bultmann, Rudolf, *The History of the Synoptic Tradition* (trans. John Marsh; Oxford, Basil Blackwell, 1968).

Burkitt, F.C., 'Review of *The Four Gospels, a Study of Origins* by B. H. Streeter', *JTS* 26 (1925), pp. 278–94.

—'Review of "The Caesarean Text of the Gospel of Mark" by K. Lake, R.P. Blake, S. New', *JTS* 30 (1929), pp. 347–56.

Burridge, Richard, *What are the Gospels? A Companion with Graeco-Roman Biography* (SNTSMS, 70; Cambridge: Cambridge University Press, 1992).

Campenhausen, Hans von, *The Formation of the Christian Bible* (trans. J.A. Baker; Philadelphia: Fortress Press, 1972).

Cancik, Hubert, 'Die Gattung Evangelium: Das Evangelium Markus im Rahmen der antiken Historiographie' in *idem* (ed.), *Markus-Philologie* (WUNT, 33; Tübingen: Mohr, 1984).

Carcopino, J., *Daily Life in Ancient Rome* (New York: Bantam, 1971).

Carney, J., *The Poems of Blathmac Son of Cú Brettan together with the Irish Gospel of Thomas and a Poem on the Virgin Mary* (Irish Texts Society, 47; Dublin: Educational Company of Ireland, 1964).

Cathcart, Kevin, and J. F. Healy, 'The Biblical and Other Early Christian Manuscripts of the Chester Beatty Library', in Cathcart and Healy (eds.), *Back to the Sources: Biblical and Near Eastern Studies in honour of Dermot Ryan* (Dublin: Glendale, 1989).

Chadwick, H., *Origen: Contra Celsum* (Cambridge: Cambridge University Press, 1953).

Charlesworth, J.H., 'Pseudonymity and Pseudepigraphy', in *ABD* V, pp. 540–41.

Collomp, P., 'Notes et étude critique. Les papyri Chester Beatty. Observations bibliologiques', *Revue d'Histoire et de Philosophie religieuses* 14 (1934), pp. 130–43.

Colwell, Ernest C., 'Method in Evaluating Scribal Habits, a Study of P45, P66, P75', in *Studies in Methodology in Textual Criticism of the New Testament* (NTTS, 9; Leiden: Brill, 1969), pp. 106–24.

Comfort, Philip W., and David P. Barrett (eds.), *The Complete Text of the Earliest New Testament Manuscripts* (Grand Rapids, MI: Baker Books, 1999).

Cook, John Granger, *The Interpretation of the New Testament in Greco-Roman Paganism* (STAC, 3; Tübingen: Mohr, 2000).

Cross, F.L., and E.A. Livingstone (eds.), *The Oxford Dictionary of the Christian Church* (Oxford: Oxford University Press, 3rd edn, 1997).

Dain, Alphonse, *Les manuscrits* (Paris, rev. edn, 1964).

Danker, Frederick W. (ed. and rev.), *A Greek-English Lexicon of the New Testament and other Early Christian Literature* (Chicago, London: University of Chicago Press, 3rd edn, 2000).

Dawson, Warren Royal, and Eric P. Uphill, *Who Was Who in Egyptology: A Biographical Index of Egyptologists, of Travellers, Explorers… from the year 1500 to the present day, but excluding persons now living* (London: Egypt Exploration Society, 1972).

de Hamel, Christopher, *The Book: A History of the Bible* (London: Phaidon, 2001).

Di Capua, F., 'Osservazione sulla lettura e sulla preghiera ad alta voce presso gli antichi', *RAAN* 28 (1953), pp. 59–99.

Dindorf, Ludwig (ed.), *Chronicon Paschale ad exemplar Vaticanum* (Bonn: Weber, 1832).

Doresse, Jean, 'Trois livres gnostiques inédits: Évangile des Égyptiens, Épître d'Eugnoste, Sagesse de Jésus Christ', *VC* 2 (1948), pp. 137–43.

—'Le Livre sacré du grand Esprit invisible ou L'Évangile des Égyptiens', *JA* 254 (1966), pp. 317–435.

Doyle, Peter, 'A Study of the Text of St. Matthew's Gospel in the Book of Mulling and of the Palaeography of the Whole Manuscript' (PhD thesis, National University of Ireland, 1967).

—'The Text of St. Luke's Gospel in the Book of Mulling', *Proceedings of the Royal Irish Academy* 73 C (Dublin: Royal Irish Academy, 1973), pp. 177–200.

Drexhage, Hans-Joachim, *Preise, Mieten, Pachten, Kosten und Löhne im römischen Ägypten bis zum Regierungsantritt Diokletans* (St. Katharinen: Scripta Mercaturae, 1991).

Dumville, D.N., *A Palaeographer's Review: The Insular System of Scripts in the Early Middle Ages*, I (Kansai University Institute of Oriental and Occidental Studies: Sources and Materials Series 20-1; Suita, Osaka: Kansai University Press, 1999).

Duval, Y.-M., *Le livre de Jonas dans la littérature chrétienne greque et latine* (2 vols.; Paris: Etudes Augustiniennes, 1973).

Ehrman, Bart D., 'Methodological Developments in the Analysis and Classification of New Testament Documentary Evidence', *NovT* 29 (1987), pp. 22–45.

Elliott, J.K., 'Textual Variation Involving the Augment in the Greek New Testament', *ZNW* 69 (1978), pp. 247–52.

—*The Apocryphal New Testament* (Oxford: Oxford University Press, 1992).

—'Thoroughgoing Eclecticism in New Testament Textual Criticism', in B.D. Ehrman and M.W. Holmes (eds.), *The Text of the New Testament in Contemporary Research: Essays on the Status Quaestionis* (SD, 46; Grand Rapids: Eerdmans, 1995), pp. 321–35.

Epp, Eldon Jay, 'The Significance of the Papyri for Determining the Nature of the New Testament Text in the Second Century: A Dynamic View of Textual Transmission', in W.L. Petersen (ed.), *Gospel Traditions in the Second Century* (Notre Dame and London: Indiana University Press, 1989), pp. 71–103.

—'The New Testament Papyri in Historical Perspective', in M.P. Horgan and P.J. Kabelski (eds.), *To Touch the Text: Biblical and Related Studies in Honor of Joseph A. Fitzmyer SJ* (New York: Crossroad, 1989), pp. 261–88.

—'The Codex and Literacy in Early Christianity and at Oxyrhynchus: Issues Raised by Harry Y. Gamble's *Books and Readers in the Early Church*', *Critical Review of Books in Religion* 10 (1997), p. 21.

Fee, Gordon D., *Papyrus Bodmer II* (P^{66}): *Its Textual Relationships and Scribal Characteristics* (SD, 34; Salt Lake City: University of Utah, 1968).

—'Codex Sinaiticus in the Gospel of John: A Contribution to Methodology in Establishing Textual Relationships', *NTS* 15 (1969), pp. 23–44.

—'Rigorous or Reasoned Eclecticism – Which?' in Eldon J. Epp and Gordon D. Fee (eds.), *Studies in the Theory and Method of New Testament Textual Criticism* (SD, 45; Grand Rapids: Eerdmans, 1993), pp. 124–40.

—'P^{75}, P^{66}, and Origen: The Myth of Early Textual Recension in Alexandria', in Eldon J. Epp and Gordon D. Fee (eds.), *Studies in the Theory and Method of New Testament Textual Criticism* (SD, 45; Grand Rapids: Eerdmans, 1993), pp. 247–73.

Fischer, B., 'Das Neue Testament in lateinischer Sprache: Der gegenwärtige Stand seiner Erforschung und seine Bedeutung für die griechische Textgeschichte', in K. Aland (ed.), *Die alten Übersetzungen des Neuen Testaments, die Kirchenväterzitate und Lektionare* (Arbeiten zur neutestamentlichen Bibel, 11; Berlin: de Gruyter, 1972), pp. 1–92; and reproduced in *idem, Beiträge zur Geschichte der lateinischen Bibeltexte* (Aus der Geschichte der lateinischen Bibel, 12; Freiburg: Herder, 1986), pp. 156–274.

—'Zur Überlieferung des lateinischen Textes der Evangelien', in R. Gryson and P.-M. Bogaert (eds.), *Recherches sur l'histoire de la Bible latine* (Colloque organisé à Louvain-la-Neuve pour la promotion de H.J. Frede au doctorat *honoris causa* en théologie le 18 avril 1986; Cahiers de la Revue théologique de Louvain, 19; Louvain-la-Neuve: Publications de la Faculté de Théologie, 1987), pp. 51–104.

—*Die lateinischen Evangelien bis zum 10 Jahrhundert*; 1. Varianten zu Mathäus (Freiburg: Herder, 1988), (= Vetus Latina: Aus der Geschichte der lateinischen Bibel, 13); 2. Varianten zu Markus (Freiburg: Herder, 1989), (= Vetus Latina: Aus der Geschichte der lateinischen Bibel, 15); 3. Varianten zu Lukas (Freiburg: Herder, 1990), (= Vetus Latina: Aus der Geschichte der lateinischen Bibel, 17); 4. Varianten zu Johannes (Freiburg: Herder, 1991), (= Vetus Latina: Aus der Geschichte der lateinischen Bibel, 18).

Fox, Robin Lane, 'Literacy and Power in Early Christianity', in A.K. Bowman and G. Wolf (eds.), *Literacy and Power in the Ancient World* (Cambridge: Cambridge University Press, 1994), pp. 126–48.

Frei, Hans, *The Eclipse of Biblical Narrative: A Study in 18th and 19th Century Hermeneutics* (New Haven: Yale University Press, 1974).

Frickenschmidt, Dirk, *Evangelium als Biographie: Die Vier Evangelien im Rahmen antiker Erzählkunst* (Tübingen: Franke Verlag, 1997).

Gamble, Harry Y., *The New Testament Canon: Its Making and Meaning* (Philadelphia: Fortress Press, 1985).

—*Books and Readers in the Early Church: A History of Early Christian Texts* (New Haven and London: Yale University Press, 1995).

Gardiner, Alan, *The Library of A. Chester Beatty: Description of a Hieratic Papyrus with a Mythological Story, Love-Songs and other Miscellaneous Texts* (London: privately printed, 1931).

—*Hieratic Papyri in the British Museum. Third Series: Chester Beatty Gift* (London: British Museum, 1935).

Geer, Thomas C. Jr, 'Analyzing and Categorizing New Testament Greek Manuscripts: Colwell Revisited', in Bart D. Ehrman and Michael W. Holmes (eds.), *The Text of the New Testament in Contemporary Research: Essays on the* Status Quaestionis (SD, 46; Grand Rapids: Eerdmans, 1995), pp. 253–67.

Gerstinger, Hans, 'Ein Fragment des Chester Beatty-Evangelienkodex in der Papyrussammlung der Nationalbibliothek in Wien', *Aegyptus* 13 (1933), pp. 67–72.

Giversen, Søren, *Apocryphon Johannis: The Coptic Text of the Apocryphon Johannis in the Nag Hammadi Codex II with Translation, Introduction and Commenta,* (ATDan 5; Kopenhagen: Munksgaard, 1963), pp. 34–40.

Glaue, P., *Die Vorlesung heiliger Schriften im Gottesdienst* (Berlin: Duncker, 1907).

Goranson, S., 'Ebionites' in *ABD*, II (New York: Doubleday, 1992), pp. 260–61.

Green, William Scott, 'What's in a Name? The problem of Rabbinic Biography', in *idem* (ed.), *Approaches to Ancient Judaism: Theory and Practice* (Brown Judaic Series, 1; Missoula, MT: Scholars Press, 1978), pp. 77–96.

Greenlee, J. Harold, *The Gospel Text of Cyril of Jerusalem* (SD, 17; Copenhagen: Munksgaard, 1955).

Glunz, Hans H., 'The Gospel Glosses in the Harleian MS 1802 (about 1140), from Armagh', in *idem* (ed.), *History of the Vulgate in England from Alcuin to Roger Bacon* (Cambridge: University Press,1933), pp. 328–41.

Griffiths, Paul J., *Religious Reading: The Place of Reading in the Practice of Religion* (New York: Oxford University Press, 1999).

Haelst, Joseph van, *Catalogue des papyrus littéraires Juifs et Chrétiens* (Paris: Publications de la Sorbonne, 1976).

—'Les Origines du Codex', in Alain Blanchard (ed.), *Les Débuts du Codex* (Turnhout: Brepols, 1989), pp. 15–16.

Handley, E.W., U. Wartenberg and R.A. Coles (eds.), *The Oxyrhynchus Papyri, Volume LXIV* (London: Egypt Exploration Society, 1997).

Harnack, Adolf von, *The Origin of the New Testament and the Most Important Consequences of the New Creation* (trans. J.R. Wilkinson; London: Williams & Norgate, 1925).

—'Das Alte Testament in den paulinischen Briefen und in den paulinischen Gemeinden', *SBAW* (1928), pp. 124–41.

—*Marcion, das Evangelium vom fremden Gott; eine Monographie zur Geschichte der Grundlegung der katholischen Kirche* (Wissenchafliche Buchgesellschaft, 1921; reprint Darmstadt 1960).

Harris, W.V., *Ancient Literacy* (Cambridge, MA: Harvard University Press, 1989).

—'Why did the Codex Supplant the Book-Roll?', in J. Monfasani and R.G. Musto (eds.), *Renaissance Society and Culture, Essays in Honor of Eugene F. Rice Jr* (New York: Italica Press, 1991), pp. 71–85.

Haslam, M.W., A. Jones, F. Mattomini and M.L. West *et al.* (eds.), *The Oxyrhynchus Papyri Volume LXV* (London: Egypt Exploration Society, 1998).

Head, Peter M., 'Observations on Early Papyri of the Synoptic Gospels, Especially on the "Scribal Habits"', *Bib* 71 (1990), pp. 240–47.

Hedley, P.L., 'The Egyptian Texts of the Gospels and Acts', *CQR* 118 (1934), pp. 23–39, 188–230.

Hendrickson, G.L., 'Ancient Reading', *CJ* 26 (1930–31), pp. 182–96.

Hengel, Martin, *Studies in the Gospel of Mark* (London: SCM Press, repr. 1997 [1983]), pp. 64–84.

—*Die Johanneische Frage: ein Lösungsversuch, mit einem Beitr. zur Apokalypse von Jörg Frey* (WUNT, 67; Tübingen: Mohr, 1993).

—*The Four Gospels and the One Gospel of Jesus Christ* (trans. John Bowden; London: SCM Press, 2000).

—'Review of J. Jervell's *Der Jude Paulus und sein Volk: Zu einem neuen Actakommentar*', (Theologische Rundschau 66 (2001), pp. 338–68.

Hering, J., 'Observations critiques sur le texte des Évangiles et des Actes de P45', *Revue d'Histoire et de Philosophie religieuses* 14 (1934), pp. 145–54.

Horton, Charles, ' "It was all a great adventure": Alfred Chester Beatty and the formation of his Library', *History Ireland* 8.2 (2000), pp. 37–42

—*Alfred Chester Beatty: from Miner to Bibliophile* (Dublin: Townhouse, 2003).

Hume, David, *A Treatise of Human Nature: Being an Attempt to Introduce the Experimental Method of Reasoning into Moral Subjects, etc.* (London: John Noon, 1739).

—*The Life of David Hume, Esq., Written by Himself* (London, W. Strahan and T. Cadell, 1777).

Humphrey, J.H. (ed.), *Literacy in the Roman World* (JRASS, 3; Ann Arbor: University of Michigan, 1991).

Hurtado, L.W., 'Codex Washingtonianus in the Gospel of Mark: Its Textual Relationships and Scribal Characteristics' (PhD thesis, Case Western Reserve University, 1973; Ann Arbor, MI: University Microfilms).

—*Text-Critical Methodology and the Pre-Caesarean Text: Codex W in the Gospel of Mark* (SD, 43; Grand Rapids: Eerdmans, 1981).

—'The Earliest Evidence of an Emerging Christian Material and Visual Culture: The Codex, the *Nomina Sacra* and the Staurogram', in Stephen G. Wilson and Michel Desjardins (eds.), *Text and Artifact in the Religions of Mediterranean Antiquity: Essays in Honour of Peter Richardson* (ESCJ, 9; Waterloo: Wilfrid Laurier University Press, 2000), pp. 271–88.

Huston, Hollis W., 'Mark 6 and 11 in P[45] and in the Caesarean Text', *JBL* 74 (1955), pp. 262–71.

Judge, E.A., *The Social Pattern of Christian Groups in the First Century* (London: Tyndale, 1960).

—'The Early Christians as a Scholastic Community', *JRH* 1 (1960–61), pp. 125–37.

Jülicher, Adolf, Walter Matzkow and Kurt Aland, *Itala: Das Neue Testament in Altlateinsicher Überlieferung* (Berlin: de Gruyter, 1938–63).

Junack, K., 'Abschreibpraktien und Schreibergewohnheiten in ihrer Auswirkung auf die Textuberlieferung', in E.J. Epp and G.D. Fee (eds.), *New Testament Textual Criticism: Its Significance for Exegesis (Essays in Honor of Bruce Metzger)* (Oxford: Clarendon Press, 1981), pp. 277–95.

Junack, K., *et al.* (eds.), *Das Neue Testament auf Papyrus. II. Die paulinischen Briefe*, 1 (ANTF, 12; Berlin: de Gruyter, 1989).

Kelhoffer, James A., *Miracle and Mission: The Authentication of Missionaries and their Message in the Longer Ending of Mark* (WUNT, 2.112; Tübingen: Mohr, 2000).

Kennedy, Brian P., *Alfred Chester Beatty and Ireland 1950-1968: A Study in Cultural Politics* (Dun Laoghaire: Glendale Press, 1988).

Kenyon, Frederic G., *Our Bible and the Ancient Manuscripts Being a History of the Text and its Translations* (London: Eyre & Spottiswoode, 1895).

—*Recent Developments in the Textual Criticism of the Greek Bible* (London: Oxford University Press, 1933).

—*The Chester Beatty Biblical Papyri: Descriptions and Texts of Twelve Manuscripts on Papyrus of the Greek Bible, Fasciculus I: General Introduction* (London: Emery Walker, 1933); *Fasciculus II: The Gospels and Acts, Text* (London: Emery Walker, 1933); *Fasciculus II: The Gospels and Acts, Plates* (London: Emery Walker, 1934); *Fasciculus III: Pauline Epistles and Revelation, Text* (London: Emery Walker, 1934); *Fasciculus III: Pauline Epistles and Revelation, Plates* (London: Emery Walker, 1936); *Fasciculus III Supplement: Pauline Epistles, Text* (London: Emery Walker, 1936); *Fasciculus III Supplement: Pauline Epistles, Plates* (London: Emery Walker, 1937).

—Review of Sanders' Edition, *American Journal of Philology* 57 (1936), pp. 91–95.

—*The Text of the Greek Bible* (ed. A.W. Adams; London: Duckworth, 3rd edn, 1975).

Kilpatrick, G., 'The Bodmer and Mississippi Collection of Biblical and Christian Texts', in *GRBS 4* (1963), pp. 33–47.

Kim, Young Kyu, 'Palaeographical Dating of P^{46} to the Later First Century', *Bib* 69 (1988), pp. 248–57.

Knox, B.M.W., 'Silent Reading in Antiquity', *GRBS* 9 (1968), pp. 421–35.

Koester, H., *Ancient Christian Gospels* (London: SCM Press; Valley Forge, PA: Trinity International, 1990).

Köhler, W.-D., *Die Rezeption des Matthäusevangeliums in der Zeit vor Irenäus* (WUNT, 2.24 (Tübingen: Mohr, 1987).

Kraus, Thomas J., '*Ad fontes*: Gewinn durch die Konsultation von Originalhandschriften am Beispiel von *P. Vindob. G* 31974', *Bib* 82 (2001), pp. 1–16.

Kyrtatis, D.J., *The Social Structure of the Early Christian Communities* (London: Verso, 1987).

Lagrange, M. J., 'Le group dit césaréen des manuscrits des Évangiles', *RB* 38 (1929), pp. 481–512.

—'Le papyrus Chester Beatty pour les Évangiles', *RB* 43 (1934), pp. 5–41.

Lake, Kirsopp, *Codex 1 of the Gospels and its Allies* (TS, 7.3; Cambridge: Cambridge University Press, 1902), pp. xxiii–iv.

Lake, Kirsopp and R.P. Blake, 'The Text of the Gospels and the Koridethi Codex', *HTR* 16 (1923), pp. 267–86.

Lake, Kirsopp, Robert Blake and Silva New, 'The Caesarean Text of the Gospel of Mark', *HTR* 21 (1928), pp. 207–404.

—'De Westcott et Hort au Père Lagrange et au-dela', *RB* 48 (1939), pp. 497–505.

Lake, Kirsopp and Silva Lake, *Family 13 (The Ferrar Group): The Text according to Mark with a Collation of Codex 28 of the Gospels* (SD, 11; London: Christophers, 1941).

Lake, Silva, *Family Pi and the Codex Alexandrinus* (SD, 5; London: Christophers, 1937).

—*The Text of the New Testament* (repr.; London: Rivingtons, 6th rev. edn, 1959 [1928]).

Lampe, P., *Die Stat-römischen Christen in den ersten beiden Jahrhunderten: Untersuchungen zur Sozialgeschichte* (WUNT, 18; Tubingen: Mohr, 1987).

Lawlor, H.J., *Chapters on the Book of Mulling* (Edinburgh: David Douglas, 1897).

Lawton, Thomas and Linda Merrill, *Freer: A Legacy of Art* (Washington, DC: The Freer Gallery of Art, 1993).

Leloir, L., *Doctrines et methods d'Éphrem d'après les oeuvres éditées* (CSCO, 220 [Subsidia 18]; Louvain: Peeters, 1961).

—*Le témoignage d'Éphrem sur le Diatessaron* (CSCO, 227 [Subsidia 19]; Louvain: Peeters, 1962).

—*Saint Éphrem, Commentaire de l'Évangile concordant, texte syriaque* (Chester Beatty Monographs, 8; Dublin: Hodges & Figgis, 1963).

—*Ephrem de Nisibe, Commentaire de l'Évangile concordant ou Diatessaron* (Sources chrétiennes, 121; Paris: Editions du Cerf, 1966).

—*Saint Éphrem, Commentaire de l'Évangile concordant, texte syriaque (Manuscrit Chester Beatty 709), Folios Additionnels* (Chester Beatty Monographs 8(b); Louvain: Peeters, 1990).

Löhr, H., *Studien zum frühchristlichen und frühjüdischen Gebet: Eine Untersuchung zu 1 Clem 59 bis 61 in seinem literarischen, historischen und theologischen Kontext* (WUNT, 160; Tübingen: Mohr, 2003).

Lührmann, D., and E. Schlarb (eds.), Fragmente apokryph gewordener Evangelien in griechischer und lateinischer Sprache (MThSt, 59; Marburg: Elwert, 2000).

Luz, Ulrich, *Matthew 1–7* (Edinburgh: T. & T. Clark, 1989).

McCarthy, C., *Saint Ephrem's Commentary on Tatian's Diatessaron* (Journal of Semitic Studies Supplements, 2; Oxford: Oxford University Press, 1993), pp. 9–14.

McCartney, E.S., 'Notes on Reading and Praying Audibly', *CP* 43 (1948), pp. 184–87.

McCormick, Michael, 'Typology, Codicology and Papyrology', *Scriptorium* 35 (1981), pp. 331–34.155

—'The Birth of the Codex and the Apostolic Lifestyle', *Scriptorium* 39 (1985), pp. 150–58.

McGurk, Patrick, 'The Irish Pocket Gospel Book', *Sacris Erudiri* 8 (1956), pp. 249–70.

—*Latin Gospel Books from A.D. 400 to A.D. 800* (Les Publications de Scriptorium, 5; Paris and Brussels: Éditions 'Érasme'; Antwerp-Amsterdam: Standaard, 1961).

—'The Gospel Text', in P. Fox (ed.), *The Book of Kells. MS 58 Trinity College Library Dublin* (Lucerne: Fine Arts Facsimile Publications of Switzerland, 1990), pp. 37–152.

McNamara, M., 'The Echternach and Mac Durnan Gospels: Some Common Readings and their Significance', *Peritia* 6-7 (1987–88), pp. 217–22.

—*Studies on Texts of Early Irish Latin Gospels (A.D. 600-1200)* (Instrumenta Patristica, 20; Steenbrugge & Dordrecht: Kluwer, 1990).

—'The Celtic-Irish Mixed Gospel Text: Some Recent Contributions and Centennial Reflections', *Filologia mediolatina* 2 (1995), pp. 69–108.

—'Irish Gospel Books and Related Texts', *Proceedings of the Irish Biblical Association* 23 (Dublin: Irish Biblical Association Publications, 2000), pp. 60–66.

—'Bible Text and Illumination in St Gall Stiftsbibliothek Codex 51, with Special Reference to Longinus in the Crucifixion Scene', in M. Redknap, N. Edwards *et al.* (eds.), *Pattern and Purpose in Insular Art* (Proceedings of the Fourth International Conference on Insular Art held at the National Museum & Gallery Cardiff 3–6 September 1998; Oxford: Oxbow Books, 2001), pp. 191–202.

Malherbe, J., *Social Aspects of Early Christianity* (Philadelphia: Fortress Press, 2nd edn, 1983).

Martin, Victor, *Papyrus Bodmer II: Évangile de Jean Chap. 1-14* (Cologny-Geneve: Bibliotheca Bodmeriana, 1956).

—*Papyrus Bodmer II: Évangile de Jean, Supplément, Chaps. 14-21* (Cologny-Geneva: Bibliotheca Bodmeriana, 1958).

Martin, V., and J.W.B. Barns (eds.), *Papyrus Bodmer II: Supplement, Nouvelle édition augmentée et corrigée* (Cologny-Geneva: Bibliotheca Bodmeriana, 1962).

Martin, V., and Rodolf Kasser, *Papyrus Bodmer XIV* (Cologny-Geneva: Bibliotheca Bodmeriana, 1961).

Martini, C.M., *Il Problema della recensionalità del codice B alla luce del papiro Bodmer XIV* (Rome: Pontifical Biblical Institute, 1966).

Meeks, W., *The First Urban Christians* (New Haven: Yale, 1983).

Merk, A., 'Codex evangeliorum et actuum ex collectione papyrorum Chester Beatty', *Miscellanea Biblica* II (1934), pp. 375–406.

Merkel, H., *Die Widersprüche zwischen den Evangelien* (WUNT, 13; Tübingen: Mohr, 1971).

Metzger, B.M., 'The Caesarean Text of the Gospels', in *idem* (ed.), *Chapters in the History of New Testament Textual Criticism* (NTTS, 4; Leiden: Brill, 1963), pp. 42–72.

—'Explicit References in the Works of Origen to Variant Readings in New Testament Manuscripts', in J.N. Birdsall and R.W. Thomson (eds.), *Biblical and Patristic Studies in Memory of Robert Pierce Casey* (Freiburg: Herder, 1963), pp. 78–95.

—*The Text of the New Testament: Its Transmission, Corruption and Restoration* (Oxford: Clarendon Press, 2nd edn, 1968).

—*The Early Versions of the New Testament: Their Origin, Transmission and Limitations* (Oxford: Clarendon Press, 1977).

—'St. Jerome's Explicit References to Variant Readings in Manuscripts of the New Testament', in Ernest Best and R. McL. Wilson (eds.), *Text and Interpretation: Studies in the New Testament Presented to Matthew Black* (Cambridge: Cambridge University Press, 1979), pp. 179–90.

Millar, Eric, *The Library of A. Chester Beatty: A Descriptive Catalogue of the Western Manuscripts* (Oxford: Oxford University Press, 1927).

Millard, A., *Reading and Writing at the Time of Jesus* (Sheffield: Sheffield Academic Press, 2000).

Mizzi, J., 'The Old-Latin Element in Jn. I,29-III,26 of Cod. Sangallensis 60', *Sacris Erudiri* 28 (1978–79), pp. 33–62.

Moore, Stephen D., *Literary Criticism and the Gospels: The Theoretical Challenge* (New Haven: Yale University Press, 1989).

Neirynck, Frans, 'Q: From Source to Gospel', *ETL* 71 (1995), pp. 421–30.

Nestle, [E]-[K] Aland, *NovT Graece et latine* (Stuttgart: Deutsche Bibelgesellschaft, 26th edn, 1984).

Ohlig, K.–H., *Die theologische Begrundung des neutestamentlichen Kanons in der alten Kirche* (KBANT; Dusseldorf: Patmos, 1972).

Pagels, Elaine, *The Gnostic Gospels* (New York: Random House, 1979).

Patterson, Steven J., and James M. Robinson, *The Fifth Gospel: The Gospel of Thomas Comes of Age* (Harrisburg, PA: Trinity Press International, 1998).

Pietersma, Albert, 'The Chester Beatty Papyri', in *ABD* [on CD-Rom].

Pestman, P.W., 'Who were the owners, in the "Community of Workmen", of the Chester Beatty Papyri', in R.J. Demaree and Jac. J. Janssen (eds.), *Gleanings from Deir El-Medina* (Leiden: Nederlands Instituut voor het Nabije Oosten, 1982).

Petersen, William L., *The Diatessaron and Ephrem Syrus as Sources of Romanos the Melodist* (CSCO, 475 [Subsidia 74]; Louvain: Peeters, 1985).

—*Tatian's Diatessaron: Its Creation, Dissemination, Signifiance and History in Scholarship* (VCSup, 25; Leiden: Brill,1994), pp. 35–83.

Plooij, D., *A Primitive Text of the Diatessaron* (Leyden: Sijthoff, 1923).

Quinn, K., 'The Poet and his Audience in the Augustan Age', *ANRW* 30.1, pp. 75–180.

Rawson, E., *Intellectual Life in the Late Roman Republic* (London: Duckworth, 1985).

Richards, E.R., *The Secretary in the Letters of Paul* (WUNT, 42; Tübingen: Mohr, 1991).

Rittmueller, J., 'The Gospel Commentary of Máel Brigte ua Máeluanaig and its Hiberno-Latin Background', *Peritia* 2 (1983), pp. 185–214.

—'Afterword: The Gospel of Máel Brigte', *Peritia* 3 (1984), pp. 215–18.

Roberts, C.H., *An Unpublished Fragment of the Fourth Gospel in the John Rylands Library* (Manchester: Manchester University Press, 1935).

—*Manuscript, Society and Belief in Early Christian Egypt* (Schweich Lectures, 1977; London: British Academy [Oxford University Press], 1979).

Roberts, C.H., and T.C. Skeat, *The Birth of the Codex* (London: Oxford University Press for the British Academy, 1983, reprint 1987).

Robbins, G., 'Eusebius' Lexicon of Canonicity', *StPat* 25 (1993), pp. 134–41.

Robinson, James M., 'Q 12.49-59: Children against Parents—Judging the Time—Settling out of Court', in S. Carruth (ed.), *Documenta Q: Reconstructions of Q through Two Centuries of Gospel Research Excerpted, Sorted, and Evaluated* (Leuven: Peeters, 1997), pp. 119–21.

—'The Pre-Q Text of the (Ravens and) Lilies: Q 12.22–31 and P. Oxy. 655 (Gos. Thom. 36)', in Stefan Maser (ed.), *Text und Geschichte: Facetten theologischen Arbeitens aus dem Freundes- und Schülerkreis. Dieter Lührmann zum 60. Geburtstag* (MThSt, 50; Marburg: Elwert, 1999), pp. 143–80.

—'A Written Greek Sayings Cluster Older than Q: A Vestige', *HTR* 92 (1999), pp. 61–77.

—'Excursus on the Scribal Error in Q 12.27', in J.M. Robinson, Paul Hoffmann, and John S. Kloppenborg (eds.), *The Critical Edition of Q: Synopsis including the Gospels of Matthew and Luke, Mark and Thomas with English, German, and French translations of Q and Thomas* (Minneapolis: Fortress Press; Leuven: Peeters, 2000), pp. xcix–ci.

Robinson, James, M. (ed.), *The Nag Hammadi Library in English* (Leiden: Brill, 1977).

Robinson, James M., and Christoph Heil, 'Zeugnisse eines schriftlichen, griechischen vor-kanonischen Textes: Mt 6,28b a*, P.Oxy. 655 I, 1–17 (EvTh 36) und Q 12,27', *ZNW* 89 (1998), pp. 30–44.

—'Noch einmal: Der Schreibfehler in Q 12,27', *ZNW* 92 (2001).

—'The Lilies of the field: Sayings 36 of the Gospel of Thomas and Secondary Accretions in Q 12.22b-31', *NTS* 47 (2001).

Robinson, James M., and Marvin W. Meyer (eds.), *The Nag Hammadi Library in English* (trans. members of the Coptic Gnostic Library Project of the Institute for Antiquity and Christianity, James M. Robinson, Director; Leiden: Brill, 1977).

Royse, James R., 'Scribal Habits in Early Greek New Testament Papyri', (ThD thesis, Graduate Theological Union; Berkeley, CA, 1981).

—'Scribal Tendencies in the Transmission of the Text of the New Testament', in Bart D. Ehrman and Michael W. Holmes (eds.), *The Text of the New Testament in Contemporary Research: Essays on the Status Quaestionis* (SD, 46; Grand Rapids: Eerdmans, 1995), pp. 239–52.

Saenger, P., 'Silent Reading: Its Impact on Late Medieval Script and Society', *Viator* 13 (1982), pp. 367–414.

Salzmann, J.C., *Lehren und Ermhanen: Zur Geschichte des christlichen Wortgottesdienstes in den ersten drei Jahrhunderten* (WUNT, 59; Tübingen: Mohr, 1994).

Sanders, Henry A. (ed.), *A Third-Century Papyrus Codex of the Epistles of Paul* (University of Michigan Studies; Humanistic Series, 38; Ann Arbor: University of Michigan, 1935).

Sato, Migaku, *Q und Prophetie: Studien zur Gattungs- und Traditionsgeschichte der Quelle Q* (WUNT, 2.29; Tübingen: Mohr, 1988).

Sayce, A.H., *Reminiscences* (London: Macmillan, 1923).

Schenke, Hans-Martin, *Das Philippus-Evangelium* (Nag-Hammadi-Codex II,3) (TU, 143; Berlin: Akademie Verlag, 1997).

Schenkeveld, D.M., 'Prose Usages of *AKOUEIN* "To Read" ', *CQ* 42 (1992), pp. 129–41.

Schlusser, M., 'Reading Silently in Antiquity', *JBL* 111 (1992), pp. 499.

Schmidt, Carl, *Pistis Sophia* (translation and notes by Violet MacDermot; The Coptic Gnostic Library; NHS, 9; Leiden: Brill, 1978).

Schneemelcher, Wilhelm (ed.), *Neutestamentliche Apokryphen in deutscher übersetzung* (1. Band, *Evangelien*, 6 Aufl; Tübingen: Mohr–Siebeck, 1999).

Scholes, R. and R. Kellogg, *The Nature of Narrative* (London: Oxford University Press, 1966).

Schwemer, Anna Marie, *Studien zu den frühjüdischen Prophetenleben* (2 vols.; Texte und Studien zu Antiken Judentum, 49 and 50; Tübingen: Mohr, 1995–96).

Skeat, T.C., 'The Lilies of the Field', *ZNW* 37 (1938), pp. 211–14.

—'Irenaeus and the Four-Gospel Canon', *NovT* 34 (1992), pp. 194–99.

—'A Codicological Analysis of the Chester Beatty Papyrus Codex of Gospels and Acts (P45)', *Hermathena* (*A Trinity College Dublin Review*) 155 (1993), pp. 27–43.

—'The Origin of the Christian Codex', *ZPE* 102 (1994), pp. 263–68.

—'The Oldest Manuscript of the Four Gospels?', *NTS* 43 (1997), pp. 1–34.

Skeat T.C., and B.C. McGing, 'Notes on Chester Beatty Biblical Papyrus I (Gospels and Acts), *Hermathena* (*A Trinity College Dublin Review*) 150 (1991), pp. 21–25.

Slusser, Michael, 'Reading Silently in Antiquity', *JBL* 3.3 (1992), p. 499.

Stuhlmacher, P., *Das paulinische Evangelium* (FRLANT, 95; Göttingen: Vandenhoeck und Ruprecht, 1968).

Stanton, G.N., 'The Fourfold Gospel', *NTS* 43 (1997), pp. 317–46.

—'Jesus Traditions and Gospels in Justin Martyr and Irenaeus', in J.-M. Auwers and H.J. de Jonge (eds.), *The Biblical Canons* (Leuven: University Press, 2002).

—*Jesus and Gospel* (Cambridge: Cambridge University Press, 2004).

Starr, R.J., 'Reading Aloud: *Lectores* and Roman Reading', *CJ* 86 (1991), pp. 337–43.

Stevensen, J. (ed.), *A New Eusebius* (London: SPCK, 1957).

Stock, B., *The Implications of Literacy: Written Language and Models of Interpretation in the Eleventh and Twelfth Centuries* (Princeton: Princeton University Press, 1983).

Streeter, B.H., *The Four Gospels: A Study of Origins* (London: Macmillan, 1926).

—'The Washington MS of the Gospels', *HTR* 19 (1926), pp. 165–72 .

—'The Washington MS and the Caesarean Text of the Gospels', *JTS* 27 (1926), pp. 144–47.

—'Origen, Aleph and the Caesarean Text', *JTS* 36 (1935), pp. 178–80.

—'Codices 157, 1071 and the Caesarean Text', in R.P. Casey, S. Lake and A.K. Lake (eds.), *Quantulacumque: Studies Presented to Kirsopp Lake* (London: Christophers, 1937), pp. 149–50.

Stuhlmacher, P., *Das paulinische Evangelium* (FRLANT, 95; Göttingen: Vandenhoeck & Ruprecht, 1968).

Talbert, Charles H., 'Biographies of Philosophers and Rulers as Instruments of Religious Propaganda in Mediterranean Antiquity', in *ANRW* II, 16.2 (1978), pp. 1619–51.

Tarelli, C.C., 'Some Linguistic Aspects of the Chester Beatty Papyrus of the Gospels', *JTS* 39 (1938), pp. 254–59.

—'The Chester Beatty Papyrus and the Caesarean Text', *JTS* 40 (1939), pp. 46–55.

—'The Chester Beatty Papyrus and the Western and Byzantine Texts', *JTS* 41 (1940), pp. 253–60.

—'Some Further Linguistic Aspects of the Chester Beatty Papyrus of the Gospels', *JTS* 43 (1942), pp. 19–25.

Theissen, G., *The Social Setting of Pauline Christianity: Essays on Corinth* (trans. John Schutz; Philadelphia: Fortress Press, 1982).

Thompson, Edward, *Introduction to Greek and Latin Palaeography* (Oxford: Clarendon Press, 1912).

Thornton, C.-J., *Der Zeuge des Zeugen: Lukas als Historiker der Paulusreisen* (WUNT, 56; Tübingen: Mohr, 1991).

Tischendorf, C., *Evangelium Palatinum* (Leipzig: Brockhaus, 1847).

Tolbert, Mary Ann, *Sowing the Gospel: Mark's World in Literary-Historical Perspective* (Minneapolis: Fortress Press, 1989).

Tonder, I.P. van, 'An Assessment of the Impact of Second-Century Heretical Christian Movements on the Formation of the Catholic Christian Canon of Scripture' (dissertation, Cambridge University, 2000).

Tracy, David, *The Analogical Imagination: Christian Theology and the Culture of Pluralism* (London: SCM Press, 1981).

Tuckett, C.M., ' "Nomina Sacra": Yes and No?' in J.-M. Auwers and H.J. de Jonge (eds.), *The Biblical Canons* (Leuven: University Press, 2003).

Turner, E.G., *The Typology of the Early Codex* (Philadelphia: University of Pennsylvania Press, 1977).

—*Greek Papyri: An Introduction* (Oxford: Clarendon Press, 2nd edn, 1980).

—*Greek Manuscripts of the Ancient World* (ed. P. Parsons; London: University of London Institute of Classical Studies, 2nd edn, 1987).

Turner, Martha Lee, *The Gospel according to Philip: The Sources and Coherence of an Early Christian Collection* (NHMS, 38; Leiden: Brill, 1996).

Verey, C., 'Notes on the Gospel Texts', in C.D. Verey, T. Julian Brown and E. Coatsworth (eds.), *The Durham Gospels, together with Fragments of a Gospel in Uncial. Durham, Cathedral Library, MS A. II. 17* (Copenhagen: Rosenkilde & Bagger, 1980), pp. 68–108.

Wachtel, K., and K. Witte (eds.), *Das Neue Testament auf Papyrus*. II. *Die paulinischen Briefe*, II (ANTF, 22; Berlin: de Gruyter 1994).

Waldstein, Michael and Frederik Wisse (eds.), *The Apocryphon of John: Synopsis of Nag Hammadi Codices II.1: III,1 and IV,1, with B6 8502.2* (The Coptic Gnostic Library; NHMS, 33; Leiden: Brill, 1995).

Walker, G.S.M., *Sancti Columbani Opera* (Scriptores Latini Hiberniae, 2; Dublin Institute for Advanced Studies, 1970).

Weber, R., *et al.*, *Biblia Sacra iuxta Vulgatam Versionem* (Stuttgart: Württembergischer Bibelanstalt, 1969).

Wegener, G.S., *6000 Years of the Bible* (trans. Margaret Shenfield; London: Hodder & Stoughton, 1963).

Westcott, Brooke F., and Fenton John A. Hort, *The New Testament in the Original Greek* (Cambridge and London: Macmillan, 1881).

—*The New Testament in the Original Greek: Introduction and Appendix* (Cambridge and London: Macmillan, 1882).

White, A.H., 'The Problem of the Caesarean Text', *Journal of the Manchester University Egypt and Oriental Society* 24 (1942–45; published 1947), pp. 39–59.

Wilder, Amos, *Early Christian Rhetoric: The Language of the Gospel* (Cambridge, MA: Harvard University Press, 1971).

—*Jesus' Parables and the War of Myths: Essays in Imagination in the Scriptures* (London: SPCK, 1982).

Wilken, R.L., 'Collegia, Philosophical Schools, and Theology', in S. Benko and J.J. O'Rourke (eds.), *The Catacombs and the Coliseum: The Roman Empire as the Setting of Primitive Christianity* (Valley Forge, PA: Judson, 1971), pp. 268–91.

—*The Christians as the Romans Saw them* (New Haven: Yale University Press, 1984).

Wilson, A.J., *The Life and Times of Alfred Chester Beatty* (London: Cadogan, 1985).

Wohleb, L., 'Ein Beitrag zur Geschichte des lauten Lesens', *Philologus* 85 (1929), pp. 111–12.

Wood, C.M., *The Formation of Christian Understanding: An Essay in Theological Hermeneutics* (Philadelphia: Westminster Press, 1981).

Wordsworth, J., and F.J. White, *Nouum Testamentum Domini Nostri Iesu Christi latine secundum editionem Sancti Hieronymi. Pars Prior – Quattuor euengalia* (Oxford: Clarendon Press, 1889–98).

Zahn, Th., *Grundriss der Geschichte des neutestamentlichen Kanons* (Leipzig: Deichert, 2nd edn, 1904), pp. 1–14.

—*Geschichte des neutestamentlichen Kanons* (Erlangen: Deichert, 1888–92), I, pp. 122–25.

Zuntz, Günther, 'Reconstruction of One Leaf of the Chester Beatty Papyrus of the Gospels and Acts (P45)', *Chronique d'Égypte* 51 (1951), pp. 191–211.

—*The Text of the Epistles: A Disquisition upon the Corpus Paulinum* (Schweich Lectures of the British Academy, 1946; London: Oxford University Press for the British Academy, 1953).

—'Ein Heide las da Markusevangelium', in Hubert Cancik (ed.), *Markus-Philologie* (WUNT, 33; Tübingen: Mohr, 1984).

INDEX OF AUTHORS